CW00732890

The Machine Knitters' Guide to
DOUBLE JACQUARD

The Machine Knitters' Guide to
DOUBLE JACQUARD

• BETTY BAILEY •

CASSELL

This book is dedicated to machine knitters worldwide, both known to the author and unknown. It is written in the hope and belief that it will add to the sum of knowledge in this expanding craft.

A CASSELL BOOK

First published in the UK 1992 by Cassell
Villiers House 41/47 Strand LONDON WC2N 5JE

Copyright © 1992 Betty Bailey Bee Gee Bee Machine Knits
Photography copyright © 1992 Kitchenham Limited

Distributed in the United States
by Sterling Publishing Co., Inc.
387 Park Avenue South, New York, NY 10016–8810

Distributed in Australia
by Capricorn Link (Australia) Pty Ltd
P.O. Box 665, Lane Cove, NSW 2066

British Library Cataloguing in Publication Data
Bailey, Betty 1923–
 The machine knitters' guide to double jacquard
 1. Knitting, Machine
 I. Title
 746.432

 ISBN 0–304–34131–2

Typeset by Columns of Reading

Printed and bound by Courier International Ltd., East Kilbride.

Photography by Grahame Austin, AMPA, LIBPP

FRONTISPIECE
The Brother/Knitmaster garments from Chapters 1 and 2.

Contents

Acknowledgements

The author is grateful to the many people who have helped and encouraged her in the writing of this book, first to the yarn spinners and distributors who donated yarn for the garments featured: Amber UK, Greendale Mills, Windhill, Shipley, West Yorkshire; Argyll Wools Ltd, Pudsey, West Yorkshire; Atkinson Yarn, Terry Mills, Ossett, West Yorkshire WF5 9SA; F.W. Bramwell & Co. Ltd, Unit 5, Metcalf Drive, Altham Lane, Altham, Accrington, Lancashire BB5 5TU; James C. Brett (Yarns), Clyde Street, Bingley, West Yorkshire; Denys Brunton Designer Yarns, Moorland Mills, Law Street, Bradford Road, Cleckheaton, West Yorkshire BD19 3QR; Celandine Ltd, 44 Kirkgate, Otley, West Yorkshire LS21 3HJ; T. Forsell & Son Ltd, Blaby Road, South Wigston, Leicester LE8 2SG; King Cole Ltd, Merrie Mills, Old Souls Way, Bingley, West Yorkshire BD16 2AX; Many-a-Mickle, Hacking Street, Darwen, Lancashire BB3 1AL; T.E. Stanley, The House of Corbiere, Corbiere, Weston Road, Weston-upon-Trent, Derbyshire DE7 2BH (sole distributor of Tamm yarns); Studley Wools, Stockhill Road, Greengates, Bradford, West Yorkshire BD10 9TE; Waterwheel Yarns, Thomas B. Ramsden & Co. (Bradford) Ltd, Westgate Common Mills, Alverthorpe Road, Wakefield, West Yorkshire WF2 9NR.

Also to Joan and Sue, who helped to check the script and sew up garments; to other knitting friends, old and new, from clubs, classes and Saturday teach-ins; to the models, including John, Vicar of St Mark's Church, Highcliffe, Dorset, Helen, his wife, and Nicholas and Kate, two of their children, and the following friends from the congregation – Katharine, Nicola, Jessica, Anne, Diane, Simon, Dominic, Janet, Lisa, Sarah, Wendy, Kirsty, and Ruby and Sarah who were in the previous book; to those who hosted the photography, John and Helen for the use of the Vicarage, Brian and Pam, Lisa and Ray for the use of their homes and gardens; to Grahame Austin for his professional skill with the photography and for his patience; to Aisin (UK) Ltd, for the loan of a Toyota 950 knitting machine; and to her publishers, especially all those responsible for production and marketing.

All the photographs were taken specially for the book by Kitchenham Limited of Bournemouth. The line illustrations (garment blocks), punch card diagrams, electronic charts and needle diagrams are from the originals prepared by the author on her Amstrad PCW8256 with enlarged memory using Locomotive software, LocoScript 2.

Preliminaries

Having launched *The Machine Knitter's Guide to the Ribber* I decided to write a sequel to cover the rib fabrics and techniques I did not have room for in the first book. I started with Double Jacquard – known in the US as double bed Fair Isle – but the book grew and grew and became a book exclusively about Double Jacquard, written for the three makes of Japanese knitting machines. There are patterns, lots of them. Many of you have asked me for patterns because so few are written for this fabric.

Of course, some experts would ask 'Do you not use your charting device?', and so do I – up to a point. There is room for both patterns and charters. The latter are fine when the fabric is unpatterned, but when the pattern is complicated I like to fit it sensibly into the garment shape. You will see what I mean when you work through Chapter 6. The same also applies to many of the other garments, for I cannot bear to have odd bits of patterns – two or three stitches past the end of the punch card width against the sleeve head, just where it shows most. Remember that knitwear has a great deal of stretch, and a few stitches more or less make very little difference to the fit of a garment. It's a case of swings and roundabouts – take off a stitch or two here, add a row or two there.

What makes all the difference to the look of a garment is a sensible arrangement of the pattern. That is why I test-knit and complete all the garments myself. What a job! Of course, I knit only the one size required by the particular model, but I try out all the others on the empty needles and make sure they fit, adjusting them if they do not. I have recommended this to you several times in the following chapters.

In the first paragraph I could have said 'these fabrics', because Double Jacquard is not confined to the one type given in your ribber instruction books, as you will see from the chapter headings. Double Jacquard is a collective term for a great variety of fabrics.

The variety is made even greater because two types of machine, Brother and Knitmaster, operate in one way, and the other type, Toyota, knitting Simulknit, operates quite differently. Whichever machine you own, your aim should be to exploit its potential to the full. That has been one of my aims here. I have dealt with the main types of Double Jacquard fabric (there are still more) and have applied the techniques to all the machines whenever it is possible to do so. Because of this Toyota knitters will find here some stitches which are completely new. I hope that all knitters who make full use of this book will learn new techniques. There are some particularly interesting ones for the Brother 850 ribber.

Those of you with older machines have not been forgotten. Knitmaster 321 and Brother 830 are still very popular – I frequently use an 830, which was my first machine – and there are special ways in which they can be 'stretched' to do, with your help, things which more modern machines do automatically.

Then there are the electronic machines. Since they were first invented they have developed almost beyond recognition, and I have no doubt that they will go on developing. As you probably know, they vary considerably in the amount of information which needs to be entered into the 'works' in order to produce the complete pattern. For that reason the pattern charts I have given you are whole pattern repeats. You may need to use them just as they are. In some cases you will all need the whole chart – the cat, for instance – while in other designs, some of you will only need a small section – the patterns in Chapter 4, for example. There are two important points here. First, these patterns are suitable now, for all users of the older and current electronic machines. Second, they will not be outdated by any developments on main bed machines yet to come. But, and it is a big but, you must know your own machine, exactly how to programme it and what short cuts to programming you can take.

Notice one more thing. I have not referred here to mylar sheets as such, but to electronic charts. If your machine uses mylar sheets copy the charts on to them. If you have one of the other pattern programmers enter the information on the chart into it. The charts have been divided into sections of 5 stitches by 5 rows. This is the same as Brother mylar sheets. Unfortunately Knitmaster's mylar sheets are not the same. Be careful – *your* stitches are in sixes.

There are two other important variations in the machines – there is the matter of double length patterns combined with Double Jacquard, and there is the way the pattern faces when finished. Be sure you know, but just in case you do not, the information is given at relevant places in the text.

Double Jacquard fabrics are very suitable for the cut-and-sew method of garment construction, although Tuck Jacquard is difficult to use in this way because of its tendency to run. I have used the method for the necklines of the rose jumper in Chapter 10 and both jackets in Chapter 12, and for the shoulders and neckline of the Toyota waistcoat in Chapter 7. There are several books on this subject to which you can refer if you need more help than is given in the patterns. Do use a roller foot on your sewing machine, and put 2 rows of machining inside the cutting line for fine yarns and for tuck patterns.

Those of you who know me, personally or through print, will by now have gathered that I cannot bear poor sewing up. Some of these garments require even more care than usual. This is particularly true of the reversible ones. I used single crochet on one side of both jackets. Be careful, in the case of double length ribbed cuffs, to reverse the mattress stitching so that the seam does not show on the turned-back section.

The measurements shown on the garment blocks allow the standard 5cm (2in) *ease*, the term used for the difference between body measurement and garment size. It is important to check with the person for whom you are knitting if this is sufficient for their taste. The present fashion is for looser knitwear, and you may have to knit a larger size. If that is the case, do check that the length and sleeve length, both of which increase with size, are not too great. You may need to recalculate some of the shaping, or you could draw the size and length on your charter. Remember that patterns are there to help you, and can be followed exactly only if the person suits the block size, and that does not often happen.

The method of calculating rows and stitches is very simple. For example, consider a tension swatch measuring 28 stitches and 38 rows to 10cm. In this instance 1cm = 2.8 stitches and 3.8 rows. Therefore, to calculate any width, multiply the width in centimetres by 2.8, and to calculate any length, multiply the length in centimetres by 3.8. Round up or down to a whole number, remembering to adjust the stitches and rows to fit in with the pattern.

For Toyota knitters there are some ideas for extending the use of Simulknit. These are the result of much experimenting, and they are described in Chapters 3, 5, 7, 8, 9 and 10. For knitters with Brother 850 ribbers there is a new idea for the use of the 1 × 1 slip facility. This is explained in Chapter 12, and it also has a bearing on shaping, which is dealt with in Chapter 3.

I am most grateful to the yarn spinners and merchants who gave me yarns with which to knit the garments. Inevitably, between the writing and knitting and the publication there is a considerable length of time. During that time, some of the yarns I have used will have disappeared from the market, and others will not be available to knitters in other countries. For that reason I have given stocking stitch tension swatch measurements for all the yarns used. This will enable you to find substitutes where necessary. I have not given you the quantities of yarn required for each garment. A rough estimate based on the fact that Double Jacquard takes about 70 per cent more than the same type of garment knitted on the single bed will tell you how many cones of each yarn to buy.

I have dealt with many variations on the theme of Double Jacquard, but by no means all of them. There is not enough space for everything, so it has been necessary to be selective. Apart from the limitations of space, it is, of course, impossible to deal with everything relevant to my subject. There are still discoveries and inventions to be made. Knitters will go on inventing and perfecting variations on all the stitches available to them as long as there are knitting machines. I commend the habit of trying out things. Look at knitwear in the shops. Try to see how the stitches were formed. Stand and sketch the pattern so that you can sit down at your machine when you get home and work out yet another stitch.

Lastly, for all of you, will you treat this book as a course book, a text book, and think of me, as so many have kindly told me they do in the first book, as your personal tutor sitting beside you to help you to make the most of your knitting machines? I hope that you will all enjoy this book and profit from it. Happy knitting!

– 1 –
An Introduction to Double Jacquard and to Colour Changers

– FULL NEEDLE RIB STRIPED SLIPOVER TO KNIT –

The yarn used for the garments shown in colour photographs 1 and 2 is Sterling (65 per cent acrylic, 35 per cent wool) by Argyll: 884 navy (1), 771 white (2), 779 deep rose (3) and 778 pink (4). The measurements for the tension swatch are:

Full needle rib   28 stitches and 38 rows = 10cm   Tension 5/5
Stocking stitch   30 stitches and 36 rows = 10cm   Tension 7

Why Jacquard?

Jacquard knitting is a very wide subject, the principles of which, once understood, can lead to many exciting design possibilities. The name Jacquard derives from a nineteenth-century French weaver, Joseph Marie Jacquard, who invented a punch card attachment for the loom. These cards were designed to select warp threads mechanically, making the weaving of multicolour designs much quicker. Subsequently, manufacturers of knitting machines have made use of punch cards, and, more recently, silicon chips, for the selection of needles for all types of patterns, but the name itself is restricted in machine knitting to some of the fabrics having two or more colours.

Jacquard Fabrics Related to Knitting Machines

There are two types of Jacquard fabric, both of which have a number of variations. The fabric most commonly known as Fair Isle is well known to both hand and machine knitters. It is a patterned fabric having a knit-side and a purl-side, as does stocking stitch. It is sometimes called Knit-in, Slip-knit or Skip-knit, and sometimes Jersey Jacquard, and it is knitted either by hand or on single bed machines.

In this book we are concerned with the same type of pattern knitted on both beds. This is often known as Double Jacquard, Double Bed Fair Isle, Rib Jacquard or Multicoloured Rib. It has a great advantage over single bed Fair Isle in that there are no floats of yarn on the reverse side, because the main bed pattern is backed with rib bed knitting.

When single bed Fair Isle is produced, both the main yarn and the contrast yarn are knitted into each row in one carriage movement. Each carriage movement is one complete design row, represented by one line on the punch card or on the electronic machine pattern selector. In punch card machines the main or background yarn knits stitches which are represented by blank spaces on the punch card, and the contrast yarn knits stitches which are represented by holes. Yarns can be changed over in the feeds to reverse the effect.

It is similar with electronic machines. Main colour stitches are represented by unmarked squares on the pattern chart, and contrast colour stitches by marked ones. When a reversal of colours is required, yarns are not changed over; instead the reversing switch is used. This has the effect of making the marked squares behave like unmarked ones and vice versa and is just one of the more sophisticated controls available to knitters using these machines.

When Brother or Knitmaster ribbers are used for double bed work, whether on punch card or electronic machines, it is not possible to knit two colours in one design row with just one carriage movement. This is because the ribber arm has only one yarn feed and can, therefore, carry only one colour at a time. For this reason, with these machines, it is necessary to break down the pattern so that either the background colour stitches or the contrast ones are knitted. This means that it needs two carriage movements, one in each colour, to produce one design row. In practice, groups of four carriage movements, two in each colour, are knitted, in order always to return the yarns to the colour changer, which is fixed to the left of the needle bed. The number of carriage movements made when knitting Double Jacquard on all models of these two makes of machine is, therefore, twice as many as for the same design knitted in single bed Fair Isle. Don't let that put you off – it's worth all the extra work!

Double Jacquard on the Toyota machine is knitted differently using Simulknit. The Toyota ribber is the only one dealt with in this book with a double yarn feed, so enabling both yarns to be knitted at the same time, as in single bed Fair Isle. The main bed knits the pattern using any single bed Fair Isle punch card, and the rib bed knits a plain backing in contrast yarn. All main yarn floats are sandwiched between the beds. Where the contrast yarn knits pattern stitches, the fabric is ribbed, and where the main yarn knits, it is circular. This means that where back and front are in different colours a 'blister' is formed, so leading to the technical name Blister Jacquard.

All garments in this book can be knitted in Simulknit using the single bed version of the punch card. Using the method of hand selection, all pattern charts can also be used. Pattern instructions have all been recalculated for Toyota machines to take account of the difference in row count.

Toyota knitters should note that all garments can also be knitted using any of your basic Fair Isle punch cards. You may have to adjust the number of stitches slightly to allow for variations in tension swatch measurements and for the correct joining up of the pattern.

Fabric like Simulknit can be knitted automatically on the latest Knitmaster ribber, SRP 60N, by using Auto Drive. Knitters using these machines can also choose between contrast and main yarn backing. By manually changing the rib bed setting so that it knits one colour and slips the other, Brother ribbers and other Knitmasters can do the same. The carriage movements for all these machines are twice the number used for Simulknit because only one colour is knitted at a time.

It is also possible to knit Brother- and Knitmaster-type Double Jacquard fabric on Toyotas, but the yarns need to be changed by hand, and this is a laborious process. However, it is a good idea to try out at least one or two of the tension swatches to see the type of fabric under discussion and to compare it with a Simulknit tension piece. The latter can then be used, as already suggested, to knit the garments given as projects in each chapter.

2. *The Toyota garments from Chapters 1 and 2.*

In many circumstances the patterning mechanisms of the electronic machines make it unnecessary to mark out patterns especially for Double Jacquard. The separation of the colours just described is done automatically by the machine when the Jacquard control is used. However, it is useful for knitters who own these machines to understand how a single bed Fair Isle punch card is converted for Double Jacquard, so do read the part of the next chapter which deals with this.

There are many variations on the basic Double Jacquard fabric, and a separate chapter is devoted to each of the main types and includes at least one pattern to knit as a project.

The Availability and Use of Colour Changers

The use of a colour changer for this kind of knitting is invaluable, since yarns in patterned Double Jacquard are changed every 2 rows. Double bed colour changers are available to fit all current models of Brother and Knitmaster machines. Knitters, being both adventurous and patient people, have, of course, been colour changing manually for many years. The advent of the colour changer has just served to make it quicker and easier, as well as providing parking places for the yarns not in use.

At the time of writing there is no double bed colour changer to fit Toyota machines, possibly because they have Simulknit. Where fabrics cannot be knitted easily using a Toyota machine, alternatives have been given so that, in every chapter, there is a pattern for Toyota users to knit. Do try out the new methods of using Simulknit which were developed during the writing of this book, so that its possibilities are 'stretched' much further than before. A Toyota colour changer is being developed, and Toyota knitters will then have an even greater range of patterns.

In a later chapter you will learn how to knit plain fabrics of the same weight and texture as the patterned fabric. These can be knitted plain or in horizontal stripes on any machine, even a pre-punch card one, with or without a colour changer. They are also used with border and motif patterns.

I hope that by the time you have looked at the colour photographs of the fabrics you will be knitting, you will decide that a colour changer, if it is available for your machine, is top of your knitting shopping list!

If you have a colour changer which is still in its box now is the time to get it out, set it up, thread up and learn to use it. Here is a colour changer practice garment – a striped slipover in full needle rib, which I have knitted in 4 ply yarn. The same type of yarn is used for the projects in Chapter 2. Colour photograph 1 shows the Brother/Knitmaster garments, and colour photograph 2 shows the Toyota set. There is no shaping at all in the slipover, just a slash neck with welts, yokes and armbands in 1 × 1 rib.

The arrangement of stripes used for the Brother/Knitmaster slipover is a simple one – 4 rows of each colour in turn. This colour sequence can be changed by the knitter if so desired. I have started with a different colour in each garment. Notice that the hat welts match the slipover welts. Two points to bear in mind if changes are made:

1. Check the totals of your stripe sequence and adjust the total number of rows accordingly – a small difference in total length does not matter.
2. If you knit stripes deeper than 4 rows use a side weight at the left to prevent colour changing floats tightening at that side and so distorting the shape of the piece. All knitters without colour changers might like to knit very wide stripes in order to cut out some manual work. The Toyota garment uses the colours in turn, dividing the total length into wide bands of each colour.

Knitters who are already experienced in using colour changers may wish to knit an alternative slipover in the Double Jacquard pattern which will be used in Chapter 2. Instructions for converting the pattern in this chapter are given on page 30.

To Knit the Slipover

To fit chest sizes in centimentres	46	51	56	61	66	71	76	81	86	91	96	102	107	112	117	122
in inches	18	20	22	24	26	28	30	32	34	36	38	40	42	44	46	48

Fig. 1 *Garment block for slipover. The width of both pieces is shown below*

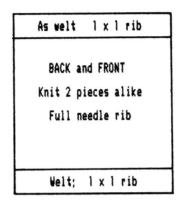

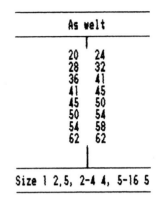

25·5 28 30,5 33
35,5 38 40,5 43
46   48 51   53,5
56   58,5 61   63,5

Back

Use colour 1 for all welts. Over width of main bed needles arrange needles of both beds for 1 × 1 welt. Cast on. Knit selvedge. RC 000. Tension 3/3.

Knit to RC

	71	79	85	93	99	107	113	121	127	135	141	149	155	163	169	177

Prepare for full needle rib.

All intermediate needles need stitches. Put them into working position and fill them with heels from opposite bed. This method avoids holes. Keep beds in full pitch while picking up heels. *Set to half pitch* before knitting. Set machine for circular knitting: MB Slip to left, RB Slip to right. Tension 5/5. Knit 2 rows. This is easier, particularly when using fine yarn, than going straight into full needle rib. Number of stitches given means stitches *on both beds throughout*, noting that there is one fewer on rib bed to comply with the end needle rule.

12	18	18	24	all other sizes

Number of stitches

Set both carriages to knit. RC 000.

	71	79	85	93	99	107	113	121	127	135	141	149	155	163	169	177

Brother/Knitmaster Knit 4 rows of each colour throughout starting with colour 2. Knit to RC

	76	92	108	124	140	156	156	172	172	188	188	204	204	220	236	236

Toyota Knit following rows in colours 1, 2, 3

	20	22	26	28	30	32	36	42	44	46	48	50	52	52	58	58

Knit in colour 4 to RC

	84	92	108	116	120	132	144	168	176	188	192	204	208	212	232	236

Neck ribbing

Rearrange stitches for rib as in welt. Transfer stitches not required across beds always in same direction. Change to colour 1. Tension 3/3. RC 000. Knit ribbing. Knit to RC   12   18   18   24   all other sizes
Tension 8/8. Knit 1 row. Cast off from bed to bed using latch tool.

Joining shoulders

Before knitting and attaching armbands join shoulder ribs for a suitable width. On smaller sizes join at least 1.5cm both sides, sewing on buttons and making button loops at one or both sides to avoid tightness in neckline.

Armbands

Over width of
main bed needles arrange needles of both beds for welt. Cast on using colour 1. Knit selvedge. RC 000. Tension 3/3.   51 61 79 89 95 95 101 101 107 107 113 117 117 129 129 135
Knit to RC
Pick up heels on both beds as before.   8   8 10 12 12 12 12 12 12 12 16 16 16 16 16 16
This time have the same number of stitches on both beds. Tension 6/6. Knit 3 rows on main bed with rib bed set to slip. Pull down loop of yarn between beds to avoid tight thread between 3rd row on main bed and 1st row on rib bed. Knit 3 rows on rib bed with main bed set to slip. Transfer all stitches to main bed. Tension 8. Knit 1 row.

Attaching main pieces

With wrong side facing, place loops of armhole edge evenly on needles, taking care to keep to straight line of stitches. Tension 10. Knit 1 row. Cast off with latch tool.

To make up

Finish off ends. Sew underarm seams. Seam ribs together at shoulders or make crochet loops and sew on buttons.

– 2 –
All-over Fair Isle Pattern Converted to Double Jacquard

– HAT AND SCARF TO KNIT –

The yarns used are the same as in Chapter 1: Sterling (65 per cent acrylic, 35 per cent wool) by Argyll: main colour 884 navy (1), contrast colour(s) one or more of 778 pink, 779 deep rose and 771 white. The tension swatch measurements are:

Fabric 1	28 stitches and 50 rows = 10cm	Tension 6/5
Fabric 2	28 stitches and 76 rows = 10cm	Tension 6/6
Fabric 3	28 stitches and 76 rows = 10cm	Tension 6/6
Fabric 4a	28 stitches and 38 rows = 10cm	Tension 5/6
Fabric 4b	28 stitches and 76 rows = 10cm	Tension 7/7
Stocking stitch	28 stitches and 36 rows = 10cm	Tension 7

The first task in this chapter is to learn about basic Double Jacquard fabric and how to make punch cards or electronic pattern charts which, when combined with the mechanism of the various machines, will achieve the desired result.

Converting a Single Bed Fair Isle Pattern for Double Jacquard

In this chapter the pattern requires the first type of Double Jacquard punch card. This is always used, with the following row sequence, when the single bed pattern changes from row to row.

Figure 2 on page 16 is the punch card for a simple Fair Isle design. For convenience, throughout the book, all numbers on the left are for Knitmaster machines, and those on the right are for Brother and Toyota machines. The starting line for Knitmaster machines is the lower one.

Toyota Machines

The single bed Fair Isle card should be punched out exactly as it is for use with Simulknit. Knitters who would like to work through all the methods changing colour manually should also punch out the converted card.

Converting the Pattern to a Double Jacquard Punch Card
This is quite easy. In the single bed card shown on the next page, the stitches which relate to the holes knit the pattern in contrast yarn and those which relate to the blanks are the background knitted in main yarn. One line of card is one design row.

For Double Jacquard the card must be rewritten so that only one colour knits in

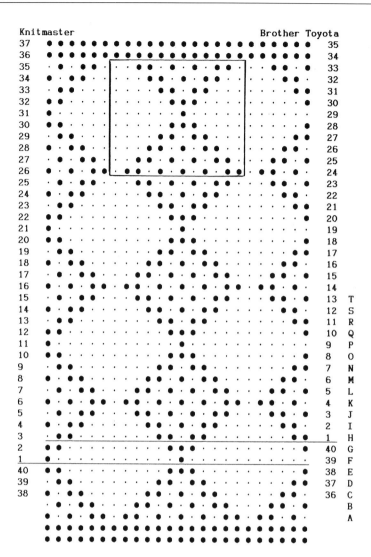

Fig. 2   *The punch card for the hat and scarf. Use this for Simulknit. Copy the section within lines for electronic machines.*

each line. Some lines will be knitting pattern and some background to pattern. Two lines of card, one pattern and one background, are needed to make one design row.

To make it easier to see what happens, two symbols have been used throughout the book to represent holes on punch cards. They are as follows:

● is used for all holes on single bed cards, for those which form pattern in Double Jacquard cards and for joining rows.

○ is used in Double Jacquard cards only for holes which form the background to a pattern row.

When you copy from a single bed Fair Isle card put a ruler across it so you can see at a glance which row you are copying. Take a new punch card and on the 2nd and 3rd rows above the 2 bottom joining rows mark in pencil the holes of rows A and B. This is what it should look like.

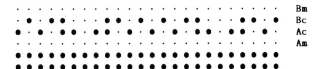

Next, miss 2 lines and mark holes for rows C and D on the next 2 lines. Continue like this, missing 2 lines and copying the next pair of rows until you have copied row T, which is the end of the 2nd pattern repeat.

Notice that a total of four pattern repeats is needed to make a long enough card for single bed Fair Isle. In the Double Jacquard card, because the colours are separated, a pattern repeat covers twice as many lines. Therefore, only two pattern repeats are needed for this particular Double Jacquard card.

What has been marked out so far represents stitches making up the pattern to be knitted by contrast yarn. The empty lines have to be marked to represent stitches which will be knitted by main yarn in order to complete each design row. That is why the 4 lines above have been shown as Am and Ac, Bc and Bm, 'm' being main yarn and 'c' being contrast yarn.

On line Am mark all spaces which are blank on line Ac. That completes the 1st design row. On line Bm mark those which are blank on line Bc, so completing the 2nd design row. If you have done this correctly, there will be a total of 24 marked spaces on each pair of lines. These marked spaces will be punched out, and, as all experienced knitters know, holes represent stitches which will knit when the punch card is in use and the machine set to slip. This is how you should have marked it.

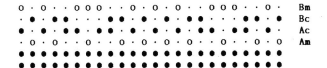

Fig. 4 *Converting a single bed Fair Isle card for Double Jacquard, step 2.*

Continue filling in empty lines. Check each pair of lines to make certain that each space is marked only once. The card finishes with a background line, Tm, after line Tc. When you are certain you have it right, punch out marked spaces and two joining rows top and bottom and cut off the spare card.

If you make a mistake and get a hole in the wrong place, first cover it on the wrong side with a small piece of sellotape. Next fill in the hole. I use typist's correcting fluid, but you can use a punched out piece of card, covering it with sellotape on both sides so that it does not become detached and end up in the works. Check your card with the one given on the next page before punching.

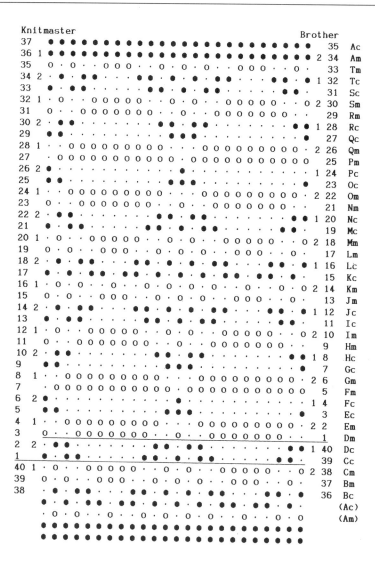

Fig. 5   *The Double Jacquard punch card for the hat and scarf.*

Patterns for Electronic Machines

The pattern repeat is the section outlined at the top of Figure 2, the single bed card: 10 rows by 12 stitches. By using this section as the repeat, the centre will be the same as on the punch card. When using a punch card or graph design for an electronic machine always use the minimum portion which works for your particular machine.

Electronic machines differ in the amount of pattern it is necessary to copy. Knitters should refer to their instruction books. Although all machines will knit patterns from whole charts, there are short cuts to chart copying, which, combined with the correct procedure, will achieve the same result.

The development of electronic machines has to date been mainly concerned with two aspects – first, the ability to programme larger and larger patterns; and second, the introduction of increased facilities for repeating patterns, up, down and across. There will undoubtedly be more developments in the future, but basic types of knitting remain the same and will be knitted on future machines as on those of today. The ease with which they are knitted depends on your having a thorough knowledge of the machine you are using.

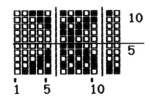

Fig. 6 *The chart for hat and scarf for electronic machines.*

Colour Changing

When the type of Double Jacquard pattern featured in this chapter is knitted on Knitmaster and Brother machines which are fitted with colour changers, the first pattern row is always knitted from right to left. This is because after that row the yarn is changed to contrast, and the colour changer is at the left. Even if you are changing colour manually with these machines, it is better to start this way, because the opening on the ribber arm makes it easier to change colour at the left.

Yarn changing on a Toyota, which at present has to be done manually, is easier if done at the right because of the way in which the ribber coupling is threaded.

Colour Change Numbers

In the Double Jacquard punch card diagram, Figure 5, you will no doubt have noticed the figures 1 and 2 alternating on both sides of the card. These are colour change numbers, 1 representing the main yarn and 2 the contrast. In the Brother Double Jacquard cards which are provided with the colour changer, numbers are printed against even-numbered lines on the left side. In the diagrams in this book numbers on the right are for Brother and Toyota, so leaving space at the left for all Knitmaster information.

On Knitmaster printed Double Jacquard cards the numbers for pairs of lines which will be knitted in main yarn are enclosed in rectangles on the right. Unmarked lines on those cards are knitted in contrast yarn. If you use Knitmaster's own make of blank punch card to make cards for the patterns in this book you will not need to mark in colours for this type of Double Jacquard pattern. If, however, you use any other make of card, you will need to put in the colour change numbers given at the left of the diagrams in this book.

All knitters using unmarked cards should enter the colour change numbers which have been given for their type of machine. If you do your own pattern conversions, you will need to understand how to do this for yourself. It is not difficult if you think about how pattern knitting begins. The card is locked on line 1 and programmed as the carriage is moved from left to right. The colour in the feeder is 1, main colour. As it is already threaded before line 1 is knitted, put 1 against the line below. The card is unlocked, and line 1 is knitted. Line 2 is indicated, and it is to be knitted in colour 2, the contrast colour, so put 2 against line 2. Lines 2 and 3 will be knitted in colour 2. Continue marking alternate lines to the top of the card, including the top joining lines. These will lap over the first two pattern lines at the bottom of the card. Do not put numbers on the bottom joining lines or on the first two pattern lines.

A practical point! Use a very fine, permanent felt-tipped pen to mark in the numbers, putting them at the left of your card. If you make a mistake, use a typist's correction pen.

On mylar sheets there is a column of windows down one side. These little squares should be marked to indicate colour changes. Start at the bottom of the window strip.

Knitting Double Jacquard Tension Swatches Using Different Types of Rib Bed Backing

Several types of rib bed backing can be used for Double Jacquard knitting. Sometimes this is automatic, sometimes it is necessary to adjust the rib carriage settings manually. Most of the backings are knit, or knit and slip in various combinations. I have developed one of the knit/slip settings, Fabric 5, especially for single motif work. At the correct tension it measures exactly the same as Fabric 3, which is available in patterned knitting only to those with Brother 850 or Knitmaster SRP 60N ribbers. It is particularly useful for all other Brother and Knitmaster ribbers.

Tuck and tuck/knit backings can also be used, and these are dealt with in Chapter 11.

The first knitting project in this chapter is to make tension swatches of the fabrics described in this chapter. The second project is to use either Fabric 1 or Fabric 4a to knit the hat and scarf featured in colour photographs 1 and 2. The main colour is the one which knits the solid diamonds. I have used navy in the outfits worn by the three older children, and a different contrast colour for each section of the hats. The contrast colour has been changed from time to time in the scarves. In one scarf, worn by the child sitting on the slide, the contrast yarn was navy, and the other three colours have been used as main yarn, changing from time to time. Experiment with the pattern and note the row numbers on the card so that you know how to change colour at the beginning of a spotted or solid diamond and at the end.

All tension swatches are started as follows:

1. Arrange needles for full needle rib.
   Fabrics 1 and 2 60 main bed needles, 59 rib bed. Tension swatch is said to be 'over the width of 60 main bed needles'. All counting of needles when in full needle rib setting refers to main bed needles only. Rib bed needles within the width are included but not counted.
   Fabric 3 – Brother 850 and Knitmaster SRP 60N ribbers with Jacquard carriage RJ1 61 main bed needles, 60 rib bed. This is necessary whenever Farbic 3 is knitted on Knitmaster SRP 60N ribbers.
   Fabric 4 – Toyota and Knitmaster SRP 60N 60 main bed needles. End needles on rib bed. This means having an extra needle in working position on the rib bed (61). Carriage right.

   N.B. All Brother machines – knit full needle rib selvedge with the slide lever on I except when using fine yarns, which need position II.

2. Tension 0/0. Use waste yarn. Knit 1 row. Insert comb. Set machine for circular rows. Knit 2 or 3 rows to finish carriage left. Programme punch card on last circular row.

   N.B. Do not use end needle selection for this pattern.

Now you are going to knit the various fabrics using 4 ply yarn. Use waste yarn at the beginning and end, knitting in full needle rib at a lower tension than the Double Jacquard. When tuck stitch backings are to be knitted, use the same tension as the Tuck Jacquard pattern.

When each sample is finished, transfer the rib bed stitiches to the main bed. Leave the ribber, comb and weights in position. Knit 1 row at tension 10. Push all needles to holding position. Remove the comb and weights. Cast off with latch tool. Label your samples, not forgetting to mark the tension.

A permanent method of marking tension is to knit about 6 rows of stocking stitch before the row at tension 10. On the 3rd or 4th row make holes to indicate tension. It is important that the holes are read from the right side of the fabric. In this, and in most Double Jacquard fabrics, the wrong side is facing, so start to the right of centre with the main bed number, and, if the rib bed number is different, put it to the left of centre. The following tension swatches are illustrated on the next page.

Fabric 1: Rib Bed Knitting Throughout Work

Carriage settings:	Main bed: slip/part/empty ← →
	Rib bed: knit ← →
Tension:	6/5
Fabric formation:	Main bed – Double Jacquard: 2 rows selected needles both colours = 2 rows pattern
	Rib bed: 2 rows both colours = 4 rows in 2 row stripes
Advantage:	Automatic setting
Disadvantage:	Unbalanced fabric: twice as many rows on rib bed causes main bed stitches to be elongated. This is partially overcome by lowering tension on rib bed to at least one whole number lower than main bed.
Machines:	All ribbers

Fabric 2: Rib Bed Set to Knit Alternate Rows

Carriage settings:	Main bed: slip/part/empty ← →
	Rib bed: knit → slip ←
Tension:	6/6
Fabric formation:	Main bed – Double Jacquard: as above
	Rib bed: 1 row both colours = 2 rows in single row stripes
Advantages:	Balanced fabric: equal rows on both beds
	Automatic setting
Disadvantage:	Long floats make it unsuitable for single motif work
Machines:	All ribbers

Fabric 3: Rib Bed Set for 1 × 1 Slip – Brother 850 and Knitmaster SRP 60N Fitted with Jacquard Ribber Carriage RJ1

Needle arrangement: Uneven number of needles on main bed, even number on rib bed: essential

Both end needles on main bed

Right end rib bed needle on unmarked space, therefore left on marked space

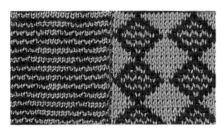

Carriage settings: Main bed: part ← →
                      Rib bed: part ← →
                                Slide lever   lιlι
                                KR change knobs lιlι
Tension: 6/6
Fabric formation: Main bed – Double Jacquard: 2 rows both colours = 2 rows
                      fabric
                      Rib bed – 1 × 1 slip: 2 rows both colours = 2 rows fabric
Advantage: Balanced fabric: equal rows on both beds
Machines: Brother fitted with 850 ribber and Knitmaster fitted with SRP
                      60N ribber with RJ1

If you are new to this stitch, do not start knitting until you have lowered the rib bed and moved the ribber carriage across on its own as suggested below. Then you can see how the needles work.

The diagram in the instruction manual shows the end needle at the right on an unmarked position on the needle tape, and the end one at the left on a marked position. It would work just as well if they were the other way round. The important thing is that each end is different. However, I suggest that, in this instance, you do as the manual says so that it becomes a habit.

Set the carriage as shown above. The 2nd needle from the carriage and alternate needles along the bed will now knit. On the 2nd row, the same thing will happen – knitting will start with the 2nd needle from the carriage. This means that, because an even number of needles is in use, all needles which did not knit in the 1st row will knit in the 2nd.

Notice that when you set the controls on the rib bed for this stitch, the marked needles knit when the carriage is moved left, and the unmarked needles knit when it is moved right. Keep this in mind – it becomes very important when increasing and decreasing.

Knit a sample of Fabric 3 in the same way as the other samples.

3.   *Fabric 1 folded to show reverse; this fabric was used for the Brother/Knitmaster hats and scarves.*

4.   *Fabric 2 folded to show reverse.*

5.   *Fabric 3 folded to show reverse; this fabric was used for the Brother/Knitmaster garments from Chapters 3 and 5.*

6.   *Fabric 4 folded to show reverse. This fabric was used for the Toyota garments from Chapters 5, 11 and 12 and would also be used by Toyota knitters for the garments from Chapters 4 and 6.*

Fabric 4: Plain-faced Jacquard

4a: Toyota Simulknit

Needle arrangement: Both end needles on rib bed
Carriage settings: Main bed: colour
                      Rib bed: E-T levers   plain
                                Simulknit levers S
                                Coupling lever   S
Main yarn in feeder 0, contrast yarn in feed S
Tension: 5/6
Fabric formation: Main bed – Double Jacquard
                      Rib bed – contrast yarn
Advantages: Balanced fabric: equal rows on both beds
                      1 carriage movement = 1 row of pattern so half the total
                      number of rows is required compared with Knitmaster machines

4b: Knitmaster SRP 60

Needle arrangement: Both end needles on rib bed

	A: Main colour backing	B: Contrast colour backing
Carriage settings:	Main bed: slip ← →	Main bed: slip ← →
	Rib bed: instal driving cam	Rib bed: instal driving cam
	Set auto-set lever to 1 before first pattern row ←	Set auto-set lever to 0 before first pattern row ←

Tension: 6/6

Fabric formation: Main bed – A and B: Double Jacquard: 2 rows selected needles both colours = 2 rows fabric

Rib bed – A or B: 2 rows knit, 2 rows slip = 2 rows fabric

Advantages: Balanced fabric: equal rows on both beds

Either colour can be used as backing

4b: Brother, other Knitmaster ribbers, Toyota ribbers without Simulknit

Needle arrangement: Both end needles on main bed

	A: Main colour backing	B: Contrast colour backing
Carriage settings:	Main bed: part/slip/empty ← →	Main bed: part/slip/empty ← →
	Rib bed: rows 1 and 4 knit rows 2 and 3 slip	Rib bed: rows 1 and 4 slip rows 2 and 3 knit

Tension: 6/6

Fabric formation: Main bed – Double Jacquard: 2 rows selected needles both colours = 2 rows fabric

Rib bed – A and B: 2 rows knit 2 rows slip = 2 rows fabric

Advantages: Balanced fabric: equal rows on both beds

Either colour can be used as backing

Machines: All ribbers

7. *Fabric 5 folded to show reverse. This is the alternative to Fabric 3 for the Brother/Knitmaster garments from Chapter 5. Instructions are on page 68.*

8. *The small border pattern from Chapter 4. The punch cards can be found on page 58.*

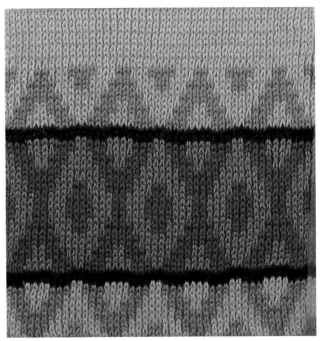

Fabric 5

This fabric has been developed for single motif work for Brother machines without an 850 ribber and for Knitmaster machines without an SRP 60N ribber with RJ1. Full details are given in Chapter 5, page 68.

A pattern repeat for Brother/Knitmaster machines is 20 rows. It is necessary to knit 2 extra rows in order to complete a diamond. This means that the number of rows must be divisible by 20 + 2, so the knitting finishes with 1 row of contrast yarn. For Toyota machines the repeat is 10 rows, so the total length must be divisible by 10 + 1 to complete a diamond.

Comparing Fabrics

Measurements

Fabric 1	28 stitches and 50 rows = 10cm	Tension 6/5
Fabric 2	28 stitches and 76 rows = 10cm	Tension 6/6
Fabric 3	28 stitches and 76 rows = 10cm	Tension 6/6
Fabric 4a	28 stitches and 38 rows = 10cm	Tension 5/6
Fabric 4b	28 stitches and 76 rows = 10cm	Tension 7/7
Stocking stitch	28 stitches and 36 rows = 10cm	Tension 7

Appearance and Texture

Fabric 1 This is looser than the other fabrics, and it has rather large, slightly distorted stitches on the right side. Notice that the diamonds are 'stretched' compared with the other fabrics. Check to see whether the main yarn shows through behind the contrast diamonds. Much will depend on the colour combination.

Fabric 2 This is a much firmer fabric. Floats of main yarn behind the solid diamonds do not show through in this sample, although this could be a problem with some colour combinations. This fabric looks better than Fabric 1 because there are the same number of rows back and front.

Fabric 3 This, too, is a firmer fabric, very evenly knitted. Despite the firmness, however, it still has quite a lot of elasticity. Another similar sample, knitted at tension 5/5, is firmer still, and would be very suitable for outdoor garments such as jackets and coats. Its measurements are 32 stitches and 86 rows = 10cm.

Fabrics 4a and 4b These are very smooth fabrics, with a good texture.

Yarns for Jacquard

A very warm fabric, ideal for some outdoor garments and for warm pullovers, is produced by 4 ply yarn. There is a method of reducing the backing to make a lighter weight fabric, and this is explained in Chapter 9 when multicoloured Double Jacquard is discussed. The method can also be applied to two-colour fabrics. The Scottie dog sweater shown in Chapter 6 was made lighter by using brushed acrylic yarn for the dogs on a pure wool background. Also suitable are 3 ply and 2 ply yarns, and so are industrial yarns, used one- or two-stranded. The table below shows the comparative stitch and row requirements for 10cm knitted in the same pattern in all the fabrics. Remember that these measurements will vary slightly with different makes and colours of yarn. They are meant as a guide only, and *not to save you knitting tension swatches*.

Deciding what tensions to use can be a problem, especially on the ribber, because you cannot see what the fabric is like as you knit. Try knitting a 'feeler strip'. Cast on over about 40 main bed stitches. Start with the tension you think is most likely to be right and knit 24 rows. Using your transfer carriage, put all the stitches on the main bed. Knit a few rows of stocking stitch, recording the tension. Let the bed down and have a look. If the fabric feels right, stop there and knit a tension swatch. If it is boardlike, the tensions need to be higher, if it is raggy, they need to be lower. Commonsense and experience will tell you by how much to change the tension. Often one dot is enough. With your rib carriage on tension 0, knit 1 row to come back to full needle rib setting. Change the tension and try again. Repeat until you are satisfied that you have it right.

Yarn	Fabric 1 Tension	Sts	Rs	Fabric 2 Tension	Sts	Rs	Fabric 3 Tension	Sts	Rs	Fabric 4a Tension	Sts	Rs	Fabric 4b Tension	Sts	Rs
4 ply	6/5	28	50	6/6	28	76	6·/6·	28	76	5/6	28	38	7/7	28	76
3 ply	4··/4··	30	66	4··/4··	30	86	5/5	30	86	3/4	30	42	6/6	30	84
2 × 2/30	3/2	32	70	3/3	32	92	3·/3·	32	92	2/3	32	46	5/5	32	92

You may like to try an experiment I have just completed. I knitted a number of tension swatches in a variety of Double Jacquard patterns using the same kind of yarns. I worked to the tensions given and knitted each pattern in the various fabrics. All the measurements were almost the same as in the above table. This means that any Double Jacquard design can be substituted in a garment pattern written for Double Jacquard, provided the same yarn is used. This is an important fact to remember.

Both increasing and decreasing are needed from time to time. The following instructions will help you. Knit practice samples.

Increasing

Fabrics 1, 2 and 4 – All Ribbers
At the carriage end bring 1 needle on both beds to upper working position to ensure that both knit in the next row. See Figure 7 on the next page.

Fabric 3 – Brother 850, Knitmaster SRP 60N with RJ1
When the first increase or decrease has been made there will no longer be an even number of stitches on the bed. This means that the end needles will no longer fit in with the former pattern of marked and unmarked stitches. Adjustments must be made to keep the stitch formation correct. The diagrams and pictures on the next page show how to proceed. Notice that main bed needles are pushed to upper working position and that rib bed ones are pushed only to working position.

On no account push increased rib bed needles to upper working position or to holding position – only to working position. You will see why in the next chapter.

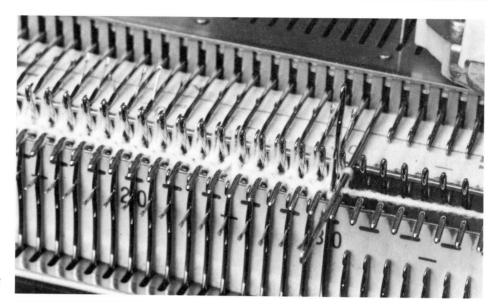

Fig. 7 *Increasing one stitch on both beds at carriage end. Fabric 1, 2 and 4.*

Figs 8 and 9 *Before increasing; the right end of the work is shown. Fabric 3.*

Fig. 10 *1st increase – 1 stitch is increased on main bed, nothing on the rib bed; the extra stitch is marked *.*

Fig. 11 *One main bed needle is pushed out to the upper working or holding position depending on the circumstances; the row is then knitted.*

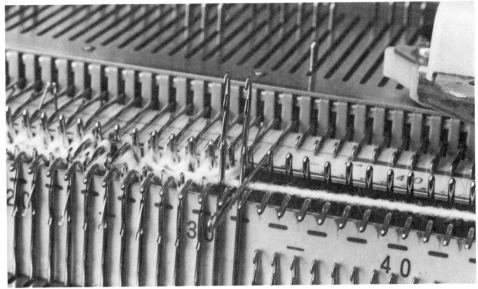

```
      ✻
MB ,,,,,,,,,,,| | | | | | | | | |
RB ,,,,,,,,,,| ⊥ | ⊥ | ⊥ | ⊥ | ⊥ |
                              ✻ ✻
```

Fig. 12 *2nd increase – 1 stitch is increased on the main bed, 2 stitches on the rib bed. Extra stitches marked *.*

Fig. 13 *One main bed needle and two rib bed needles are pushed to the upper working position. When the row is knitted the rib bed needles will knit the first 2 stitches, and then the correct sequence – i.e., slip, knit – from right to left across the row.*

Decreasing

Fabrics 1, 2 and 4 – All Ribbers
Transfer 1 stitch on both beds to the next working needle, bringing the needles with 2 stitches to upper working position so that they knit in the next row.

Fabric 3 – Brother 850 Knitmaster SRP 60N with RJ1
When decreasing at the right end, the rib bed needle must always be an unmarked one. Remember to leave the end needle in working position. *Do not push it up.*

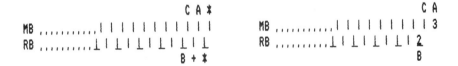

```
                    C A ✻
MB ,,,,,,,,,,,| | | | | | | | | |
RB ,,,,,,,,,,| ⊥ | ⊥ | ⊥ | ⊥ | ⊥ |
                    B + ✻
```

```
                    C A
MB ,,,,,,,,,,,| | | | | | | | | 3
RB ,,,,,,,,,,| ⊥ | ⊥ | ⊥ | ⊥ | 2
                            B
```

Fig. 14 FAR LEFT
1st decrease – 1 stitch is decreased on the main bed, 2 stitches on the rib bed; the stitches marked * are transferred to A, the stitch marked + is transferred to B.

Fig. 15 LEFT
Numerals 3 and 2 indicate the number of stitches on needles A and B respectively after this decrease and before knitting the next row.

Fig. 16 *Hang the side weight and push out the end main bed needle to make sure it knits.*

```
                                    C
MB ,,,,,,,,,,,| | | | | | | | 2
RB ,,,,,,,,,,⊥ | ⊥ | ⊥ | ⊥ | ⊥
```

Figs 17 and 18   *2nd decrease – 1 stitch is decreased on the main bed only by moving the end stitch in one place to needle C where there are now 2 stitches.*

3 pieces measure 39 43 45 47 48 when joined together

Fig. 19   *Block for section of hat.*

Fig. 20   *The correct way of inserting the comb in order to hang loops on the main bed needles. * To release the rib bed loops, run the rib bed carriage across on its own, then push the rib bed needles to non-working position.* In the photograph a few rib bed loops have been released manually.*

To Knit the Hat

The hat is knitted in three pieces, each using navy as the main yarn and a different contrast yarn. The pattern is given for Fabrics 1 and 4a. The ribbed band for Fabric 1 is added afterwards. With Fabric 4a the band is the reverse side of Simulknit and is included in the length. Note that a starting row is given so that there is a complete diamond at the top.

To fit head: circumference in centimetres	41.5	48	54.5
in inches	16.5	19	21.5

Piece 1

Fabric 1

Bring needles of both beds to working position over following number of main bed needles   39   45   51
Position needles so that odd needle is at right to make the pattern symmetrical. Tension 0/0
With waste yarn knit zigzag row.
Hang weights. Set rib bed to slip. Tension as sample throughout.
Knit several rows in waste yarn, 1 row with nylon cord, 2 rows with main yarn. Carriage left. Pick up heels from main bed stitches

Fig. 21 *The incorrect way of inserting a comb. Try working from * to * as for Figure 20 and see what happens.*

and place on rib bed needles. Knit 2 circular rows, rib bed then main bed. During 2nd row programme pattern at row

1	9	1

Set carriages for Double Jacquard. Use navy and contrast 1. Knit straight to RC

| 62 | 74 | 82 |

Decrease 1 stitch on both beds at both ends: next row and every following 4th row ×

| 9 | 10 | 12 |

Knit 2 rows. Decrease in same way: next row and every alternate row ×

| 9 | 10 | 11 |

Fabric 4a

Arrange needles of both beds for Simulknit. Main bed needles as Fabric 1. End needles on rib bed. Main yarn. Cast on. Finish selvedge with carriage left. Tension 5/6. Knit 8 circular rows. Tension 4/4. Knit 1 row full needle rib, programming pattern at row

| 6 | 6 | 1 |

Set for Simulknit. Contrast 1 in feeder S. Knit straight to RC

| 65 | 75 | 81 |

Decrease 1 stitch on both beds at both ends: next row and every alternate row ×

| 9 | 10 | 12 |

Knit 1 row. Decrease in same way: next row and every following row ×

| 9 | 10 | 11 |

Both fabrics

Stitches remaining

| 3 | 5 | 5 |

Thread stitches on to a length of double yarn.

Pieces 2 and 3

Knit as before using the other two contrast yarns.

Ribbed welt

Brother/Knitmaster machines Before knitting welt join two seams with 2 rows double crochet using main yarn. Pick up loops of 1st row of main yarn stitches. Remove waste yarn. Arrange stitches for 1 × 1 rib. Insert comb and hang weights. Use same colour as welt of slipover in Chapter 1.

Tension 3/3. Knit in rib to RC   24   28   32
If a double welt is required, knit more rows. Tension 10/8. Knit 1
row. Cast off with latch tool.

To make up

Fabric 1
Join 3rd seam and welt.

Fabric 4a
Join all seams as for Fabric 1, reversing joining side on brim.

Both fabrics
Thread all remaining stitches on to one double length of yarn. Pull up tightly and
secure on wrong side. Make a bobble to match welt (Fabric 4a – tubular edge). Sew
on.

To Knit the Scarf

Knit over width of 61 main bed needles in same stitch pattern to desired length,
knitting to the end of a pattern.

Fabric 1
1 metre = 502 rows; 1.25 metres = 625 rows; 1.5 metres = 750 rows

Fabric 4a
1 metre = 381 rows; 1.25 metres = 477 rows; 1.5 metres = 571 rows

Rearranging the Colours

The colour arrangement can be varied as follows:

   Centre diamonds spotted: centre needle is no. 1 right of 0
   Centre diamonds plain: centre needle is no. 6 left of 0
   Solid diamonds in navy: navy yarn in Feeder A; 1; 0
   Solid diamonds in any other colour: navy yarn in Feeder B; 2; S

Feeders: Brother – A and B; Knitmaster – 1 and 2; Toyota – 0 and 5.

An Extra Garment to Knit

The slipover pattern from Chapter 1 can very easily be used to knit a Double Jacquard
top to match the hat and scarf just completed. The stitches are the same. The
approximate row calculation is as follows:

Fabric 1	1⅓ times given length
Fabrics 2, 3 and 4b	Twice given length
Fabric 4a	Given length

Add enough rows to complete a diamond and so end the pattern correctly.

– 3 –

Plain Fabrics to Match the Texture of Double Jacquard Patterned Fabrics

– JACKET AND SKIRT TO KNIT –

The yarn for the jacket is: 2 ply (2/16) Botany wool from Many-a-Mickle, and the colour is Aran. The tension swatch measurements are:

32 stitches and 96 rows (Toyota 48 rows) = 10cm   Tension 4/4
Stocking stitch   28 stitches and 40 rows = 10cm   Tension 7

There may well be times when you want to knit a plain garment with a Double Jacquard pattern on one part of it – a border, perhaps, or a yoke – or you may wish to have a vertical stripe of pattern or a motif. In all these cases the fabric surrounding the patterned area needs to be of the same type and texture as the fabric of the pattern itself.

In this chapter the first task is to knit fabrics to match in weight and texture the patterned fabrics knitted in Chapter 2. One of them, Fabric 3, which can be knitted by all types of machine, will then be used for knitting the jacket shown in colour photograph 9. A pattern is also given for a matching skirt. In the following three chapters plain and patterned Double Jacquard fabrics will be combined.

The fabrics described in Chapter 2 were:

Fabric number	Main bed design rows	Carriage movements	Rib bed actions				Rib bed backing rows
			1	2	3	4	
1	2	4	Knit	Knit	Knit	Knit	4
2	2	4	Slip	Knit	Slip	Knit	2
3	2	4	Knit/slip alternate stitches				2
4a	2	2	Knit	Knit			2
4b	2	4	Knit	Slip	Slip	Knit	2

The chart is a reminder that these fabrics can be divided into two groups: Fabric 1 in which there are 4 backing rows on the rib bed to 2 main bed rows, and Fabrics 2, 3, 4a and 4b in which the backing and main bed are balanced. This means that you need to know how to knit two types of plain Jacquard in order to match each group.

Punch Card Machines: Making the Punch Card

In the patterned punch card, lines 2 and 3 were pattern rows, and lines 1 and 4 filled in the background.

In plain fabric the 'pattern' is all knitted in one colour, so it is knitted on every main bed needle in main yarn in lines 2 and 3. Because every stitch is going to knit there is no 'filling in' to do in lines 1 and 4. They remain blank.

Fig. 22   *Making a Double Jacquard punch card with the knitting sequence for Fabric 1.*

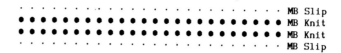

Remember! When the carriage is set to slip, part or empty, holes will knit and blanks will slip.

Plain Double Jacquard to Match the Fabrics from Chapter 2

Fabric 1

Use a plain Double Jacquard punch card with the main bed set to slip and the rib bed set to knit. The plain fabric will match the patterned sample in both weight and texture because there will be 2 main bed rows to 4 rib bed rows.

Fabric 2

This sample was knitted with the setting altered so that the rib bed slipped to the left and knitted to the right.

Fig. 23   *A punch card with the knitting sequence for Fabric 2.*

Notice that in the 1st row neither bed knits. This means that there will be a long float right across the row. Knitting back to the right can prove difficult as there is a tendency for the yarn to catch and for stitches at the left to drop off. The 1st row float ought to be held down by the stitches of the next row, but sometimes it lifts above some of the needles. To make it easier to start knitting the 2nd row, push the rib bed needle at the opposite end to the carriage to upper working position or to holding position before knitting the 1st row. That stitch will then knit and hold the yarn in place. This fabric will match the second pattern sample.

Observe the row sequence carefully. There must be one row in which both beds knit or the fabric will be circular knitting. That is why, in this setting, there is also one row in which both beds slip. Use side weights. This is a possible piece of knitting, but not greatly to be recommended.

An alternative, when patterned and plain areas occur in the same garment, is to continue knitting the pattern punch card using the main yarn only. The textures then match exactly. Why not try it?

Fabric 3

Brother 850 and Knitmaster SRP 60N with RJ1
This fabric was backed by 1 × 1 slip setting. To use that setting for plain fabric use the plain Double Jacquard punch card for the main bed, setting the carriages as you would for patterned Double Jacquard. That is:

MB Both Part buttons/Slip levers
RB Both Part buttons/Slip levers; set for 1 × 1 selection

Other Machines
In all other machines this fabric is knitted with the beds reversed – 1 × 1 slip on the main bed and the plain Double Jacquard sequence on the rib bed.

Toyota Use two matching cones of yarn, threading one into each feed. Use the basic punch card 1, Figure 24, and machine set for Simulknit. The yarn in S feed will knit main bed needles represented by holes and all rib bed needles. The yarn in O feed will knit main bed needles represented by blanks. The resulting fabric is exactly the same as Fabric 3 knitted by Brother 850, but it is knitted using half the number of rows.

Knitmaster SRP 60 using Auto Drive Use the main yarn only. Start at the right using card 1 and main bed set to slip. Set the Auto Drive so that the rib bed knits with only one yarn, slipping the 1st and 4th rows.

```
● · ● · ● · ● · ● · ● · ● · ● · ● · ● · ● ·  MB Knit ● Slip ·  RB Slip
· ● · ● · ● · ● · ● · ● · ● · ● · ● · ● · ●  MB Slip · Knit ●  RB Knit
● · ● · ● · ● · ● · ● · ● · ● · ● · ● · ● ·  MB Knit ● Slip ·  RB Knit
· ● · ● · ● · ● · ● · ● · ● · ● · ● · ● · ●  MB Slip · Knit ●  RB Slip
```

Fig. 24 *Card 1 and row sequence for Auto Drive.*

Other Brother and Knitmaster Ribbers Use basic card 1 and set the main bed to slip. Change the setting of the rib bed manually after the 1st and 3rd rows as shown in the knitting sequence for SRP 60.

This is very useful fabric for plain or striped garments. It is the one used for the jacket in this chapter. Note that in the last three examples the fabric faces the opposite way to that of Brother 850 ribber. This will be important if you knit the skirt.

Fabrics 4a and 4b

Plain Fabric 3 can be used very satisfactorily. So, too can the method given opposite as an alternative for a match to Fabric 2 – that is, continue using the pattern punch card knitting in main yarn only.

MB Both Part buttons/Slip levers
RB Both Part buttons/Slip levers; set for 1 × 1 selection

Knitting Plain Double Jacquard with Electronic Machines

Brother Machines

Method 1 Place carriage outside the set mark. Set KC II. Push switch 7 to up position. Select any marked square on the mylar sheet. Enter its position in the memory. Programme while knitting the next row. Press in both Part buttons and proceed.

Think about this! Using switch 7 reverses the marked square to unmarked for row 1, uses it in its original state – that is, marked – for rows 2 and 3, and reverses it again for row 4. This gives the knitting sequence slip, knit, knit, slip.

Method 2 Proceed as above except that switches 6 and 7 are both pushed to the up position. Select any unmarked square and enter it. This time switch 6 acts throughout the knitting to reverse the unmarked square you entered, making it behave like a marked square. Switch 7 then deals with it in the same way as in the first method.

Knitmaster Machines

If you have been knitting in pattern, switch the machine off, then on again. Be certain you understand how to lock on to one line. This is in the instruction manual. You need to push the inspection button three times. Point cams must be in position to enclose all the knitting. N1 cam is not needed. There are three methods.

Method 1: Using a Blank Line The chosen line should be at least 12 lines above any marked square. Switch on. Lights for buttons 1 and 2 come on and the machine bleeps once. Switch on button 6. Enter the chosen line. Push the inspection button three times. Release the rib carriage. With the main carriage in slip, move it across the bed at least twice until the left light of button 1 is on. The machine will now slip rows 1 and 4 and knit rows 2 and 3.

Method 2: Using a Printed Line This time slip the carriage across until the right light of button 1 is on. The knitting sequence is the same as in Method 1.

Method 3: No Mylar Sheet Follow the steps for Method 1 without using the inspection button. The result will be exactly the same.

Knitting Tension Swatches in Plain Double Jacquard Fabric

Use the same yarn for these samples as in Chapter 2 so that measurements can be compared. Casting on and tensions are as before. Knit each sample, label it and attach it to the matching patterned sample.

Measurements of Samples Using 4 Ply Yarn

Sample 1	28 stitches and 50 rows = 10cm
Sample 2, 3 and 4b	28 stitches and 76 rows = 10cm
Sample 4a	28 stitches and 38 rows = 10cm

This is exactly what one would expect. Measurements are identical with the patterned

9. *A plain Double Jacquard jacket.*

Double Jacquard fabrics knitted similarly (page 25). This means that all garment patterns knitted in Double Jacquard fabric can easily be adapted to plain or striped fabric or to any other Double Jacquard design.

Tension Swatch for Jacket

The jacket in colour photograph 9 is designed to wear either over a summer dress or to team with a skirt to make a two-piece outfit. Patterns are given for both garments.

Knit the jacket tension swatch according to instructions for Fabric 3, using tension 4/4. After knitting the final 12 rows in waste yarn, change to main yarn again in order to practise buttonholes.

Wide Buttonholes in Double Jacquard

Continue on the tension swatch, knitting 16 rows in main yarn. Make 3 buttonholes, 6 stitches wide across the row.

Fig. 25 *Transfer for right-handed knitters.*

Fig. 26 *Transfer for left-handed knitters.*

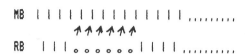

Fig. 27 *Select groups of 6 stitches on main bed. Transfer the same number of rib bed stitches to those needles. It is important to transfer rib bed stitches as shown above.*

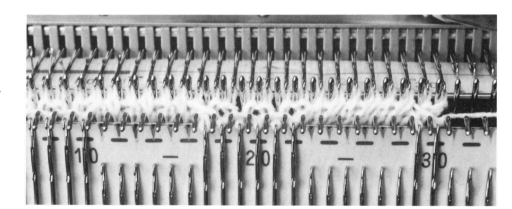

Fig. 28 *Starting at the left of group and using a spare length of yarn, cast off 6 pairs of stitches, putting the last loop on the main bed needle to right of group. Repeat for remaining groups. Remove cast-off edges from gate pegs. Directions are given for transfer in Figure 25. Knitters using Figure 26 reverse right and left.*

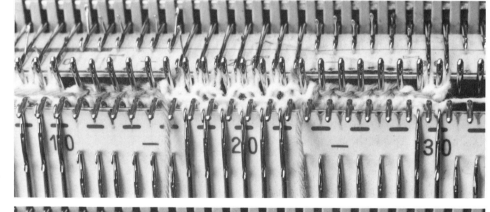

Fig. 29 *Using the same yarn, cast on again over 12 needles by winding in figure-of-eight fashion in the order shown in photograph.*

Fig. 30 *Drop the end of the yarn down between beds and anchor it firmly. Place a wire weight hanger across each cast-on edge. Hang small weights. Keep the weights in position as long as necessary when knitting buttonholes in the jacket.*

Fig. 31 *The finished buttonhole with just two ends to darn in.*

Continue on the tension swatch, knitting 16 (Toyota 8) rows after completing the buttonholes, then cast off as follows and keep the sample. Transfer all stitches to the main bed. Knit 1 row at tension 10. Cast off. Buttonholes, which can be knitted in other widths if required, will be finished off using the ends of yarn left from making them. This is better left until after washing and blocking. When breaking off yarn on garment pieces, leave enough for seaming. This will then be washed, too, which is important to allow for shrinkage.

For Brother 850 Knitters Only: Special Method of Shaping

Before we go on to knit the garment, I have an experiment for you. I must honestly tell you that I found it out quite by accident!

You will remember that in the section on increasing (page 25) you were told that on no account should you push up an end rib bed needle to upper working or holding position. Many knitters do this automatically, particularly if the needles have to be encouraged to knit because they hold a group of stitches. I did, and made a discovery which you will not find in your manual. It is a very useful discovery indeed, as you will find out if you have a go without any knitting on your machine so that you see what happens to the needles.

Lower the rib bed and use the rib carriage only. Set the carriage for 1 × 1 slip. Raise an even number of needles to working position, the end one on the right being on a marked space on the number tape. Push the carriage to the left. Watch what happens to the needles. The second and following alternate ones from the carriage end move up further than the rest. They are in unmarked tape positions. They move up to knitting position. Those in marked positions do not move up at all. They remain in slip position. Move the carriage back to the right. Again the second and following alternate needles from the carriage end move up to the knitting position, but this time they are in the marked tape position. This means that, had we been knitting, in 2 rows all needles would have knitted once, exactly as you would expect.

Now push up the end needle at the right to holding position. Move the carriage across slowly. Which needles knitted? If you are not sure, bring the carriage back and watch again. Repeat from left to right, pushing up the left end needle to holding position. Do you see now?

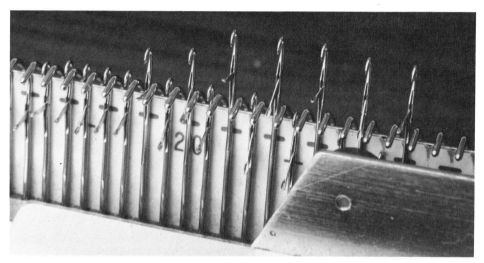

Fig. 32 *The first and alternate needles are raised to knitting position when the first needle only is pushed to holding position before knitting. The carriage on the empty lowered rib bed shows the needle positions clearly. The ones raised higher will knit. Compare this with Figure 13 on page 27.*

That is an interesting discovery! The normal working of the rib carriage can be altered simply by pushing the end needle to holding position. Now try out the effect of this on shaping. Decreasing first.

1. Arrange some needles for full needle rib. Select an even number on the rib bed, with the right-hand end one on a marked space. Cast on as for the tension swatch. Knit 20 rows, ending with the carriage at the right. Decrease 1 stitch at both ends every 10 rows. The number chosen is not divisible by 4, so decreasings will not always come on the same row of pattern repeat. Start decreasing before knitting the next row.

2. Decrease 1 stitch on both beds at both ends. The right-hand end rib bed needle is now on an unmarked position. To keep the rib bed sequence correct, it is unmarked needles – 1st, 3rd, 5th and so on – which need to be knitted as the carriage moves from right to left. To make this happen, the right-hand end needle must be pushed to holding position before knitting. Push up the needle and knit across.

3. The following row is left to right. The end needle is a marked one, and it is those which must knit. Push it to holding position and knit the row. If you examine the stitches carefully you will see that, in the last 2 rows, all rib bed needles have

knitted once. They have also knitted correctly according to direction of carriage, so the sequence of knitting has been maintained, despite having the 'wrong' needles at the ends.

4. Until the next decrease is made there is an unmarked end needle at the right and a marked one at the left. This means that for the next 8 rows the first needle at the carriage end must be pushed to holding position before each row is knitted. That ensures that the same order of knitting is kept throughout, with unmarked needles knitting from right to left, and marked ones from left to right. Knit those 8 rows. Remember! Push up first needle before knitting each row.

5. Decrease at the beginning of the next 2 rows. The needle positions are back to normal, so for 8 rows there is no need to push up the end needles. Carry on like this for 40 rows so that you get the feel of it.

Now put the row counter to 000 and try increasing. This will be done at the carriage end each time. It needs more thought than decreasing because the end rib bed needles are set to slip and so will not pick up a loop. Furthermore, on 2 rows of the pattern sequence the main bed will also slip. It is not difficult to make the main bed collect a loop, just push the end needle to holding position. However, as you now know, if you do that every time on the rib bed you will put the 1 × 1 backing wrong. You can increase in that way only when you need to change the order of knitting, which will be on alternate increasings.

Now what can be done? Both the decreasing and increasing on the jacket were done by 1 stitch on both beds every time because it makes a much smoother line than any other method. The photographs below and the next page show how I worked out the increasing. Notice that the first increase comes halfway through the pattern sequence of 4 rows, and the second increase after completing a sequence.

Fig. 33   *RC 10 – 1st increase at right. The main bed increase needle is pushed into line with the rest so that it will knit. The rib bed increase needle is pushed to holding position to change the order of rib bed knitting, so maintaining correct slip/knit formation.*

Fig. 34   *RC 11 – 1st increase at left. The main bed needles are set to slip on the next row, so the increase needle is pushed to upper working position so that it knits. The rib bed needle is pushed up as in previous row.*

Continue to push up the end rib bed needles until the next increase. Knit to RC 20. Rib bed first this time. An extra needle pushed to working position will slip, and this will give the correct sequence for this section, so the row must be knitted with the needle in that position. However, that will not give an extra stitch. If you push it to holding position you will alter the knitting sequence, and this would be wrong. The following photographs show how to increase and still have correct order of knitting.

Fig. 35   *RC 20 – 2nd increase at right. The yarn is hooked into the rib bed increase needle before the next row, leaving it in working position so that it slips. The main bed increase needle is pushed to holding position.*

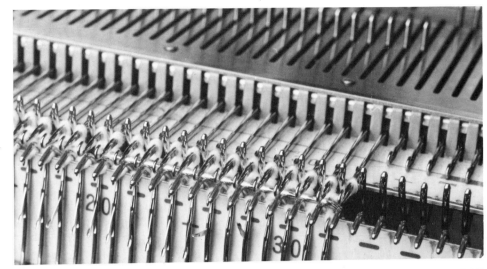

Fig. 36 *RC 21 – both increase needles at right have collected loops. Remove the loops and twist in a figure-of-eight. Hang side weights.*

Fig. 37 *RC 21 – 2nd increase at left. The end rib bed needle is dealt with as in previous row. Main bed needles have been selected to upper working position ready to knit the next row. The main bed increase needle is also pushed to upper working position.*

When increasing, remember to use the side weights, moving them up each time after the second increase.

This method of shaping was used for the armholes and sleeve heads in the jacket in this chapter. Interesting, isn't it how the rules can be bent!

To Knit the Jacket

To fit bust sizes in centimetres	66	71	76	81	86	91	96	102	107	112	117	122
in inches	26	28	30	32	34	36	38	40	42	44	46	48

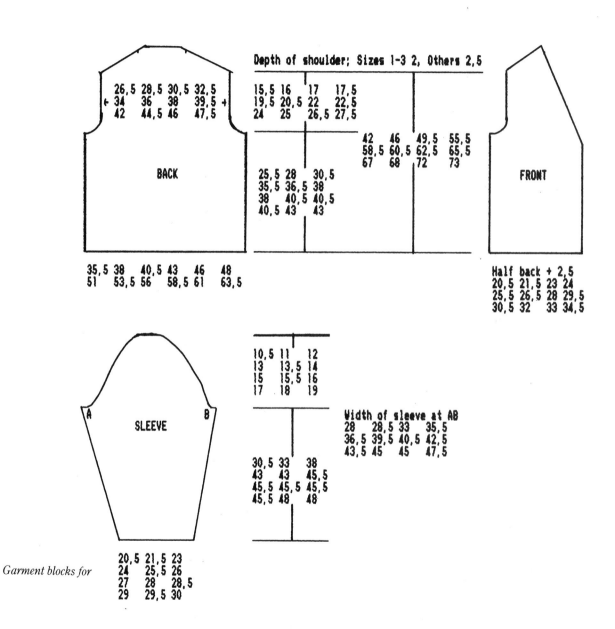

Fig. 38 *Garment blocks for jacket.*

Back

Over width of main bed needles arrange needles of both beds for full needle rib. Number of main bed needles Cast on, knit selvedge using same tensions as in swatch. Set machine for Double Jacquard using chosen method.

Number of main bed needles	113	121	129	137	145	153	161	169	177	185	193	199
Brother/Knitmaster Knit to RC	244	268	292	334	352	364	364	388	388	388	412	412
Toyota Knit to RC	122	134	146	168	176	182	182	194	194	194	206	206

Armhole shaping

RC 000. At beginning of next 2 rows cast off following stitches

5	5	5	5	5	5	5	5	6	6	6	6

Brother/Knitmaster only Knit 2 more rows
N.B. Follow decreasing instructions on pages 27 and 28.
Size 1: at beginning of next 2 rows cast off following stitches. **Brother/Knitmaster only** Knit 2 more rows

3	—	—	—	—	—	—	—	—	—	—	—

Sizes 2–12: *at beginning of next 2 rows cast off following stitches. **Brother/Knitmaster only** Knit 2 more rows.*
Repeat from * to * once more.

—	2	2	2	3	3	3	3	3	3	3	3

Brother/Knitmaster RC

8	12	12	12	12	12	12	12	12	12	12	12

Toyota RC

4	6	6	6	6	6	6	6	6	6	6	6

All sizes: at both ends of next row and every following 4th row (Brother/Knitmaster), 2nd row (Toyota), decrease 1 stitch the following number of times in all

6	6	7	8	7	7	9	10	10	11	12	13

Stitches decreased on each armhole

14	15	16	17	18	18	20	21	22	23	24	25

Stitches remaining

85	91	97	103	109	117	121	127	133	139	145	149

Brother/Knitmaster Knit to RC

148	160	164	168	188	196	212	220	232	240	256	264

Toyota Knit to RC

74	80	82	84	94	98	106	110	116	120	128	132

Shoulder shaping

At beginning of next 2 rows cast off 3 stitches the following number of times

8	6	5	7	6	7	10	8	10	7	6	5

Brother/Knitmaster Knit 2 more rows after each cast off. At beginning of next 2 rows cast off 4 stitches the following number of times

—	2	3	2	3	3	1	3	2	5	6	7

Stitches cast off for each shoulder

24	26	27	29	30	33	34	36	38	41	42	43

Stitches remaining for back neck. Cast off.

37	39	43	45	49	51	53	55	57	57	61	63

Brother/Knitmaster RC

180	192	196	204	224	236	256	264	276	288	304	312

Toyota RC

90	96	98	102	112	128	128	132	138	144	152	156

Left front

Pocket linings

Knit 2 over width of following main bed needles

25	25	25	29	29	33	33	37	37	37	41	41

Brother/Knitmaster Knit to RC

76	76	76	88	88	100	100	112	112	112	124	124

Toyota Knit to RC

38	38	38	44	44	50	50	56	56	56	62	62

Release on 6 rows waste knitted separately on both beds.

Main piece

Over width of following main bed needles cast on as for back

65	69	73	79	83	87	95	99	103	107	111	115

Brother/Knitmaster Knit to RC

76	76	76	88	88	100	100	112	112	112	124	124

Toyota Knit to RC

38	38	38	44	44	50	50	56	56	56	62	62

Insert pocket as follows:
Brother 850 Wrong side faces. Pocket at left of front.
All ribbers using 1 × 1 slip on main bed. Right side faces.

Pocket at right of front. Leave following stitches in rib
formation at pocket side of front.

12	12	12	14	14	16	16	18	18	18	20	20

Transfer rib bed stitches to main bed to match pocket size.
Cast off stitches on main bed needles as follows

25	25	25	29	29	33	33	37	37	37	41	41

Remove cast off from gate pegs. Taking care pocket lining
faces same way as front, place stitches of row
below waste knitting on needles. Pin lining to main knitting.
Use side weights at edges of pockets.

Brother/Knitmaster Knit to RC	244	268	292	334	352	364	364	388	388	388	412	412
Toyota Knit to RC	122	134	146	168	176	182	182	194	194	194	206	206

RC 000

Armhole shaping

Pocket side, as back. *At same time* slope neck edge by
decreasing 1 stitch on both beds as follows:
Brother/Knitmaster 1st row and every following 6th row
Toyota 1st row and every following 3rd row
decrease following number of times

27	28	30	33	35	36	41	42	43	43	45	47

Knit without further shaping.

Brother/Knitmaster to RC	162	168	180	198	210	216	246	252	258	258	270	282
Toyota to RC	82	84	90	94	106	108	124	126	130	130	136	142

Shoulder shaping as on back. Start at pocket side.

Right front

Knit to match left front, reversing shapings and pocket
position. *At same time* make buttonholes as practised (see
pages 35–37).

Number of buttonholes	3	3	3	4	4	4	4	4	4	4	4	4
Size of buttonholes	4	4	4	5	5	5	6	6	6	6	6	6
Stitches from front edge	4	4	4	5	5	5	8	8	8	8	8	8
Brother/Knitmaster Rows below 1st buttonhole	84	92	100	88	88	100	100	100	100	100	106	106
Rows between buttonholes	80	88	96	84	88	88	88	96	96	96	102	102
Toyota Rows below 1st buttonhole	42	46	50	44	44	50	50	50	50	50	53	53
Rows between buttonholes	40	44	48	42	44	44	44	48	48	48	51	51

Sleeve

Cast on	65	69	75	79	85	87	89	91	93	95	99	101

Increase 1 stitch both ends at following row intervals

Brother/Knitmaster	32	28	28	32	30	26	24	22	20	20	20	20
Toyota	16	14	14	16	15	13	12	11	10	10	10	10
Number of increasings at both ends	8	10	11	11	12	15	16	17	18	19	19	20
Number of stitches after increasing	81	89	97	101	109	117	121	125	129	133	137	141
Brother/Knitmaster RC at end of increasing	256	280	308	352	360	390	384	374	360	380	380	400
Knit without further shaping to RC	292	316	364	412	412	436	436	436	436	436	460	460

Toyota RC at end of increasing											
128	140	154	176	180	195	192	187	180	190	190	200
Knit without further shaping to RC											
146	158	182	106	106	118	218	218	218	218	230	230

RC 000

Sleeve head shaping

At beginning of next 2 rows cast off following number of stitches

5	5	5	5	5	5	5	5	6	6	6	6

Brother/Knitmaster Knit 2 more rows. Decease 1 stitch at both ends of next row and every following 4th row.

Toyota Decrease 1 stitch at both ends of next row and every following alternate row.

All machines Decrease following number of times in all

6	7	9	10	8	12	10	10	9	8	9	9

Brother/Knitmaster Knit 6 rows. Decrease 1 stitch at both ends of next row and every following 6th row.

Toyota Knit 3 rows. Decrease 1 stitch at both ends of next row and every following 3rd row.

All machines Decrease following number of times in all

7	7	5	5	8	3	6	7	10	13	13	15

Brother/Knitmaster Decrease 1 stitch at both ends of next row and every following 4th row.

Toyota Decrease 1 stitch at both ends of next row and every following alternate row.

All machines Decrease following number of times in all

5	6	8	9	7	11	10	10	9	8	9	9

Brother/Knitmaster Knit 2 rows. Decrease 1 stitch at both ends of next row and every following alternate row.

Toyota Knit 1 row. Decrease 1 stitch at both ends of every row.

All machines Decrease following number of times in all

5	7	9	9	10	11	12	11	10	9	9	9

Brother/Knitmaster RC											
100	112	120	128	132	136	144	148	156	164	172	184

Toyota RC

50	56	60	64	66	68	72	74	78	82	86	92

Stitches remaining

25	25	25	25	33	33	35	39	41	45	45	45

Transfer to main bed. Cast off. Knit second sleeve.

Bindings

These are knitted in stocking stitch. All machines alike. At Tension 3·· measurements were: 36 stitches and 52 rows = 10cm.

Pocket bindings

Knit 2 alike. Main bed. Cast on 11 stitches.
Tension 3··. Knit to RC

40	40	40	46	46	52	52	58	58	58	64	64

Cast off.

Main binding

Measure all round edge of garment. To calculate number of rows, multiply number of centimetres by 5.2 and allow about 20 rows extra. Knit binding in one length, starting and finishing with waste knitting. Waste yarn, spare main yarn will be unravelled after attaching.

Sleeve bindings
Knit 2 alike. Measure and knit in same way as main binding.

To make up

Wash and block all pieces. Seam shoulders, underarm and sleeve seams. Set sleeves into armholes. Sew pocket linings to inside. Finish off buttonholes. With right sides together, place bindings on outside of garment 1cm from edge. Before sewing, graft ends of main and sleeve bindings, unravelling any spare knitting. N.B. Sleeves can be shortened if necessary before attaching trims. To do this, machine a row of zigzag stitches just inside the cutting line and cut off surplus before attaching bindings. Backstitch bindings to garment, taking care to keep absolutely straight. Turn to wrong side and hem down. Sew ends of pocket bindings neatly. Steam press seams on wrong side.

Knitting a Skirt to Match

You may wish to make a complete outfit by knitting a skirt in the same fabric. Many Double Jacquard fabrics make excellent skirts because they are so firm, and they lend themselves particularly to a simple A-line using a special method of decreasing across the width on the bed, which is the wrong side. This is a method I developed some years ago for that purpose. The practice piece for the skirt will give the number of rows to 10cm. These will be different from the jacket because of the ribbed effect on the wrong side.

Practice Piece for Skirt – All Machines

Cast on over the width of 65 main bed needles. Tension 4/4 until row 81.

Brother and Knitmaster SRP 60N ribbers – main bed will be decreasing bed.

Other ribbers – rib bed will be decreasing bed.

All machines – knit 12 rows main yarn, 4 rows waste yarn, 20 rows main yarn in plain Double Jacquard. On decreasing bed, transfer every 16th stitch to the adjacent needle, putting empty needles to non-working position as follows. N.B. In the first diagram decreasing is shown on the rib bed, and in the second diagram on the main bed. Notice that this means there is 1 stitch less in one end group on the rib bed. This really does not matter.

Needle Diagram Decreasing Bed: Rows 21–40 (11–20)

Fig. 39 *Shaping on the rib bed: decrease to this needle formation then knit rows 21–40 (11–20).*

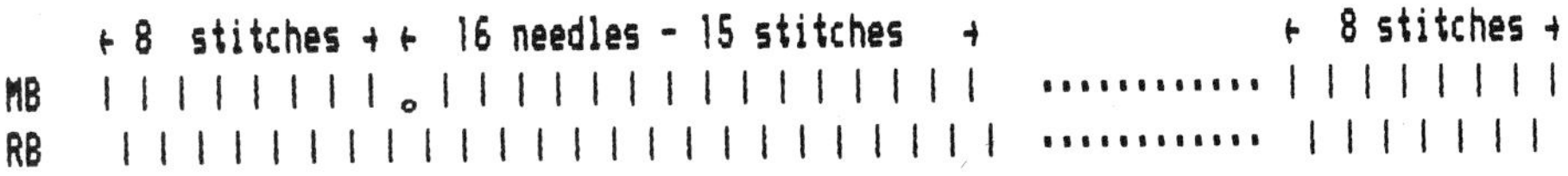

Fig. 40 *Shaping on the main bed: decrease to this needle formation then knit rows 21–40 (11–20).*

Notice the division of a group at both ends. This is necessary to join two panels together. Decreasing continues. The diagrams show the decreasing bed only to make it easier to see progression of the decreasings, in this case on the rib bed. Decreasing on the main bed, Brother 850 only, is exactly the same, except for the extra stitch at one end. Notice the end groups particularly.

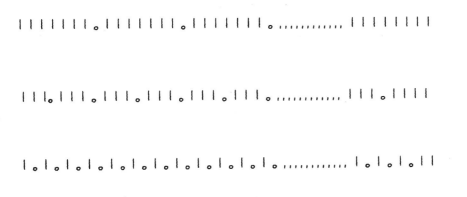

Fig. 41 *Shaping on either bed: decrease to this needle formation then knit rows 41–60 (21–30).*

Fig. 42 *Shaping on either bed: decrease to this needle formation then knit rows 61–80 (31–40).*

Fig. 43 *Shaping on either bed: decrease to this needle formation then knit rows 81–100 (41–50), at reducing tensions: 6 (3) rows at 12··/3· and 2·/3 and 8 (4) rows at 2/2··.*

Knit rows 81–100 (41–50) at reducing tensions: 6 (3) rows at 2··/3·, 6 (3) rows at 2·/3, 8 (4) rows at 2/2··.

This method shapes the section from hip to waist. The section measures the same as each of the others in length.

Make the waist band using tension 2·. Knit first on one bed, then on the other, holding down a loop of yarn between the beds when changing beds. This is necessary so that the top of the first side knitted is not joined tightly to the bottom of the second. All machines knit 10 rows on the bed that has every needle in working position, 6 rows on the 1 × 1 bed. Transfer the rib bed stitches to the main bed. Cast off loosely.

Knit a second tension swatch of fabric as it will be at the hip line, using the needle arrangement in Figure 42.

Wash and block the swatches as before. Measure the first one as follows. Lay out the tension swatch with the wrong side facing so that you can see the ladders formed by decreasing. Measure the length, excluding the waist band. From that measurement calculate the number of rows required for the skirt. Take a width measurement from the second swatch.

The first swatch measured 11cm to 100 rows knitted as described. This is 91 rows to 10cm. The second swatch measured 38 stitches to 10cm.

To Knit the Skirt

To fit waist sizes in centimetres	46	51	56	61	66	71	76	81	86	91	96	102
in inches	18	20	22	24	26	28	30	32	34	36	38	40
To fit hip sizes in centimetres	71	76	81	86	91	96	102	107	112	117	122	127
in inches	28	30	32	34	36	38	40	42	44	46	48	50
Skirt measurements at hip in centimetres	76	81	86	91	96	102	107	112	117	122	131	137
Calculating width: skirt measurement at hip × 3.8 to nearest whole number	288	308	326	346	364	388	406	426	444	464	498	520
Divide by 16: whole groups	18	19	20	21	22	24	25	26	27	29	31	32
stitches extra to whole groups*	—	4	6	10	12	4	6	10	12	—	2	8
Number of panels	2	2	2	2	2	2	3	3	3	3	3	3
Number of groups in Panel 1	9	9	10	10	11	12	9	9	9	10	11	11
Panel 2	9	10	10	11	11	12	8	9	9	9	10	11
Panel 3							8	8	9	9	10	10
Groups × 16 Panel 1	144	144	160	160	176	192	144	144	144	160	176	176
Panel 2	144	160	160	176	176	192	128	144	144	144	160	176
Panel 3							128	128	144	144	160	160

Divide extra stitches * between panels as evenly as possible, adding an extra stitch where necessary to give the uneven number needed for Brother 850.

Knit panels over following main bed needles Panel 1	145	145	163	165	183	195	145	151	149	161	177	179
Panel 2	145	163	163	181	181	193	131	151	149	145	161	179
Panel 3							131	129	145	145	161	163

Cast on. Knit selvedge. Knit each panel as tension swatch, working number of rows according to machine used and required length. Knit waistband on each panel. Cast off.

Tension	4/4	4/4	4/4	4/4	2··/3·	2·/3	2/2··
A 66cm 26in Brother/Knitmaster 600 rows Knit to RC	120	240	360	480	520	560	600
Toyota 300 rows Knit to RC	60	120	180	240	260	280	300
B 71cm 28in Brother/Knitmaster 650 rows Knit to RC	130	260	390	520	564	608	650
Toyota 326 rows Knit to RC	66	130	196	260	282	304	326
C 76cm 30in Brother/Knitmaster 690 rows Knit to RC	138	276	414	552	598	644	692
Toyota 346 rows Knit to RC	70	138	208	276	300	322	346

To line and make up

Wash and block carefully. Before sewing up, cut two or three lining pieces, using the knitting as a guide. Cut the lining 5cm wider than the panel at both sides. Seam lining and press seams. Turn top over to wrong side. Tack. Mattress stitch seams of skirt panels leaving one opening inside waistband. Pin lining to bottom of waist band stretching knitting to fit. Sew into position. Thread elastic. Leave skirt hanging for several days before hemming up lining.

– 4 –
Double Jacquard Borders
– A DROP-SHOULDER PULLOVER TO KNIT –

The yarn used for the pullover in colour photograph 10 is 4 ply, pure new wool by Forsell: 115 peat (1), 110 driftwood (2), 112 paprika (3), 113 cinnamon (4), 114 Sahara (5). The measurements for the tension swatches used in the garment are:

Fabric 1	28 stitches and 54 rows = 10cm	Tension 6/5
Fabric 4a	28 stitches and 38 rows = 10cm	Tension 6/7
Stocking stitch	30 stitches and 40 rows = 10cm	Tension 6

You have knitted a Double Jacquard pattern. You have knitted a plain (or a striped) fabric to match. The next three chapters explore ways of combining the two.

Before embarking on that subject, however, I want to deal with the question of suitable ribs or hems to use when welts are needed. Some ribs are more suitable than others because of the thickness of Double Jacquard fabric compared with stocking stitch or single bed Fair Isle. The method of making the transition from rib to full needle rib ready for knitting in pattern is also an important factor.

Types of Rib to Use with Double Jacquard Fabrics

Try out samples of all these, using the same yarn throughout. Remember to label them to show the tension.

1 × 1 Ribbing and 2 × 2 Ribbing (2 up 2 down)

Only half the needles in the width of the knitting are in working position for these ribs. This means that the rest must be filled before you can begin to knit in pattern. If empty needles are brought into working position before the first row of pattern, a row of holes will be made. Instead, fill all empty needles from the heels of stitches on the opposite bed. Put the beds into half pitch. Knit 2 circular rows, rib bed first, before commencing the pattern. This method applies to all types of rib.

These ribs are suitable with Double Jacquard when using 4 ply yarn. In thinner yarns there tends to be something of a 'ladder effect' and it is better to use one of the other ribs. The exception to this is when you are knitting with industrial yarns – then I suggest using 3 strands for the ribs and 2 for the Double Jacquard. Knit separate tension swatches in case it is necessary to work over a different number of rib bed needles for the welts.

English Rib

When the wrong side of this rib is used as the right side, the knitting resembles 1 × 1 rib, but the tucking causes the fabric to be bulkier than 1 × 1, and so it is more suitable for this particular purpose. Arrange to tuck on the bed which is to be the right side of the main fabric, so that the fat stitches which are typical of English rib are on the wrong side of the finished garment. This means, in the case of a Double Jacquard pattern, tucking on the main bed. For plain fabrics it will vary according to the choice of right side.

Knit a tension swatch to find the length to be knitted and to check which tension to use to give a smaller width measurement than the Double Jacquard. Take care that the last row is not a tuck row, as tuck stitches cannot be transferred satisfactorily for this purpose.

Fisherman's rib is not suitable because it is too wide a fabric in comparison.

Modified 1 × 1 Rib

Modified ribs are double bed fabrics knitted at half pitch, showing a rib formation on the right side and having all needles in work on the wrong side. They are not as elastic as normal ribs but are considerably more substantial because of the extra stitches.

Casting on for both these arrangements is for full needle rib. Knit the last row of selvedge on 1 × 1 bed at tension 1. This makes it easier to transfer unwanted stitches to adjacent needles.

Fig. 44 *Needle diagram for modified 1 × 1 rib using main bed side as right side of knitting.*

Fig. 45 *Needle diagram for modified 1 × 1 rib using rib bed side as right side of knitting.*

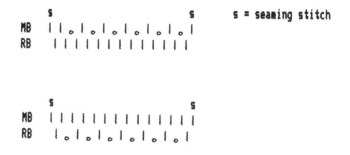

You will have noticed that this rib could be called 2 × 1 since 2 purl stitches can be seen between the columns of single knit stitches. This hardly shows in the finished garment because it is necessary to have a smaller tension on the bed which has all the stitches in work. Knit a sample over an even number of main bed needles, with the tensions as follows:

Stocking stitch tension minus 2 on the 1 × 1 bed
Stocking stitch tension minus 3 on the every needle bed.

Racked Ribs

The following points about racked ribs are common to all of them:

1. The beds are always in half pitch position.

2. In these instructions casting on starts and finishes at right.
3. There must be an even number of needles in work on both beds.
4. The selvedge cast on is zigzag and 3 circular rows; the extra rib bed needle is at the right. When casting on is by racking, for full needle rib frills only, the extra rib bed needle is at the left.

1 × 1 Rib

1. Knit the selvedge using tension 1/1 for circular rows. If you are using a Brother machine do not use Slide Lever II. Carriage right.
2. Stocking stitch tension −2. *Rack to left. Knit 1 row. Rack to right. Knit 1 row.* Repeat from * to * for the required length.

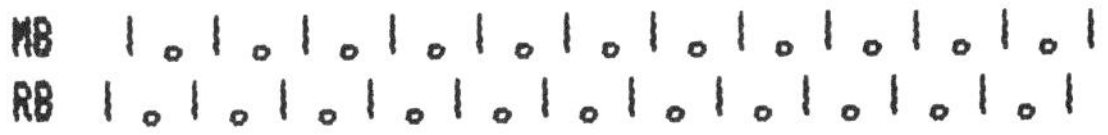

MB |₀|₀|₀|₀|₀|₀|₀|₀|₀|₀|₀|
RB |₀|₀|₀|₀|₀|₀|₀|₀|₀|₀|₀|

Fig. 46 Needle diagram for racked 1 × 1 and fisherman's rib.

Fisherman's Rib

This rib slopes due to the combination of tucking and racking. The slope can be to the left or the right, and the direction can be changed to give a zigzag effect. There are several ways of proceeding. I have given you the method I find easiest to remember.

1. Arrange and knit the selvedge as for 1 × 1. RC 000.
2. Set carriages: MB Knit ←→ Tuck RB Tuck ←→ Knit. Follow the instructions for 1 × 1 rib, knitting from * to * for 21 rows. Carriage left.
3. Change the direction of the slope by resetting carriages: MB Tuck ←→ Knit RB Knit ←→ Tuck. Knit 20 rows, racking as before. Carriage left. Cancel tuck setting. Stocking stitch tension. Release on waste knitting.

Look at the knitting from the rib bed side. In the first half, the rib slopes to the right, the opposite direction to that in which the rib bed was tucking. When the rib bed tucking was to the right the slope changed to the left. Welts can be made to slope entirely in one direction or reversed after half the knitting.

To make a vertical seam at both ends, increase or decrease 1 stitch on both beds every 4 rows, depending on the direction of tucking, as follows:

1st half Increase left, decrease right MB Knit ←→ Tuck RB Tuck ←→ Knit
2nd half Decrease left, increase right MB Tuck ←→ Knit RB Knit ←→ Tuck

Increase by pushing needles to upper working position. Use side weights.

To make a point, both ends work as follows, taking great care with weighting at the left. Increase by picking up heels.

1st half Increase left every 2 rows MB Knit ←→ Tuck RB Tuck ← → Knit
2nd half Decrease left every 2 rows MB Tuck ←→ Knit RB Knit ← → Tuck

Full Needle Rib Frill

Arrange the needles for full needle rib, with the same number on both ends and an extra needle at the *left* on the rib bed. Stocking stitch tension. Cast on by racking by working following 2 rows. Knit zigzag row, right to left. Rack to right. Knit 1 row.

Continue to knit as racked 1 × 1 rib. After releasing from the machine, stretch sideways to form a frill.

2 × 2 (2 up 1 down)

This is a very suitable rib to use. It has about one-third more needles in work than the other 2 × 2 rib, so there are not as many empty needles to fill, and it is bulkier and does not show ladders between the columns of knit and purl stitches.

Modified 2 × 2 Rib
There is a modified, and therefore less elastic, form of this rib. The purpose of slipping is to draw each pair of stitches closer together. The tension should be the same on both beds.

Fig. 47   *Needle diagram for modified 2 × 2 rib using main bed side as right side of knitting.*

Fig. 48   *Needle diagram for modified 2 × 2 rib using rib bed side as right side of knitting.*

Circular Hem

There are two types of circular hem – those with all the needles in working position on both beds, and those with some needles in non-working position in order to tighten the inside and prevent the hem sticking out. The method of knitting is the same for both, but in the second type, fewer rows are needed on the ladder side, which, as you know from single bed hems, has much more downward stretch than the stocking stitch side.

It is possible to use the single bed method to make a hem, but it is not convenient because of hanging the comb for the double bed knitting. It is far better to use the ribber from the beginning of the garment and to make a double hem.

If elastic is to be threaded through the hem it cannot be knitted as a circle, but must have both beds knitted separately. It is possible to knit only a few rows on one bed before changing to the other. When this is done on a neckband it is normal to pull down a loop of yarn between the beds to prevent an unwanted connection forming between the top of one side and the bottom of the other. If the hem is deep, this means there are a lot of ends to sew in. I have found a much easier way.

Casting On

The method is the same whether the ends are closed or open. Knit the zigzag row using the same number of needles on both beds. Do not leave any needles in non-working position at this stage. Knit 2 or 3 circular rows at tension 0/0, then 1 row of rib at tension 0/0 or 1/1, depending on the thickness of yarn. This makes a corded edge. For a smooth edge leave out the row of rib and continue in circular knitting, increasing the tension every 2 rows until the main tension is reached. Put beds to full pitch for circular knitting, remembering to go back to half pitch before knitting Double Jacquard. Continue to knit using one of the methods given below depending on the type of circular hem required. Use two cones of main yarn for a self-coloured reverse, or one cone of main yarn and one of contrast colour.

Closed Ends – All Machines

Continue with circular knitting to the required depth, using stocking stitch tension on the main bed. Some machines need the same tension on the rib bed, some need a different one. Consult your manual on this point, and, of course, test knit. Finish with 1 row of full needle rib in which you programme the pattern.

Open Ends Using All Needles

Brother and Knitmaster Machines Thread up two cones of yarn, using a colour changer if one is available. Knit the selvedge using the yarn furthest from the needle bed. Continue to use this yarn on the main bed, knitting 4 rows while slipping on the rib bed. Change to the nearer yarn and knit 4 rows on the rib bed, slipping on the main bed. The yarns will neither twist nor close the left end of the knitting. The right end is not a problem. If you change yarns manually, make sure you do not twist them. Continue in this way for the required depth and finish with 1 row of rib as in the previous example.

Toyota Set the change-over slots to the horizontal position. Insert a punch card locked on a blank row. Knit the zigzag row and 2 circular rows. Carriage left. Programme the card while knitting either the third circular row or the rib row for a corded edge. Set the machine for Simulknit. Thread a second cone of yarn into the S feed. Knit the hem on Simulknit setting, leaving the card locked. The first cone of yarn will knit on the main bed, the second on the rib bed. On the last row of the hem, left to right, programme the garment pattern. Carriage right. Change the yarn in S feed to the contrast yarn for pattern. Set the change-over slots to the vertical position.

Open Ends with Some Non-working Needles

All Machines Knit the selvedge in the same way as the previous example. Needles on the wrong side are then rearranged for 1 × 1, 2 × 1 or 3 × 1 knitting, transferring unwanted stitches along the bed, not across the beds. Tension for the bed that is knitting the ladder stitch backing must be lowered by about two whole numbers. Knit as follows, changing yarns for the beds as before:

Rows	1–4	Bed 1 stocking stitch
	5–6	Bed 2 ladder stitch
	7–12	Bed 1 stocking stitch
	13–16	Bed 2 ladder stitch

10. *The bordered pullover,*
worked in a combination of plain
and patterned Double Jacquard.

Repeat these 16 rows for the required length. Fill the empty needles with heels from the opposite bed. Finish with a rib row as before.

That gives you a good selection of edgings for your garments. Remember that the last row of the edging is the row in which you programme the Double Jacquard, so make sure it is in the right direction. For the pattern given in Chapter 3 it was left to right. In this chapter, however, it will be right to left for punch card machines, because the punch cards are different. For electronic machines start right to left as in Chapter 3. The reasons will become clear as you read on.

Designing the Pattern

I chose a bold pattern, but, having worked it out, I thought it was too deep for the smaller garment sizes, so I have given you a half-size pattern as well. If you prefer to substitute a design of your own, by all means do so, but you must, for the purpose of this chapter, choose the same type of design – that is, one with pairs of like rows. This makes a difference to the sequence of rows in Double Jacquard knitting on punch card machines, both patterned and plain.

The first step is to design a single bed Fair Isle punch card. You will see at once that it is not really suitable for single bed knitting because of the very long floats. All single bed cards in the rest of the book have only Toyota numbers on them for use with Simulknit.

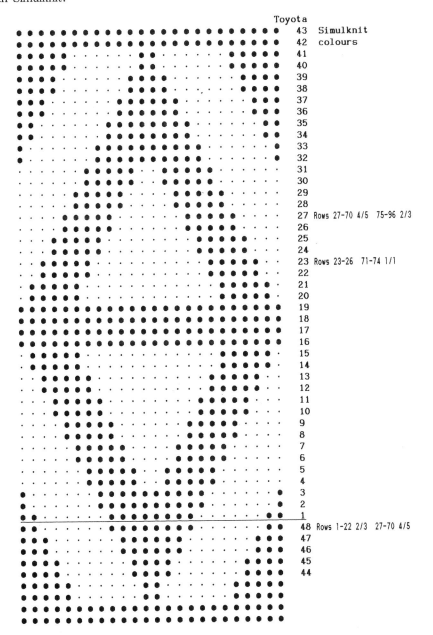

Fig. 49 *A large diamond for Simulknit.*

An Alternative Sequence for Double Jacquard

All Brother and Knitmaster Punch Card Machines

Just to remind you of the knitting sequence for the main bed given in Chapter 2:

Line 4 → Main yarn fills in background to line 3 – 2nd design row completed
Line 3 ← Contrast yarn knits pattern
Line 2 → Contrast yarn knits pattern – 1st design row completed
Line 1 ← Main yarn knits background to line 2

This sequence was used because the single bed design changed every line, making it necessary to complete each design row using both yarns before starting to knit the next one.

This time the sequence will be different because the design is made up of pairs of lines. The background of lines 1 and 2 is knitted first using the main yarn, then the pattern of lines 1 and 2 is knitted using the contrast yarn. This completes two design rows.

Fig. 50   *The Double Jacquard card for lines 1 and 2 of the large diamond.*

```
● ● ● ● ●  ·  ·  ·  ·  ·  ● ●  ·  ·  ·  ·  ·  ● ● ● ● ● c
● ● ● ● ●  ·  ·  ·  ·  ·  ● ●  ·  ·  ·  ·  ·  ● ● ● ● ● c
·  ·  ·  ·  · o o o o o o · · o o o o o o · · · · · m
·  ·  ·  ·  · o o o o o o · · o o o o o o · · · · · m
```

Look at the diagram carefully. Have you noticed something else which will need to be different this time? It is the starting place for the knitting. In Chapter 2 the knitting started at the right, with 1 row in main yarn; this time 2 rows have to be knitted in main yarn, so, because of the position of the colour changer, the 1st row is left to right.

If the whole card is punched out in the same way as the four lines above it will be very long – 92 rows, in fact. However, starting at the left means that the double length mechanism can be used. (If you do not have a double length facility, you will have to punch out double lines as above and then you may use either sequence.)

Fig. 51   *Four lines reduced to 2 and used with double length mechanism.*

```
● ● ● ● ●  ·  ·  ·  ·  ·  ● ●  ·  ·  ·  ·  ·  ● ● ● ● ● c Line 2
·  ·  ·  ·  · o o o o o o · · o o o o o o · · · · · m Line 1
```

The knitting sequence will now be:

Contrast yarn knits pattern in 2nd design row – repeat of Line 2 ←
Contrast yarn knits pattern in 1st design row   Line 2 →
Main yarn knits background to 2nd design row – repeat of Line 1 ←
Main yarn knits background to 1st design row   Line 1 →

Now convert the whole card.

Note that, to allow for using double length, colour change numbers are marked on every line, not on alternate lines as in the previous type of Double Jacquard card. Colours on the card are for the first 96 rows. The complete colour change list is: Rows 1–44: 2/3, 45–52: 1, 53–96: 4/5, 97–104: 1, 105–148: 2/3. The fabric between borders is in Sahara only.

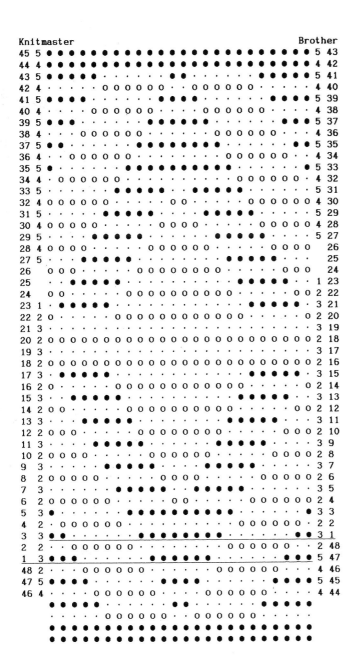

Fig. 52 *The large diamond Double Jacquard card for Brother and Knitmaster machines.*

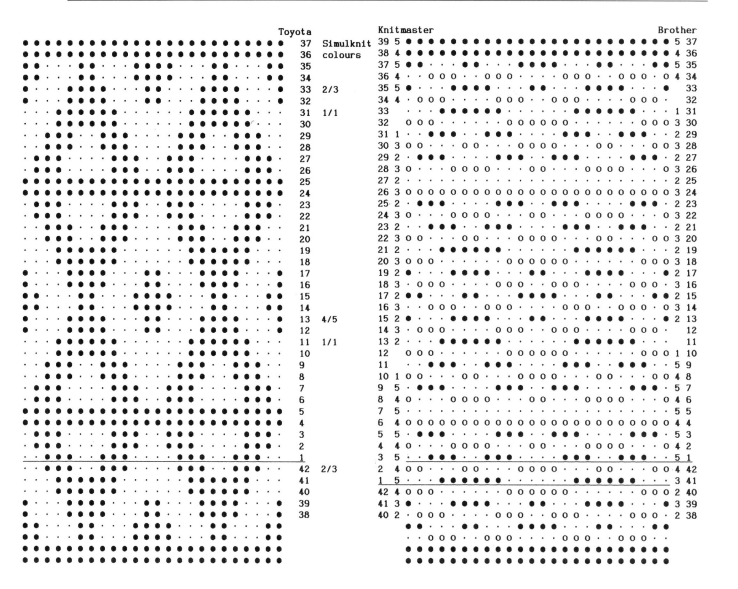

Fig. 53 ABOVE LEFT
The small diamond single bed punch card; use for Simulknit.

Fig. 54 ABOVE RIGHT
The small diamond Double Jacquard punch card for Brother and Knitmaster machines.

Electronic Machines

It is not necessary to use the alternative sequence with electronic machines. The knitting sequence is the same as in the type of design in Chapter 2.

Brother Machines Copy only one of each pair of lines for all patterns of this type. Use double length and Double Jacquard, programming from the left. Start knitting from the right with 1 row in main yarn followed by 2 rows contrast, 2 rows main.

Knitmaster Machines Double length and Double Jacquard buttons do not operate together on 500 and 560 machines. Copy each line on the electronic chart twice. If you are using a 580 enter 1 of each pair of lines and use double length and Double Jacquard buttons.

All Electronic Machines Copy the smallest section of these charts which will work for your particular machine. See page 57 for the colour sequence.

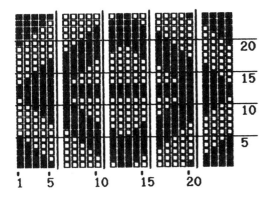

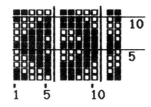

Fig. 56 *The electronic chart for the small diamond.*

Fig. 55 *The electronic chart for the large diamond.*

Plain Sections

Brother and Knitmaster Punch Card Machines

It is important to realize that when plain knitting follows or precedes a Double Jacquard pattern, the row sequence must be the same as in the pattern. Therefore, in the double row pattern we are using in this chapter the plain sequence will be as follows:

> Row 4 Main bed Main yarn knits: Rib bed Main yarn knits
> Row 3 Main bed Main yarn knits: Rib bed Main yarn knits
> Row 2 Main bed Slips   : Rib bed Main yarn knits
> Row 1 Main bed Slips   : Rib bed Main yarn knits

Use the plain Double Jacquard punch card from Chapter 3, Figure 22, joining it into a circle. Before it is programmed, lock it on the line below 1. By doing this it will start with 2 rows in which the main bed slips. This gives the knitting sequence needed to combine with any double length Jacquard pattern. Remember to change from double length to single length.

Electronic Machines

Use the method given on page 18.

Toyota Simulknit

Use either of the following methods:

1. As given for the jacket in Chapter 3 (see page 33).
2. Change the contrast yarn for second cone of main yarn. Change to small punch card, Figure 53. Knit pattern in Simulknit (see page 32).

The texture of the first method is not exactly the same as the border, and, particularly where there is a large border, as in this case, the second method, with a texture which matches it exactly, is the better one to use.

Combining Patterned and Plain Double Jacquard

Patterned Knitting Before Plain

Brother Punch Card Machines
There are several ways of proceeding depending on the type of pattern and on whether the whole punch card is used or only part of it.

1. **Complete or Part Punch Card – Double Row Type** Knit to row before last patterned row. The number of rows knitted will be divisible by 4 plus 3. Carriage right. Needles for next row will already have been selected. Change to plain card locked on line below 1. Knit last patterned row, at same time programming plain row. Break off contrast yarn. Unlock card. *Change to single length setting.* Continue knitting.
2. **Complete Punch Card – Single Row Type as in Chapter 2** Join plain card to patterned one before starting to knit. Plain knitting will carry on automatically. As soon as possible remove patterned card. Join up ends of plain card.
3. **Part Punch Card – Single Row Type as in Chapter 2** Method is the same as in 1, except that carriages will be at left when cards are changed.

Toyota Simulknit
The method of changing from the first card to the second is exactly the same as for Brother machines. The only difference is that a second cone of main yarn must be substituted for the contrast yarn used in the pattern.

The easiest way to change yarns is to break the contrast yarn just below the first feed of the yarn mast, tie the new yarn to it and pull the yarn through between the beds until the new yarn is in S feed. This saves wasting time rethreading the yarn mast, and avoids the disaster of not threading the coupling properly.

Knitmaster Punch Card Machines
1. **Complete or Part Punch Card – Double Row Type** Knit to the end of patterned knitting. Carriage left. Change to plain card locked on the line below 1. Remove yarn from feed. Uncouple carriages. Still in slip, move main bed carriage to right and back to programme pattern card. Recouple carriages. Rethread main yarn. Turn row counter back two numbers. Unlock card. *Change to single length setting.* Continue knitting.
2. **Complete or Part Punch Card – Single Row Type as in Chapter 2** Method is the same except that carriage may be right when cards are changed depending upon which side knitting started.

Plain Knitting Before Pattern

Brother Punch Card Machines

1. **Plain before Double Row Pattern** Start plain card at left on line below line 1. Knit to last but one row (rows must be divisible by 4 plus 3). Carriage right. All needles will have been selected ready for knitting last plain row. Change to pattern card locked on 1. Knit last plain row. Unlock pattern card. *Change to double length setting.* Knit pattern, working 2 rows main yarn, 2 rows contrast yarn.

2. **Plain before Single Row Pattern** Start plain card at either side on row 1. Method is the same as 1. When cards are changed, carriage will be at the opposite end to starting row.

Toyota Simulknit

Knit in Simulknit starting at the right using two cones of main yarn. Use method 2 for plain knitting already suggested (see page 59). When enough plain has been knitted and carriage is at left, turn pattern card to 1 and lock it. Knit 1 more plain row. Thread contrast yarn into right-hand side of yarn mast and S feed. Unlock card and continue.

Knitmaster Punch Card Machines

The method is the same whether the plain knitting is before or after the patterned border (see previous page).

Electronic Machines

With some machines it is possible to programme both patterned and plain Double Jacquard before beginning to knit so that the second section follows on automatically after the first. With earlier electronic machines this cannot be done. The method of changing from one pattern to another is similar to that used for the corresponding punch card machine.

Knitting a Sample

2 × 2 Rib, Large Border, Plain Fabric, Small Border

Arrange needles of both beds for 2 × 2 ribbing over the width of 60 main bed needles. The pattern is given in Fabric 1 for Brother/Knitmaster machines and Fabric 4a for Toyota. Make a sample.

1. Cast on and knit selvedge.
2. Knit 20 rows. Carriage right. Fill empty needles. Set machine for circular knitting, rib bed to knit first. Knit 2 rows. Programme large border pattern from this chapter. (If you are using Toyota Simulknit increase 1 stitch at both ends of the rib bed so that end stitches are on that bed. These stitches are seaming stitches. If you are using Brother or Knitmaster punch card machines remember to use double length for borders and single length for plain knitting.)
3. Set machine for Double Jacquard. Fabric 1 is the most suitable for Brother and Knitmaster machines because the yarn is a substantial one. Knit once through the large border pattern, changing to plain as instructed according to the machine being used. Row count at end of border is 48 for Toyota machines, 96 for Brother

and Knitmaster machines. N.B. In some machines pattern change-over is one row earlier.

4. Change to plain Double Jacquard knitting. Knit 40 rows Toyota, 80 rows other machines. Change to small border pattern. Knit small border, 22 rows Toyota, 44 other machines. Transfer all stitches to main bed. Cast off.

To Knit the Pullover

Colour Changing

N.B. Row count in brackets is for Toyota

1a. One diamond after welt on body pieces, and at cuff ends of sleeves

1st border

Small	Large	Colours
Rows 25–44 (13–22)	55–96 (27–44)	4/5
21–24 (11–12)	45–54 (23–26)	1
1–20 (1–10)	1–44 (1–22)	2/3

1b. One small diamond below yoke, and at beginning (i.e. top) of sleeves

Rows 25–44 (13–22)	2/3
21–24 (11–12)	1
1–20 (1–10)	4/5

2. Two diamonds in any position: either 1st or 2nd border

2 small	2 large	
Rows 69–88 (34–44)	149–192 (75–96)	4/5
65–68 (32–34)	141–148 (71–74)	1
25–64 (13–32)	53–140 (27–70)	2/3
21–24 (11–12)	45–52 (23–26)	1
1–20 (1–10)	1–44 (1–22)	4/5

Arrangement of Borders

The garment illustrated is a large size and so has the full border patterns. In smaller sizes there is a different pattern arrangement. Find the size you are knitting in the table below, then note the required colour changes from the one above.

Brother/Knitmaster

Size	1st border	2nd border
1–2	1a small	1a small
3–5	2 small	1a small
6–7	2 small	2 small
8–14	1a large	2 small

Toyota

Size	1st border	2nd border
1–2	2 small	1a small
3–7	2 small	2 small
8–14	2 large	2 large

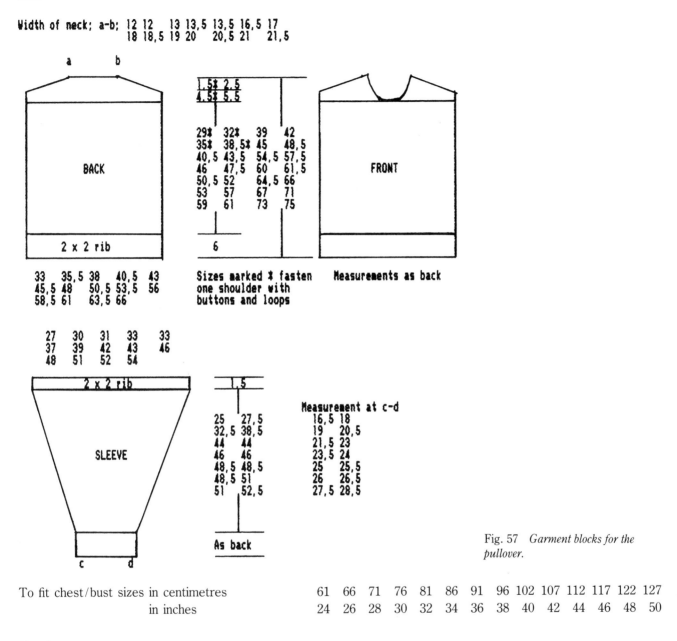

Width of neck; a-b: 12 12   13 13,5 13,5 16,5 17
18 18,5 19 20   20,5 21   21,5

a   b

BACK

2 x 2 rib

33   35,5 38   40,5 43
45,5 48   50,5 53,5 56
58,5 61   63,5 66

1,5 2,5
4,5 5,5

29   32   39   42
35   38,5 45   48,5
40,5 43,5 54,5 57,5
46   47,5 60   61,5
50,5 52   64,5 66
53   57   67   71
59   61   73   75

6

Sizes marked ‡ fasten
one shoulder with
buttons and loops

FRONT

Measurements as back

27   30   31   33   33
37   39   42   43   46
48   51   52   54

2 x 2 rib

SLEEVE

1,5

25   27,5
32,5 38,5
44   44
46   46
48,5 48,5
48,5 51
51   52,5

Measurement at c-d
16,5 18
19   20,5
21,5 23
23,5 24
25   25,5
26   26,5
27,5 28,5

c   d

As back

Fig. 57 *Garment blocks for the*
pullover.

To fit chest/bust sizes in centimetres

in inches

| 61 | 66 | 71 | 76 | 81 | 86 | 91 | 96 | 102 | 107 | 112 | 117 | 122 | 127 |
| 24 | 26 | 28 | 30 | 32 | 34 | 36 | 38 | 40 | 42 | 44 | 46 | 48 | 50 |

Back

All machines Cast on and knit welt in 2 × 2 rib
over width of following main bed needles
N.B. For all ribbing on back, front and sleeve tops
all needles are in WP on RB, alternate needles
including end ones on MB. Tension 4/4. Knit to RC

Carriage left (Toyota: right). Arrange needles for
Double Jacquard filling empty needles from heels.
Increase where necessary to
(Toyota: end needles on rib bed). Knit 2 circular
rows programming pattern.

94 102 110 114 122 130 138 142 150 158 166 174 178 186

20 20 20 20 30 all other sizes

96 102 110 116 124 130 138 144 152 160 166 174 180 188

Fabric 1 Knit 1st border. RC

Change to plain Double Jacquard. Knit to

Commence 2nd border. Rows for 2nd border

RC at end of 2nd border

Fabric 4a Knit 1st border. RC

Change to plain Double Jacquard. Knit to

Commence 2nd border. Rows for 2nd border

RC at end of 2nd border

All machines Rearrange stitches for rib as welt.

RC 000. Colour 1. Tension 3/3. Knit to RC

44	44	88	88	88	88	88	96	96	96	96	96	96	96
104	116	132	148	160	176	144	152	164	172	176	196	208	216
44	44	44	44	44	44	88	88	88	88	88	88	88	88
148	160	176	192	204	220	232	240	252	260	264	284	296	304
44	44	44	44	44	44	44	96	96	96	96	96	96	96
92	100	86	92	118	130	134	142	150	158	160	176	190	202
22	22	44	44	44	44	44	44	44	44	44	44	44	44
110	122	134	144	154	166	174	180	192	198	202	216	224	232
18	18	18	18	22	22	22	22	22	22	22	22	22	22

Shoulder shaping

Stitches for each shoulder

Cast off following stitches at beginning of next 8 rows (Sizes 1–4) 12 rows (Sizes 5–14)

31	34	36	39	43	43	45	46	50	53	55	58	60	64

11 stitches ×

10 stitches ×

9 stitches ×

8 stitches ×

7 stitches ×

—	—	—	—	—	—	—	—	—	—	—	—	—	4
—	—	—	3	—	—	—	—	—	—	1	4	6	2
—	2	4	1	—	—	—	—	2	5	5	2	—	—
3	2	—	—	1	1	3	4	4	1	—	—	—	—
1	—	—	—	5	5	3	2	—	—	—	—	—	—

Stitches remaining for back neck

RC

34	34	38	38	38	44	48	52	52	54	56	58	60	60
26	26	26	26	34	34	34	34	34	34	34	34	34	34

Transfer to main bed. Tension 7. Knit 1 row.

Release on waste knitting.

Front

Knit as back to end of pattern. Divide for neck. Set both beds to HP. Transfer following stitches to main bed

18	18	20	20	20	22	24	26	26	28	30	30	30	30

Rearrange stitches both sides for rib as welt. Knit in rib decreasing 1 rib bed stitch and main bed stitches as necessary on alternate rows. Decrease by putting stitches to HP on both beds. Use side weights. Number of rib bed stitches decreased

Knit straight to RC

8	8	9	9	9	11	12	13	13	13	13	14	15	15
26	26	26	26	34	34	34	34	34	34	34	34	34	34

At same time shape shoulder as back. Knit other side reversing shaping. Thread stitches of curve on to spare yarn. N.B. They are not transferred to main bed as they are all required for neckline. Release centre stitches on waste yarn.

Neckband

Seam 1 shoulder before knitting neckband. Hang comb on main bed. Number of stitches

Knit 6 rows waste yarn, 1 row nylon cord.

Tension 6. Knit 4 rows colour 1. Full pitch.

94	94	106	106	106	118	126	138	138	142	142	146	154	154

Transfer stitches to rib as welt. Knit 3 rows (sizes 1–6), 4 rows (sizes 7–14) at each of following tensions: 4·/4·, 4/4, 3··/3··, 3·/3·, 3··/3··, 4/4, 4·/4·. Transfer stitches to main bed. Pick up purl loops from first rib row and place on main bed needles. Knit 1 row tension 7, 3 rows tension 6. Pick up loops of 1st stocking stitch row and place on main bed needles. Knit 1 row tension 9. Place stitches of back and front neck and loops from straight sides of front neck on needles. Tension 10. Knit 1 row. Release stitches on waste knitting. Backstitch through last row.

Sleeves

All fabrics Knit sleeves downwards. Cast on over following main bed needles

74	86	86	94	94	102	110	118	122	130	134	142	146	150
76	86	88	94	94	104	110	118	122	130	136	144	146	150

Knit in rib as welt for 8 rows. Increase to main bed stitches. Arrange for full needle rib as before. Knit 1 row programming pattern, knitting patterns in reverse order of size and colour.

Fabric 1 Commence 2nd border. Rows for 2nd border

44	44	44	44	44	44	88	88	88	88	88	88	88	88

Change to plain Double Jacquard. Knit to RC

84	96	76	104	132	132	144	136	148	148	148	160	160	168

Commence 1st border. Rows for 1st border

44	44	88	88	88	88	88	96	96	96	96	96	96	96

At the same time decrease both ends of both beds at RC

9	8	9	10	13	11	10	9	9	8	8	7	7	7

and at same row intervals following number of times

14	17	17	18	16	19	22	25	26	29	31	34	34	36

Knit to RC

128	140	164	192	220	220	232	232	244	244	248	256	256	264

Fabric 4a Commence 2nd border. Rows for 2nd border

22	22	44	44	44	44	44	44	44	44	44	44	44	44

Change to plain Double Jacquard. Knit to RC

52	60	80	102	124	124	132	80	88	88	90	98	98	104

Knit 1st border. RC

44	44	44	44	44	44	44	96	96	96	96	96	96	96

At the same time decrease both ends of both beds at RC

6	6	7	8	10	8	8	7	7	6	6	6	6	5

and at following row intervals

6	6	7	8	10	8	8	7	7	6	6	6/7	6/7	5/6

Number of stitches decreased both ends

14	17	17	18	16	19	22	25	26	29	31	34	34	36

Knit to RC

96	104	124	146	168	168	176	176	184	184	186	194	194	200

All machines Stitches remaining

48*	52*	54	58	62	66	66	68*	70	72*	74	76*	78	78

Decrease 1 stitch both ends sizes marked*. Change to rib. Knit cuff as welt. Tension 10/8. Knit 1 row. Cast off with latch tool.

To make up

Wash and block all pieces. Seam second shoulder and ends of neckband. Sew sleeves to body. Sew underarm and side seams.

– 5 –
Single Motifs Knitted in Double Jacquard

– A DROP-SHOULDER JUMPER TO KNIT –

In this chapter single motifs will be knitted using the patterning mechanisms of the various machines. The toy soldier, 24 stitches wide, is for punch card machines, and there are two cats for electronic machines, one 40 stitches by 84 lines, the other 60 stitches by 128 lines. The design of a garment and the size of the motif are interdependent, and the cat has been given in two sizes so that it can be used on smaller garments.

The yarn for the garments shown in colour photographs 11, 12 and 13 is Bramwell's Ivette, which is 3 ply (70 per cent acrylic, 30 per cent wool). The colours for the cat are dove (main yarn) and black with red in the back and sleeves. The toy soldiers are knitted in red and black on a background of pampas (main yarn). Small amounts of thicker white, pink and green yarns are needed to embroider details. Use very narrow white ribbon for the soldiers' belts and braces. The cat needs a bell hung on a red crocheted chain, plastic whiskers (which are available from craft shops), and green metallic thread for the eyes.

The tension swatch measurements for the fabrics for which the pattern is written are:

Fabric 3	32 stitches and 76 rows = 10cm	Tension 5/5
Fabric 5	32 stitches and 76 rows = 10cm	Tension 1·/1
Fabric 4a	32 stitches and 38 rows = 10cm	Tension 2/3
Stocking stitch	32 stitches and 48 rows = 10cm	Tension 3

Instructions for Fabric 5, which is illustrated on page 23, are given on page 68.

If you are going to make an effective single motif garment using a punch card design you may need more than one motif, or you may need to place motifs in various positions on the garment. One small motif on its own could look insignificant, although this depends very much on the shape and size of the garment.

Toyota machines, which knit two colours in the same row, are dealt with separately from Brother and Knitmaster machines, which knit only one colour at a time. Toyota knitters will use the specially adapted single bed punch card for the toy soldier, set the machine for Simulknit, which is Fabric 4a, and follow the instructions on page 68. Knitters using Brother 830 or Knitmaster 321 machines will also follow separate instructions, since those machines do not have single motif facilities (see page 73).

11.   *The Brother/Knitmaster toy soldier jumper.*

Fabrics for Single Motif Garments

Not all the fabrics described in Chapter 2 are suitable for single motif knitting because the motif looks better in a balanced fabric so that it does not appear stretched. Fabric 1, being unbalanced, did not prove satisfactory for the toy soldier. The long stitches on the right side, combined with the vertical design, did not give a pleasing appearance to the knitting. Fabric 2, which is balanced, is not suitable because of the long floats either side of the motif. A modified form of these two fabrics, Fabric 5, is very suitable, although it is a little slower to knit as it is not fully automatic. It can be knitted on any Brother or Knitmaster ribber.

Fabric 5

There are 3 rows on the rib bed to 2 design rows on the main bed. The row sequence is as follows:

Row	Main bed pattern panel	Main bed side panels	Yarn	Rib bed	Direction
4	Background to 2nd design row	Knit	Main	Knit	→
3	Pattern of 2nd design row	Slip	Contrast	Knit	←
2	Pattern of 1st design row	Slip	Contrast	Knit	→
1	Background to 1st design row	Knit	Main	Slip	←

The left slip knob of the rib carriage is changed whenever the colour is changed. It is pushed up when changing to main yarn and down when changing to contrast yarn. It is important to test-knit to find the best tension to use. Notice that floats occur only in row 1 when the main yarn slips across those main bed needles which will be knitted in contrast yarn in row 2. There are no floats in the side panels, and the stitches of both beds are linked on one of the main yarn rows.

Fabric 3 is excellent for all motif work, but in patterned knitting it is available only to Brother 850 and Knitmaster SPR 60N ribbers with RJ1. Fabrics 4a and 4b produce stocking stitch on both beds on either side of the motif. This effect can be modified in 4a for Toyota, and instructions for this follow. The same modification could be used with the Auto Drive of the SRP 60 ribber, but it is slow to knit because a good deal of hand selection is necessary. Fabric 5 is quicker and better for earlier Knitmaster and Brother ribbers.

Making Punch Cards and Knitting Samples

Toyota Simulknit

The toy soldier single bed punch card, Figure 58, is used for Simulknit. For the moment ignore the top and bottom sections and think about the soldier himself. You will see the reasons for plain and spotted parts as you knit.

Motifs in Toyota Simulknit

Toyota machines have blocking mechanisms for knitting single motifs, combined with a means of positioning the motif in any punch card position in the width of the knitting. These are very simple and effective in single bed work, but for Simulknit it is not entirely straightforward. In fact, your manual tells you not to try it, but there is a way, as you will see! This is the stitch formation which would be knitted using Simulknit for a motif.

Side panel	*Patterned section*	*Side panel*
R. 2 MB knit MC RB knit CC	Knit pattern row 2 CC & MC	MB knit MC RB knit CC
R. 1 MB knit MC RB knit CC	Knit pattern row 1 CC & MC	MB knit MC RB knit CC

The stitch formation of the side panels is just separate pieces of stocking stitch on both beds knitted in two colours, one on each bed. This would not be satisfactory as there would be no link between beds except at the motif and end stitches.

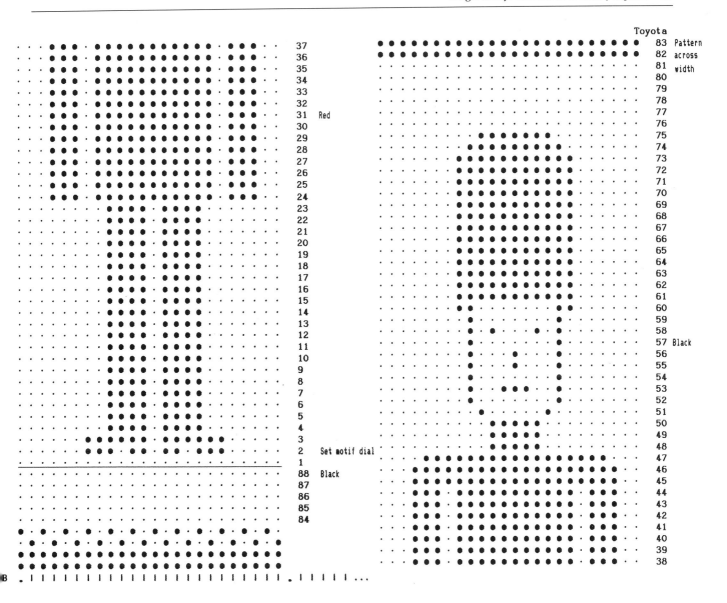

Fig. 58 *The punch card and needle diagram for the Simulknit toy soldier.*

I have experimented with my Toyota and have found a method that does enable you to use your Magic Motif with Simulknit. It is completely automatic and is suitable for any size of garment. Notice the difference between the jumper in colour photograph 11, which was knitted using a Brother 850 ribber, and the one shown in colour photograph 12, which was knitted using Simulknit. My method for Simulknit motifs is to divide up the knitting into boxes, putting the motif in one of them. This is how the Toyota knitting is planned. Use the method with any motif.

Knitting a Practice Motif

1. The motif will be knitted in the centre, dial position 3. For practice, use 75 main bed needles after the welt. Set the left change-over slot in vertical position, and the right one in horizontal position. Knit in Simulknit using side weights. The 2 end stitches on rib bed are seaming stitches.

12.   *The Toyota toy soldier –
notice the box effect. This method
has been developed by the author
to enable Toyota knitters to knit
Simulknit motifs.*

2. Knit the welt, finishing carriage right, programming pattern on last row. Arrange the main bed needles like this:

Fig. 59   *Needle diagram for
Simulknit motif and boxes.*

```
+      24 stitches    ++       24 stitches     ++      24 stitches      +
⋕ ⋕                   ⋕ ⋕                       ⋕ ⋕                      ⋕ ⋕
I₀IIIIIIIIIIIIIIIIIIIIIIII₀IIIIIIIIIIIIIIIIIIIIIIII₀IIIIIIIIIIIIIIIIIIIIIIII₀I
+ Plain panel 24 sts,  ++  Motif 24 stitches   ++ Plain panel 24 sts,  +
```

3. Set machine for Simulknit. Thread contrast yarn. Set motif dial so that the first 8 rows are knitted right across. The 2 1 × 1 rows are the bottom division of the box. Vertical 1 × 1 lines are formed because of end needle selection by the left change-over slot. Change to selected position for the toy soldier, in this case 3, at the row marked on the card. Remember to change the motif dial to all-over immediately knitting of soldier is complete.

4. Knit through the card once. Watch how the vertical box sides are formed. When the carriage is moved left, main bed needles both sides of needles in non-working position are selected to upper working position. This is because the left change-over slot is vertical. When the selector cam encounters a needle out of work it behaves as if it had reached the end of a row. Needles marked * will, therefore, be brought to upper working position on alternate rows, knitting in contrast yarn and so forming a link between the two beds. When the carriage is moved to the right these needles are not selected because the right change-over slot is horizontal.

What would happen if both change-over slots were vertical? How would you alter the bottom of the punch card to match? (The answer is at end of chapter.)

The contrasting vertical lines suggest that a drop-shoulder garment is the most suitable shape to knit. However, in sizes where there are part plain panels at either side, a square armhole is suggested so that there are vertical contrast lines next to the sleeves. The sleeves and back have horizontal and vertical stripes, knitted in contrast colour 1. I used the first 3 rows on the punch card and the same needle diagram to obtain a matching fabric, both after the motif on the front and on the other pieces. This is how it works.

1. Programme card on row 1. RC 000.
2. *Unlock. Knit 2 rows. They will be knitted in 1 × 1 Simulknit. Lock card on row 3, which is plain.
3. Knit plain to RC 87. Vertical stripes will continue to knit. Turn card back to row 1 and lock. Knit 1 more row.*
4. Repeat from * to * as necessary.

Rectangles can be made shorter if preferred, and there could be more vertical lines – it is your choice when you design a garment. This method of knitting motifs automatically lends itself to quilting. The motifs can be arranged alternately, in draught-board formation, and the other rectangles filled with pre-cut terylene wadding as the knitting progresses. You could make a lovely quilted pram cover.

Brother and Knitmaster Punch Card Machines

Converting the Card

Fabrics 3 and 5 require twice as many rows to 10cm as Fabric 4a does. This means that all three fabrics need exactly the same number of design rows. Card conversion is, therefore, easy. It involves converting the Toyota toy soldier himself, not the top and bottom sections. The soldier takes up 74 rows, so the converted card will have 148 rows and is shown on the next page.

Knitting the Motifs

Methods of knitting motifs vary according to the machine used. Having made your punch card, study the section to which your machine belongs, and knit a practice motif.

Before you knit the motif you must understand how the main bed should operate to obtain the desired result. The motifs are in panels 24, 40 or 60 stitches wide. At both sides of the panel there is plain Double Jacquard fabric, knitted, on the main bed, in background colour only. Think again about the knitting sequence of the main bed for Double Jacquard:

Row 4 Background to 2nd design row knitted in main colour
Row 3 2nd design row knitted in contrast colour
Row 2 1st design row knitted in contrast colour
Row 1 Background to 1st design row knitted in main colour

Unless you prevent it, this patterning will happen right across the knitting, just as it did in the all-over pattern for the hat and scarf in Chapter 2. The machine must be made to knit as follows:

	Side panel	*Patterned section*	*Side panel*
Row 4 MC	Knit *all* stitches	Knit background	Knit *all* stitches
Rows 2/3 CC	Slip	Knit pattern	Slip
Row 1 MC	Knit *all* stitches	Knit background	Knit *all* stitches MC

The way in which this is done depends on whether machines have automatic motif knitting accessories, which are known as blocking mechanisms. They prevent all main bed pattern knitting except in the chosen section. All electronic machines and most modern punch card machines have this facility. The Brother 830 and Knitmaster 321 do not, and they are dealt with separately.

Brother 840, Knitmaster 323 and Later Punch Card Models
Set the machine for single motif knitting. No needles will be selected in the side panels, and they must, therefore, be made to knit when the main colour is used.

	Side panel	*Motif*	*Side panel*
Row 4 MC	Push *all* needles to upper working position so that they knit	Leave as selected to knit background	Push *all* needles to upper working position so that they knit
Rows 2/3 CC	No needles will be selected	Leave as selected to knit pattern	No needles will be selected
Row 1 MC	Push *all* needles to upper working position so that they knit	Leave as selected to knit background MC	Push *all* needles to upper working position

Brother 830 – Fabric 5, or 3 if using 850 ribber
Needles will be selected right across width in all 4 rows. Using needle pusher, rearrange needles as follows:

	Side panel	*Motif*	*Side panel*
Row 4 MC	Push all unselected needles to upper working position so that they knit	Leave as selected to knit background	Push all unselected needles to upper working position so that they knit
Rows 2/3 CC	Push all selected needles to working position so that they do not knit	Leave as selected to knit contrast	Push all selected needles to working position so that they do not knit
Row 1 MC	Push all unselected needles to upper working position	Leave as selected	Push all unselected needles to upper working position

Fig. 60   OPPOSITE PAGE
The toy soldier punch card for Brother/Knitmaster machines.

Push in both Part buttons. The needles in working position will not knit, while those in upper working position will knit. By altering needle positions in this way, knitters using this machine can achieve the same results as those who have later models.

It is important to understand what happens when these actions are taken. Brother and Toyota machines both work by what is known as pre-selection; Knitmaster machines do not. Pre-selection means that as a row is knitted needles for the next row are selected as follows: needles represented by holes are put into upper working position, while needles represented by unpunched spaces are put into working position. What happens when the row is knitted depends upon the type of knitting in progress:

When two yarns are in use, in single bed Fair Isle and Simulknit, holes knit contrast yarn, blanks knit main yarn.

In Double Jacquard, using one yarn only or alternate colours, and slip setting, holes knit and blanks slip.

When tuck setting is used, holes knit and blanks tuck.

If the position of any needle is altered manually before the following row is knitted, it will work according to the position in which you place it. In this way, you, the knitter, can take personal charge and override what the patterning mechanism of the machine, combined with the carriage controls, instructs it to do.

Knitmaster 321 – Fabric 5 only

Needles in all Knitmaster machines, whether represented by holes or unpunched spaces, remain in working position until the carriage passes over them. Selection takes place during the row which is being knitted, not in the preceding one. This means that, in side panels, it is not possible to cancel the selection of needles represented by holes on the punch card in the same way as in the Brother 830. Another method has to be found to prevent contrast stitches of pattern knitting right across the work in the 2 middle rows of each group of 4 rows.

It is, however, possible to make sure that the side panel needles, represented by unpunched spaces, knit in the first and last rows of each group by pushing all needles outside the motif forwards to either C or D position.

The method to use for this machine is to combine punch card selection and hand selection. The card needs to be punched specially, as follows, working from the Double Jacquard punch card.

1. Punch out only the rows which are to be knitted in main yarn. They are those marked ○.
2. Leave lines in between unpunched. They ·are those marked ● in Figure 60.

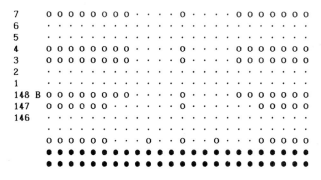

Fig. 61 *The first few rows of the punch card for use with Knitmaster 321 machines. Copy this on to your card and then punch out all the Os in the card in Figure 60.*

13. *The aristocratic cat jumper; a motif for electronic machines.*

Method of Knitting If left to its own devices the machine would knit and slip automatically according to the punch card. There would be no toy soldier, only a peculiar outline, because all stitches in contrast rows would be slipped. Make the machine do what you want it to do as follows:

1. **Main Yarn** Rows 1, 4, 5, 8, 9, 12 . . . Push all needles outside the width of the motif to C or D so that they knit in main yarn.
2. **Contrast Yarn** Rows 2, 3, 6, 7, 10, 11 . . . Use the diagram of the Double Jacquard punch card on page 72 as a guide to selecting needles in motif panel by bringing forward those marked ● to C or D. Stitches of the toy soldier will knit and all others will slip.

The methods for both the Brother 830 and the Knitmaster 321 are somewhat time-consuming, but once a rhythm is established the knitting is quite easy.

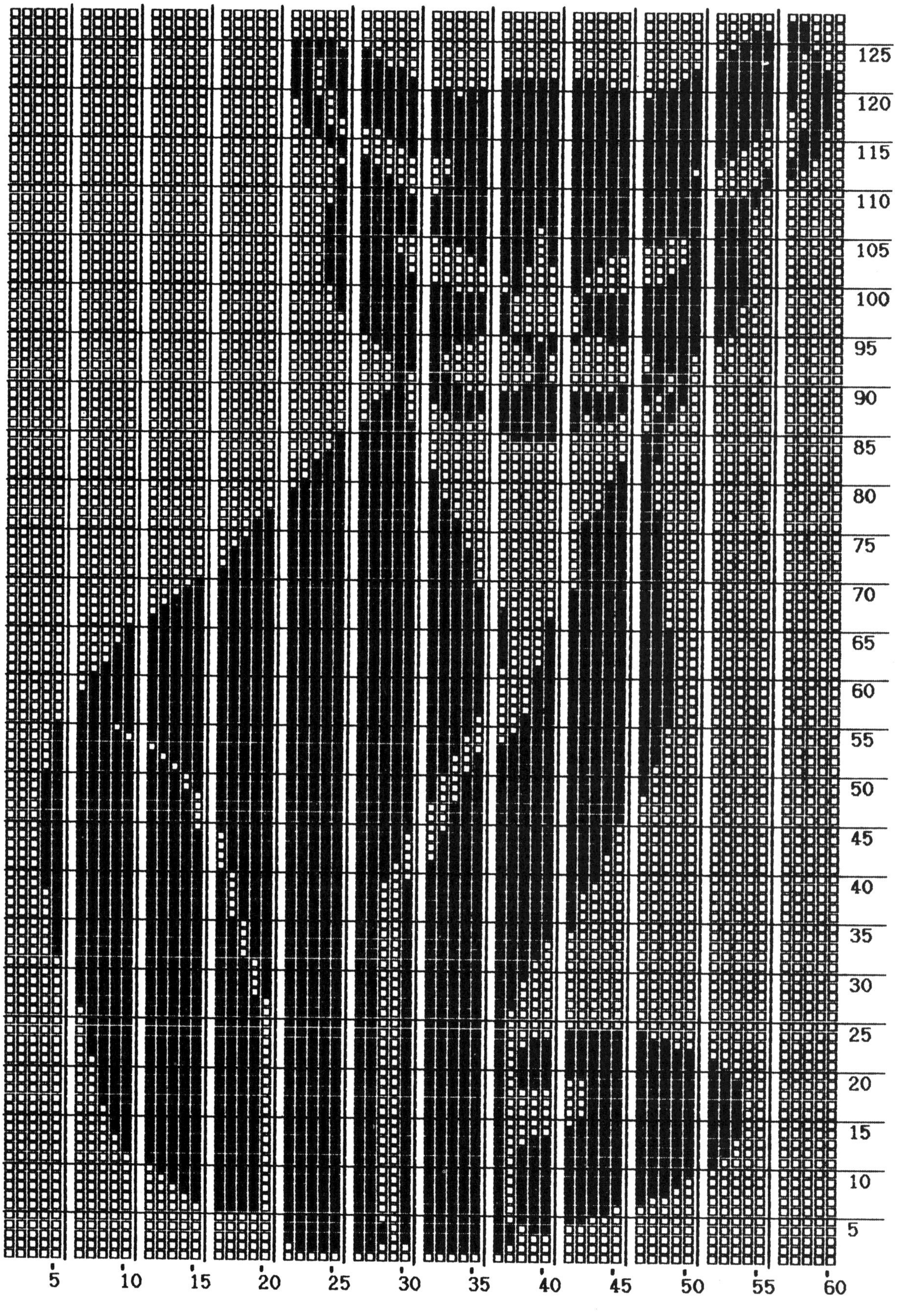
125
120
115
110
105
100
95
90
85
80
75
70
65
60
55
50
45
40
35
30
25
20
15
10
5
5
10
15
20
25
30
35
40
45
50
55
60

Designing for Electronic Machines

The two cats measure approximately 36cm and 23cm. If you make designs yourself remember that the size required on the electronic chart is much smaller than the actual knitting. My charts are 23cm and 15cm high, which is about 64 per cent of the height of the knitted motifs in this particular yarn. When planning this type of garment, work out the number of rows which will be needed for the front from your plain Double Jacquard tension swatch. Then decide how big the motif is to be and calculate the number of rows it will need. Make your drawing to fit the required space on the electronic chart. If you are not a skilled artist, find a suitable picture and have it enlarged or reduced by a photocopier to the size you need for the chart. Trace it on to the copy chart over a sheet of carbon paper, then square off the edges for the stitches and rows.

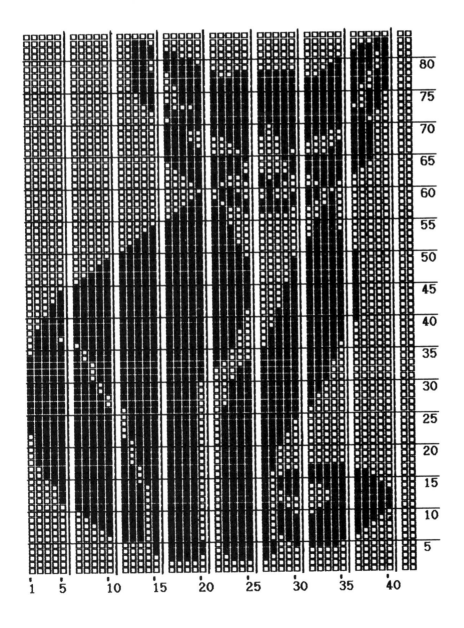

Fig. 62 OPPOSITE PAGE
The electronic chart for the large cat.

Fig. 63 *The electronic chart for the small cat.*

To Knit the Jumper

The project for this chapter is a drop-shoulder, slash-neck jumper with a motif on the front. The large cat design on the jumper shown in colour photograph 13 is suitable for sizes from 81cm (32in), but the smaller cat is better for jumpers below that size.

I decided to introduce red and black blocks and stripes into the back and sleeves of the Brother/Knitmaster garments. To knit the stripes, just change colour when using the plain Double Jacquard setting. Blocks need a punch card for the soldier jumper, and an electronic chart for the cat one. You may wish to do something different with your garment.

Fig. 64 *The punch card for blocks for sleeves of Brother/Knitmaster back and sleeves.*

Fig. 65 *The electronic chart for blocks for sleeves and back of cat jumper.*

Plan the position of the motif, remembering that the front, when hanging on the machine, is wrong side facing. When there are a lot of plain rows to be knitted you must decide how many you want to see below and above the motif. I think two-thirds below and one-third above is about right.

When you knit Fabric 4a notice that the vertical lines on the jumper front are the same colour as the motif itself. On the sleeves and back I have used red only.

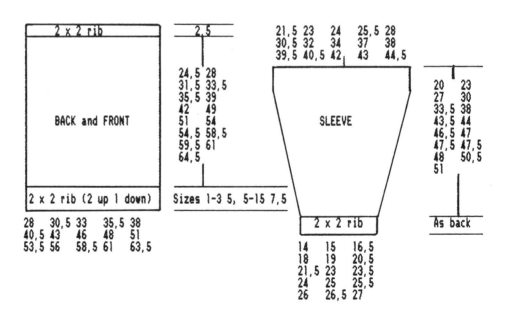

Fig. 66 *Garment blocks for jumpers.*

To fit chest/bust sizes in centimetres	51	56	61	66	71	76	81	86	91	96	102	107	112	117	122
in inches	20	22	24	26	28	30	32	34	36	38	40	42	44	46	48

Front

Toyota Before knitting set left change-over slot to vertical, right to horizontal.

All fabrics Over width of following main bed needles arrange needles of both beds for 2 × 2 rib (2 up 1 down)

	86	95	101	110	119	125	134	143	149	158	167	173	182	191	197

Cast on. Tension 1/1. Main yarn. Knit to RC

	24	24	24	24	24	30	30	30	30	30	30	30	30	30	30

Increase 1 or 2 stitches as necessary to give
Pick up heels of stitches across the beds to

	87	95	103	111	119	127	135	143	151	159	167	175	183	191	199

give full needle rib arrangement. For Fabric 4a rearrange needles according to diagram on page 70. Knit 1 row FNR programming as follows:

Brother/Knitmaster Plain Double Jacquard
Toyota Simulknit punch card. Set tension for chosen fabric.

Brother/Knitmaster Knit plain Double Jacquard to RC Toy soldier

	20	40	60	72	—	—	—	—	—	—	—	—	—	—	—
Small cat	8	24	40	52	60	80	—	—	—	—	—	—	—	—	—
Large cat	—	—	—	—	8	28	40	72	88	104	108	124	128	138	156

Knit motif. When motif is complete change to plain Double Jacquard. Knit to RC

	188	212	240	254	268	296	320	372	388	412	416	444	452	464	492

Continue at †

Toyota Toy soldier – knit in pattern as follows. Knit 3 rows of pattern right across. Lock card on plain row. Knit to RC

	11	19	23	29	—	—	—	—	—	—	—	—	—	—	—

Turn card back to Row 1. Lock. Knit 1 row. Release card. Knit 1st 2 rows of pattern right across.

Knit motif (86 rows) in centre only to RC

	102	110	114	120	—	—	—	—	—	—	—	—	—	—	—

Knit 1st 2 rows of pattern right across. Lock card after next row which is plain.

Knit plain to RC

	112	128	136	148	162	178	200	214	224	230	244	250	254	276	278

Finish with 1st 2 rows of pattern. RC

	114	130	138	150	164	180	202	216	226	232	246	252	256	278	280

N.B. Numbers of rows are given for all sizes, but full details of horizontal lines are for the toy soldier only. For any other motif they would need to be worked out individually. Continue at †

† **All fabrics** Transfer stitches for rib
decreasing 1 or 2 stitches where necessary.
Knit rib as for welt to RC
Tension 6/6. Knit 1 row. Cast off in rib by
dropping bed 1 place, and latching stitches off
from bed to bed. Alternatively, release on
waste knitting and cast off using latch tool
through loops of last row.†

12	12	12	18	18	18	18	18	18	18	18	18	18	18	18

Back

All fabrics. Stitches and rows are as front.
Fabric 3 Knit plain Double Jacquard in main
yarn to where motif started on front.
Programme for blocks.
Soldier * col. 1 (pampas), col. 2 (red): 36
rows; col. 1 (black), col. 2 (pampas): 20 rows
*. Repeat from * to * once, then 1st 36 rows
again.
Large cat * col. 1 (dove), col. 2 (black): 36
rows; col. 1 (red), col. 2 (dove): 72 rows *.
Repeat from * to * once then 1st 36 rows
again.
Small cat * col. 1 (dove), col. 2 (black): 24
rows; col. 1 (red), col. 2 (dove): 48 rows *.
Repeat from * to * once then 1st 24 rows
again.
Change to plain Double Jacquard. Knit to RC
Cast off.

188	212	240	254	268	296	320	372	388	412	416	444	452	464	492

Fabric 4a Knit sections 1 and 2 as front.
Knit 42 plain rows, 1st 2 rows of card, 42
plain rows. Knit section 4 of front.
All fabrics Knit from † to †.

Sleeves

Welt as back/front. Cast on
Knit welt. Increase as before to
Arrange stitches for FNR.

44	47	53	56	59	65	68	74	74	77	80	80	83	83	86
45	47	53	57	59	65	69	75	75	77	81	81	83	85	87

Brother/Knitmaster Soldier – place a motif
on both sleeves starting at RC
At top of sleeve knit stripes as required
except size 1 where motif takes most of
length and remainder is plain.

0	0	12	20	—	—	—	—	—	—	—	—	—	—	—

Brother/Knitmaster Cat – knit block pattern on back starting immediately after welt. Start and finish with black. Knit blocks to RC 96 for small cat, 252 for large cat. Follow with plain Double Jacquard finishing with stripes as required.

All designs *At same time* increase 1 stitch both ends both beds following number of times

at following row intervals

Number of stitches

Knit to RC

12	13	13	12	16	16	17	17	22	22	23	24	25	26	27
10	12	14	16	14	16	16	16	14	14	14	14	14	14	14
69	73	79	81	91	97	103	109	119	121	127	129	133	137	141
152	174	204	228	254	288	332	336	352	356	360	360	364	384	388

Toyota Arrange needles of main bed with 11 in WP, 1 in NWP. Make both ends alike. *Knit 3 rows of pattern. Lock card. Knit to RC

Turn card back to row 1. Lock. Knit 1 row. Release card*. Knit from * to * right across, following number of times. Knit 2 more rows. *At same time* increase 1 stitch both ends both beds following number of times

at following row intervals

Number of stitches

Knit to RC

17	19	19	21	—	—	—	—	—	—	—	—	—	—	—
4	4	5	5	—	—	—	—	—	—	—	—	—	—	—
12	13	13	12	16	16	17	17	22	22	23	24	25	26	27
5	6	7	7	7	8	9	8	7	7	7	7	7	7	6
69	73	79	81	91	97	103	109	119	121	127	129	133	137	141
74	82	102	112	124	144	168	168	178	178	178	190	190	198	198

All fabrics Transfer stitches to main bed. Using main yarn finish by one of these methods: (1) Tension 10+. Knit 1 row. Cast off with latch tool. Sew to body. (2) Tension 8. Knit 1 row. Release on waste knitting. Join to body on machine.

To make up

Prepare all pieces. Join shoulder seams to leave adequate neck opening. Make loops and sew on buttons on smaller sizes. Join sleeves to body. Sew up side and sleeve seams.

Toy soldier Sew on ribbon for belt and braces. Use Swiss darning to embroider face pink. Embroider features. Gloves are white Swiss darning.

Cat Embroider white parts of fur on body and face. Sew details on paws. Embroider eyes green, then sew radial stitches with metallic thread on top. Sew black pupil in centre. Crochet short red chain and hang bell. Push whiskers through from back of work sewing down on wrong side to fix.

Answer to question on pages 69–71: vertical lines of boxes would be unbroken, not 1 × 1. First two lines of punch card would be punched right out to give solid horizontal box lines.

– 6 –
Animals Great and Small

– A DROP-SHOULDER JUMPER
WITH RIBBED YOKE TO KNIT –

The yarn for the jumper in colour photograph 14 is, for the dogs, AngoraLook by King Cole white (1) and black (48); the main yarn is Anti-Tickle 4 ply wool by King Cole, royal blue (21). The measurements for the tension swatch used for the garment are:

Fabrics 2, 3 and 4b	28 stitches and 70 rows	= 10cm	Tension 7/7
Fabric 4a	28 stitches and 35 rows	= 10cm	Tension 5/6
Stocking stitch	30 stitches and 40 rows	= 10cm	Tension 7
Rib (2 up 1 down)	48 rows	= 10cm	Tension 4/4

Animals are frequently knitted in Fair Isle on the main bed only. If they are large designs, they are often knitted using the intarsia method, which has the merit of doing away with floats, although it is rather slow to knit. Designs which have rows and rows of animals can be knitted as single bed Fair Isle. However, this results in long floats, which ought to be neatened by one of several time-consuming methods. It seems extraordinary that more knitters do not convert their designs to Double Jacquard and knit without floats. As you saw in Chapter 2, conversion is not such a fearsome task – not nearly as fearsome as all those floats!

This type of pattern clearly comes into the category of alternating patterned and plain Double Jacquard, but some special features need to be considered. First, let us not have beheaded dogs, tail-less cats, scoop-backed pigs and so on. One can expect little better from the cut-and-sew methods used commercially, but we are seeking perfection. In the jumper shown in the colour photograph there are only whole dogs; not a chopped off tail in all 106 of them! It was knitted on an electronic machine, and this does give more scope for variation. We will deal with electronics first, then consider how to adapt the design to a punch card machine.

Electronic Machines

First, find out from the basic pattern for the thickness of yarn you intend to use how many stitches you will need for the back and front. You will have some idea, from the jumpers of this type now on the market, how wide an animal you want to knit, and from that you can find out how many will fit into the width of the garment. It is much better to fill the space available, making the design continuous around the whole jumper, than to have a plain strip at both sides. You must, therefore, work out how many spare stitches there are and divide them as evenly as possible among the spaces between the animals. However many plain stitches there are between the animals, you need only half that number plus one for seaming at both sides.

14. *The Scottie dog jumper: 106 whole dogs!*

There are a number of problems to solve when you knit this kind of garment, and it will probably help you to know how I tackled the job. Then you can do likewise, using a different animal if you wish!

When I started to plan the jumper I could not find a Scottie dog which was wide enough. I wanted fairly large dogs, and, not being an artist, ended up drawing and knitting at least half-a-dozen, until I had the right shape. Because I wanted them to walk closely head to tail all round, I did not, on the body of the jumper, have any extra background stitches between dogs. There are three stitches underneath the tip of the tail, between the rear end of one and the nose of the next, and that was sufficient space. It all worked out very conveniently with a 28-stitch pattern; five dogs on the back, five dogs on the front.

Next, I had to work out the length, and think out what to do in the area of the front neck to avoid decapitation and other unpleasant mutilation! The actual dog took up 23 lines on the mylar sheet, plus 1 plain row to make the necessary even number. That was 48 rows on the row counter. By allowing a quarter of that depth, 6 lines on the pattern chart, 12 on the row counter, between each procession I was able to start the front neck immediately above the seventh dog. If I had knitted an eighth set of dogs, the neckline would have halved one dog each side, and some of the tails would have disappeared in the shoulder line. I was determined this should not happen, so I settled for stopping the pattern immediately after the seventh set. The 12 rows of plain knitting were omitted and ribbed yokes knitted to match the 2 × 2 welts. Having planned the front, the back was easy.

The sleeves needed more thought. The top was wide enough for four dogs, but that would have been too many for the wrist. Two dogs with wider spaces between, or three with no extra space was the right size for the wrist, which was to be gathered into a cuff to be attached afterwards. I felt it would not look right to start with two or three dogs at the bottom, and have four at the top, and a rough sketch confirmed this. I considered a winding trail of dogs climbing the sleeve, but turned that down too.

There had to be the same number of dogs in each set, anything else looked wrong. The only solution was to have three dogs and put the extra stitches into the background either side of each dog, so making the distances between noses and tails progressively wider.

Because the jumper was to be a drop-shoulder style, the sleeves were shorter than the body and needed six sets of dogs. I worked out how many stitches there would be at the beginning of each set, and divided the extra stitches evenly, resetting the machine to allow for this each time a new set of dogs was started. With the newer machines all these consecutive programmes can be entered at the beginning. In fact, it all worked out very easily. I needed only two extra stitches at both sides of the dogs in each set. The pattern for the first set was therefore 28 stitches wide, the second 32, the third 36, the fourth 40, the fifth 44, and the sixth 48. When I put the final design on to the mylar sheet, I put it in the middle of the width, leaving room for the increased space either side. The centre dog remained in the same position, and the ones at either side fanned out as the sleeve grew longer.

The only adjustment to the setting which I needed to remember was to make the white dogs 'about face', and the next set of black dogs face back in the first direction.

The eyes were glass beads with silver inside, and the collars were very narrow satin ribbon, threaded through with the double-ended bodkin, and stitched on the wrong side. Amazingly, it took 6.5m of ribbon!

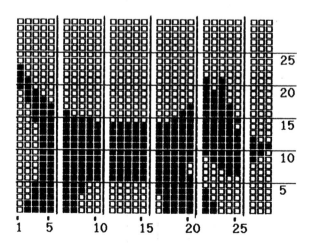

Fig. 67   *The electronic chart for the Scottie dog.*

Plain Sections Between Rows of Dogs

As we have already seen, there must be an even number of lines in a design which is to be used for Double Jacquard. If this is not so, when the number of lines is doubled to allow for knitting one colour at a time, the total rows knitted will not work out as groups of four.

There are 7 lines of main yarn knitting above each dog in the design. As it is such a short piece it is better to continue to change colour every 2 rows. The first of the 7 rows counts as part of the design section. Bearing that in mind, let us see what happens when we knit the last 2 design lines, 23 and 24.

Line	RC	Action of Jacquard switch	Main bed	Yarn
24	48	Reverses printed line	Knits all stitches	→ Main
24	47	Knits as printed	Slips all stitches	← Contrast
23	46	Knits as printed	Knits design to complete line 23	→ Contrast
23	45	Reverses printed line	Knits background to line 23	← Main

Now what about the next 6 lines? Each pair will behave in the same way. This is what will happen if we leave the machine set as it is, using just the Jacquard switch/button.

Line	RC	Action of Jacquard switch	Main bed	Yarn
26 28 30	52 56 60	Reverse line, blank to marked square	Knits all stitches	→ Main
26 28 30	51 55 59	Knits as it is, blank	Slips all stitches	← Contrast
25 27 29	50 54 58	Knits as it is, blank	Slips all stitches	→ Contrast
25 27 29	49 53 57	Reverses line, blank to marked square	Knits all stitches	← Main

That is not the same row sequence as in the plain garment in Chapter 4, but it is in the correct proportion of 2 knit rows to 2 slip rows. The continuity of the knitting is maintained throughout the garment.

When I worked out the pattern in the many sizes I have given, I realized that the smaller dog would fit better on smaller garments.

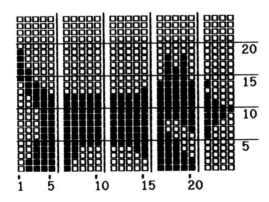

Fig. 68 *The electronic chart for the small Scottie dog.*

Punch Card Machines

Punch card machines are not as flexible as electronic ones. The width of the design is limited to 24 stitches, including plain ones at either side of the animal. Because the punch card positions are fixed, it is inevitable that there will be extra plain stitches at the edges in some sizes. When I checked through standard patterns, I found that about one-third of the garment sizes have a number of back and front stitches that is very nearly divisible by 24. Minor adjustments to make this exact, and the addition of two seaming stitches is, of course, permissible. This has been done in the patterns given here, and the necklines have been altered to compensate.

Where extra plain stitches have to be included at the sides it is important to prevent them knitting in pattern and to make them knit in the main yarn, just as in the last chapter. Refer to pages 73–75 to remind you how to do this for your machine. Notice that when there is an uneven number of dogs, the knitting will be central on the needlebed; when there is an even number it will have to be placed off-centre.

In Toyota machines turn the change-over slot to the vertical position so that end needles are selected and therefore knit in contrast yarn. With these machines there is no problem in dealing with any spare stitches either side of the dogs. Just use the motif dial to select the particular pattern blocks you will be using for the dogs.

Planning the length is the same as for the electronic machines. Round necks or slash necks are the most suitable for this type of pattern. V-necks remove too much of the front and are less satisfactory when it comes to fitting in the design. Always consider the front first, so that the number of plain rows between the animals can be adjusted in order to complete the last animal before the neckline starts. If necessary, the length of a garment must be altered slightly to fit in a reasonable number of plain rows between the animals. Never have fewer than 8, remembering that the rows of fabric are only half that number. If you wish to substitute another animal or any other motif, follow the garment pattern and, if necessary, adjust the rows to suit. Remember to work it all out before you start knitting!

When you convert a single bed punch card for Double Jacquard it is necessary to have an even number of lines on the single bed card. Unless this rule is observed the lines on the resulting Double Jacquard card will not be divisible by four. This is essential in order to keep to the correct knitting sequence. In this case, because the design changes in single line steps, the main bed sequence is the same as described in Chapter 3:

	Plain	Patterned
Line 4	Slips	Knits background to line 3 in main yarn
Line 3	Knits	Knits design of line 3 in contrast yarn
Line 2	Knits	Knits design of line 2 in contrast yarn
Line 1	Slips	Knits background to line 2 in main yarn

To understand how to put this into practice, examine the Toyota Scottie punch card design in Figure 69 and convert it for Double Jacquard.

You will notice that the card has been divided by horizontal lines into four sections. Each dog is 19 lines of pattern and 1 plain line to make an even number. Each plain section is 4 lines. Because punch card machines cannot reverse patterns as electronic ones do, there are two dogs on the card, one facing each way.

Toyota Simulknit

The Scottie dogs themselves will be knitted on both beds because they are in contrast yarn. As with the motifs in Chapter 5, it will be necessary to change the contrast yarn

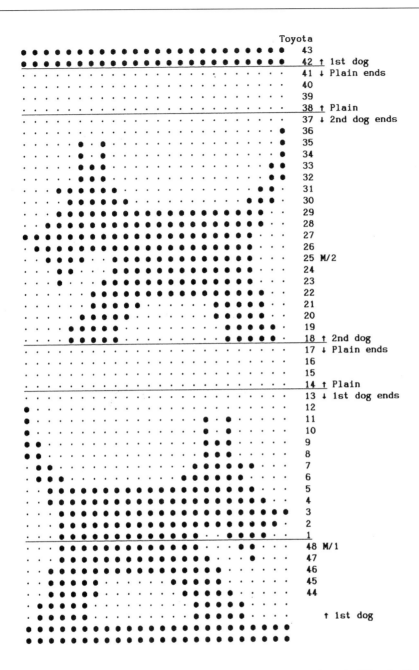

Fig. 69 *The Toyota punch card for Simulknit Scottie dogs.*

from time to time. Since the plain section is only 4 rows, continue knitting in the two yarns, which will give a tubular effect.

If you had a large area of knitting between the sets of dogs a different method would be needed. The plain section would be punched out with a small single bed Fair Isle design such as card 1, Figure 24. Two cones of main yarn would then be used to knit self-coloured Simulknit.

Facing Right or Facing Left?

This is the first design in this book which is not symmetrical. How will it appear when it is knitted? As far as these dogs are concerned, it probably does not matter which way the first row faces, but it would matter if there were letters or figures, so it is necessary to know.

> All punch card machines and all Brother electronic machines reverse the image. The first row of dogs would face left.
>
> Knitmaster electronic machines do not reverse the image so the dogs would face right as in the design chart.

Electronic machines can change the direction of a design by using the reversing switch or button. Punch cards must be punched the opposite way to the way you want the finished design to face. The easiest way to do this is to turn the card over and mark and punch on the wrong side.

Making the Double Jacquard Punch Card

Using the same method as before, it is easy to convert to Double Jacquard. Unfortunately that would produce a 96-line card, which is really unnecessary work. As I am sure you prefer knitting to punching cards, I am giving you a short cut. Knit to the end of the first plain section, then turn the card over for the second half. Make the card as shown opposite, putting the starting line for your machine on both sides, then follow the instructions for your machine.

Of course, if the thought of all that frightens you, convert the two-dog card. Leave off the joining rows after the first dog and go straight on punching out the pattern again. Remember to reverse the second dog, and finish, after the second plain section, with joining rows, which will be lines 92 and 93 on Knitmaster cards and lines 90 and 91 on Brother cards.

Using Half-length Punch Card and Reversing Card for Second Dog

Brother Machines
Start knitting at right. Knit to RC 47. Carriage left. The needles for row 48 will be selected during row 47. In fact, all needles will be selected to B position because row 48 is a row in which the main bed does not knit. Turn the card over and lock it on line 1. Knit row 48, and at the same time line 1 will be selected. Release the card. Knit to RC 95. Turn the card back to the first side and lock it as before. Make a row count chart so you know when to turn the card over.

Knitmaster Machines
Start knitting at the right. Knit to RC 48. Carriage right. First dog and plain section completed. Detach ribber carriage from main carriage. Turn card and lock on line 1. Move main carriage over to the left and back right and re-couple with ribber.

It is not necessary to remove the yarn because the main carriage is set to slip for the whole of the knitting. Do not try to programme with the carriage in the Release

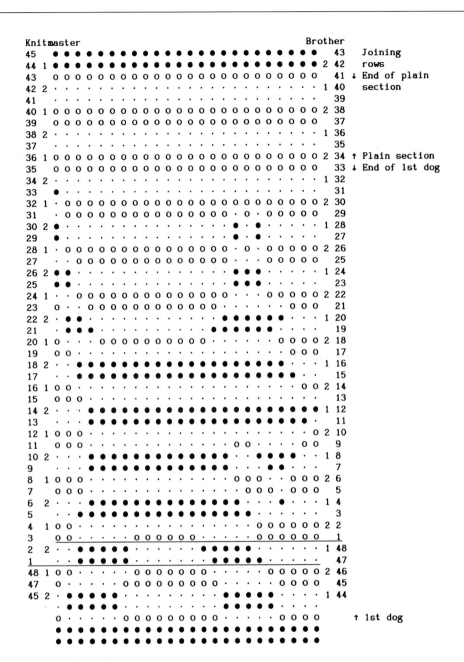

Fig. 70 *The Double Jacquard punch card for one Scottie dog; follow the instructions to make him face the other way.*

position. It must be in slip. Tension the yarn by pulling it down at the back before you knit the next row.

Turn the row counter back to 48. Release the card. Knit to RC 96, then turn back to the first side. Make a row count chart so you know when to turn the card over.

To Knit the Jumper

The Scottie dog has been designed for Fabrics 2, 3, 4a and 4b. Fabric 1 should not be used because the dogs will not be in the correct proportion. This is always a problem when knitting something realistic like the toy soldier in Chapter 5.

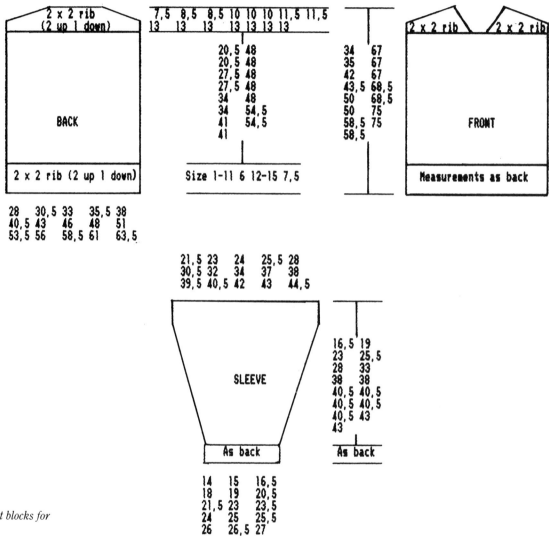

Fig. 71   *Garment blocks for jumper.*

To fit chest/bust sizes in centimetres	51	56	61	66	71	76	81	86	91	96	102	107	112	117	122
in inches	20	22	24	26	28	30	32	34	36	38	40	42	44	46	48

Back

Punch card machines Before casting on check on number of spare stitches. These are the stitches outside the punch card blocks. Place the extra stitch at the right. Make this check with the stitches which will be in position after the welt, noting that in some sizes there is an increase.

All machines Cast on for 2 × 2 rib (2 up 1 down) over width of following main bed needles

	77	83	92	98	107	113	122	125	134	143	149	155	161	170	176

Tension 4/4. Knit in rib to RC

	24	24	24	24	24	24	24	24	24	24	24	30	30	30	30

Punch card machines Increase if necessary. Stitches for pattern

	79	85	93	99	107	113	123	127	135	143	149	155	163	171	177
Number of dogs	3	3	3	4	4	4	5	5	5	5	6	6	6	7	7
Spare stitches – smaller number at left	7	13	21	3	11	17	3	7	15	23	5	11	19	3	9

Electronic machines Increase if necessary
24-stitch dogs – stitches for pattern

	78	84	92	98	107	114	122	126	136	143	151	156	163	170	176
Number of dogs	3	3	3	4	4	4	5	5	5	5	6	6	6	7	7
Width of pattern repeat	26	28	30	24	26	28	24	25	27	28	25	26	27	24	25
Spare stitches	—	—	2	2	3	2	2	1	1	3	1	—	1	2	1
28-stitch dogs – stitches for pattern										143	150	156	162	170	176
Number of dogs										5	5	5	5	6	6
Width of pattern repeat										28	30	31	32	28	29
Spare stitches										3	—	1	2	2	2

All machines Number of sets of dogs in length

	3	3	4	4	5	5	6	6	7	7	7	7	7	8	8

Fabrics 2, 3 and 4b Rows for dogs = Number of dogs × 48

	144	144	192	192	240	240	288	288	336	336	336	336	336	384	384

Fabric 4a Rows for dogs = Number of sets of dogs × 24

	72	72	96	96	120	120	144	144	168	168	168	168	168	192	192

All machines Change to main colour only. Transfer stitches for rib as for welt decreasing to original number of stitches where necessary.

Yoke

RC 000. Tension 4··/4··. Knit in rib to RC

	24	28	28	32	32	32	32	36	36	36	42	42	42	42	42

Shoulder shapings

Cast off stitches on alternate rows at both sides. N.B. In all shapings number of stitches means main bed needle positions together with rib bed stitches within width.

Groups as follows

9	10	11	9	9	10	9	9	9	10	10	11	12	12	12
9	9	10	8	9	10	9	9	9	10	10	11	11	12	12
8	9	10	8	9	9	8	8	9	10	10	11	11	12	12
—	—	—	8	9	9	8	8	9	9	10	10	11	11	12
—	—	—	—	—	—	8	8	9	9	10	10	11	11	12

Total stitches each shoulder

26	28	31	33	36	38	42	42	45	48	50	53	56	58	60

Stitches remaining for back neck

27	29	31	33	35	37	39	43	45	47	49	49	51	55	57

Total rows yoke and shoulders

30	34	34	40	40	40	42	46	46	46	52	52	52	52	52

Transfer back neck stitches to main bed. Tension 7. Knit 1 row. Release on waste knitting.

Front

Knit as back to yoke. RC 000.

Neck shaping

Put stitches for centre neck into holding position as follows

15	17	15	17	19	21	19	23	25	27	25	25	27	31	29

Put all stitches left of centre into holding position. Work on stitches at right. Knit 2 rows. Wrap inside stitches throughout decreasing. Decrease 2 stitches at neck edge on alternate rows following number of times

3	3	4	4	4	4	5	5	5	5	6	6	6	6	7

RC

8	8	10	10	10	10	12	12	12	12	14	14	14	14	16

Knit in rib to RC

24	28	28	32	32	32	32	36	36	36	42	42	42	42	42

Shoulder shaping

Knit as for back.

Left front yoke

Knit in same way as right front, reversing shapings. Transfer centre neck stitches to main bed. Pick up stitches from sides of neckline and place on main bed needles.

Number of stitches both sides

10	10	12	13	14	15	16	15	16	16	18	18	19	18	19

Tension 7. Knit 1 row. Release on waste knitting. Seam 1 shoulder before knitting neckband.

Neckband

Knit waste yarn zigzag row over width of
following main bed needles

74 80 86 92 98 104 110 118 122 128 134 134 140 146 152

Insert comb. Release rib bed loops to hang
comb on main bed needles only. Knit several
rows waste yarn and 1 row with nylon cord.
Tension 7. Knit 3 rows main yarn. Arrange
stitches for rib as welt, picking up heels to
complete layout. Knit 4 rows at each of the
following tensions: 4··/··, 4·/4·, 4/4.
Knit 12 more rows, reversing tension
settings. Transfer stitches for stocking stitch.
Pick up purl loops of 1st row of rib and place
on main bed purl needles. Tension 7. Knit 3
rows. Place loops of 1st row of stocking stitch
on needles. Tension 8·. Knit 1 row. Wrong
side facing. Place neckline stitches on same
needles. Tension 10. Knit 1 row. Release on
waste knitting. Fasten off by backstitching
through loops of last main yarn row.

Sleeves

All machines 24-stitch dogs – arrange
needles for full needle rib over width of
following main bed needles

50 50 50 50 50 74 74 74 74 74 98 98 98 98 98

Using waste yarn knit zigzag row. Hang comb
so that rib bed stitches can be released.
Release them and knit several rows waste
yarn, 1 row with nylon cord on main bed,
finishing carriage right.
Main yarn. Knit 2 rows main bed,
programming pattern on 2nd row. Pick up
heels to make full needle rib setting. Knit in
pattern starting with 12 row plain section all
sizes, except sizes 81cm and 86cm, which
start with 1st row of dogs.

Number of dogs in width

2 2 2 2 2 3 3 3 3 3 4 4 4 4 4

Increase 1 stitch on both beds at both ends of
next row and every following number of rows
following number of times

20 16 16 14 12 32 32 24 24 16 44 32 28 24 20
5 7 9 11 14 6 8 11 15 16 6 8 10 11 13

Total stitches

60 64 68 72 78 86 90 96 104 106 110 114 118 120 124

N.B. Further instruction for electronic
machines concerning the width of each set of
dogs (see also page 84).

Electronic machines 24-stitch dogs –

Set 2 26 stitches	54	54	54	54	54	80	80	80	80	80	104	104	104	104	104
Set 3 28 stitches	—	—	58	58	58	86	86	86	86	86	110	110	110	110	110
Set 4 30 stitches	—	—	62	62	62	92	92	92	92	92	122	122	122	122	122
Set 5 32 stitches	—	—	—	—	—	98	98	98	98	98	130	130	130	130	130
Set 6 34 stitches	—	—	—	—	—	—	104	104	104	104	138	138	138	138	138

All machines 24-stitch dogs –

Total rows	136	152	186	200	220	260	304	304	320	320	332	332	332	348	348
Sets of dogs	2	2	3	3	3	4	5	5	5	5	5	5	5	5	5

Electronic machines Number of 28-stitch dogs

Number of 28-stitch dogs	4	4	4	4	4	4
Set 1 Width of each dog	32	32	32	30	30	30
Total stitches	98	98	98	122	122	122
Set 2 Width of each dog	34	34	34	32	32	32
Total stitches	114	114	114	130	130	130
Set 3 Width of each dog	36	36	36	34	34	34
Total stitches	120	120	120	138	138	138
Set 4 Width of each dog	38	38	38	36	36	36
Total stitches	126	126	126	144	144	144
Set 5 Width of each dog	40	40	40	38	38	38
Total stitches	132	132	132	154	154	154
Set 6 Width of each dog	—	—	—	—	40	40
Total stitches	—	—	—	—	160	160

Welts

Knit 2 pieces alike. Cast on over width of following main bed needles

39	43	47	49	55	57	61	63	65	67	69	71	73	75	77

Knit to RC

18	24	24	30	30	30	30	30	30	30	30	30	30	30	30

Set machine for circular knitting. Tension 5/5. Knit 12 rows circular waste knitting. Release from machine. Replace on needles of main bed. Unravel waste knitting. Wrong side facing, place loops from 1st stocking stitch row of sleeve on same needles. Take care to spread extra stitches evenly across row. Tension 10. Knit 1 row. Tension 6. Release on several rows waste knitting. Seam together by backstitching through loops.

To make up

Block all pieces, steam pressing lightly. Sew shoulder seams and ends of neckband. Sew tops of sleeves to armhole edges matching centres. Sew sleeve and underarm seams. Sew on beads for eyes. N.B. If the jumper is for a small child it is safer for the eyes to be embroidered. Thread ribbon for collars overlapping ends on wrong side. Oversew ribbon joins.

– 7 –

Embossed Double Jacquard with Main Bed Patterning

– SKIRT, WAISTCOAT AND JUMPER TO KNIT –

The yarn for the Brother/Knitmaster outfit in colour photograph 15 is 2/30 HB Acrylic from Atkinson used two-stranded HB16: orphelia (1), HB12 light grey (2), HB24 fuchsia (3) and HB10 lavender (4). The yarn for the Toyota outfit in colour photograph 16 is 2/16 Botany Wool from Many-a-Mickle used singly: jade (1) and porcelain (2). For the Brother/Knitmaster fabrics shown in colour photograph 18 the tension swatch measurements are:

Skirt, waistcoat   34 stitches and 56 rows = 10cm   Tension 4/4
Jumper   32 stitches and 52 rows = 10cm   Tension 4

For the Toyota fabrics shown in colour photograph 17 the tension swatch measurements are:

Waistcoat   34 stitches and 48 rows = 10cm   Tension 1/2
Skirt   40 stitches and 64 rows = 10cm   Tension 1·/1·
Jumper   32 stitches and 52 rows = 10cm   Tension 1

Embossed Double Jacquard is a form of relief knitting in which some knit stitches are raised on the purl background of the other bed. This effect is usually obtained by leaving groups of main bed needles in non-working position while knitting a Double Jacquard pattern. However, as we shall see, there are versions which can be knitted with groups of stitches on the rib bed instead.

There are several variations of this stitch, so the subject has been divided into two chapters. In this one we shall deal with embossed Double Jacquard which incorporates patterning on the main bed, and in the next chapter the stitches will be based on plain Double Jacquard fabric or on small Fair Isle patterns from the basic set. Many examples are given with adaptations for different makes of machine.

The projects in this chapter are an embossed Double Jacquard skirt, a matching waistcoat and a plain or striped jumper. In addition to the projects, which use the main stitches featured, try out samples of all the stitches described which are suitable for your machine. By doing this, and by knitting the garments, you will gain considerable experience and be able to design your own stitch patterns.

Patterns for Punch Card Machines

With a punch card machine a narrow pattern, about 12 to 16 stitches wide, is needed to leave room for the group of non-working needles on the main bed. Suitable designs can often be found in older books and magazines which deal with push button machines using narrow patterns.

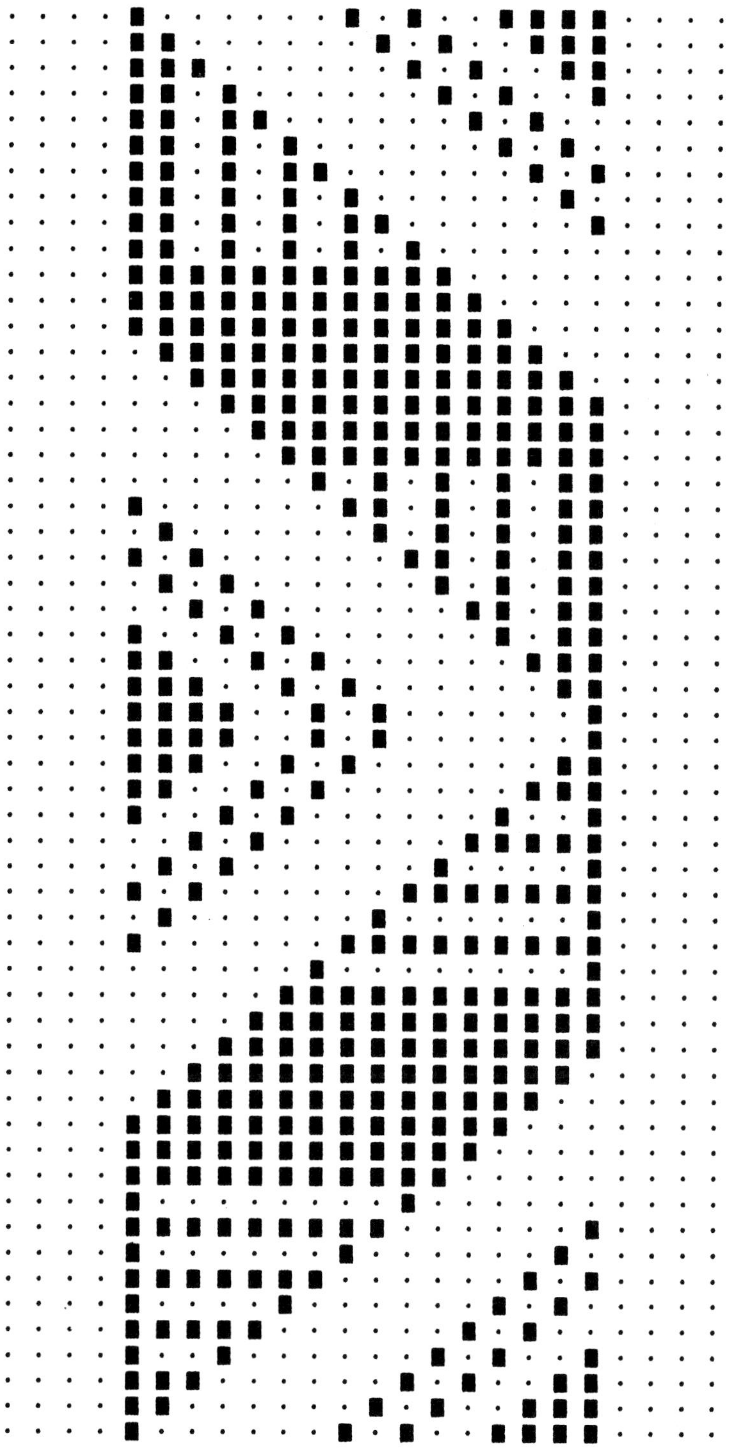

Toyota

Fig. 72 *The pattern chart for the Brother/Knitmaster waistcoat.*

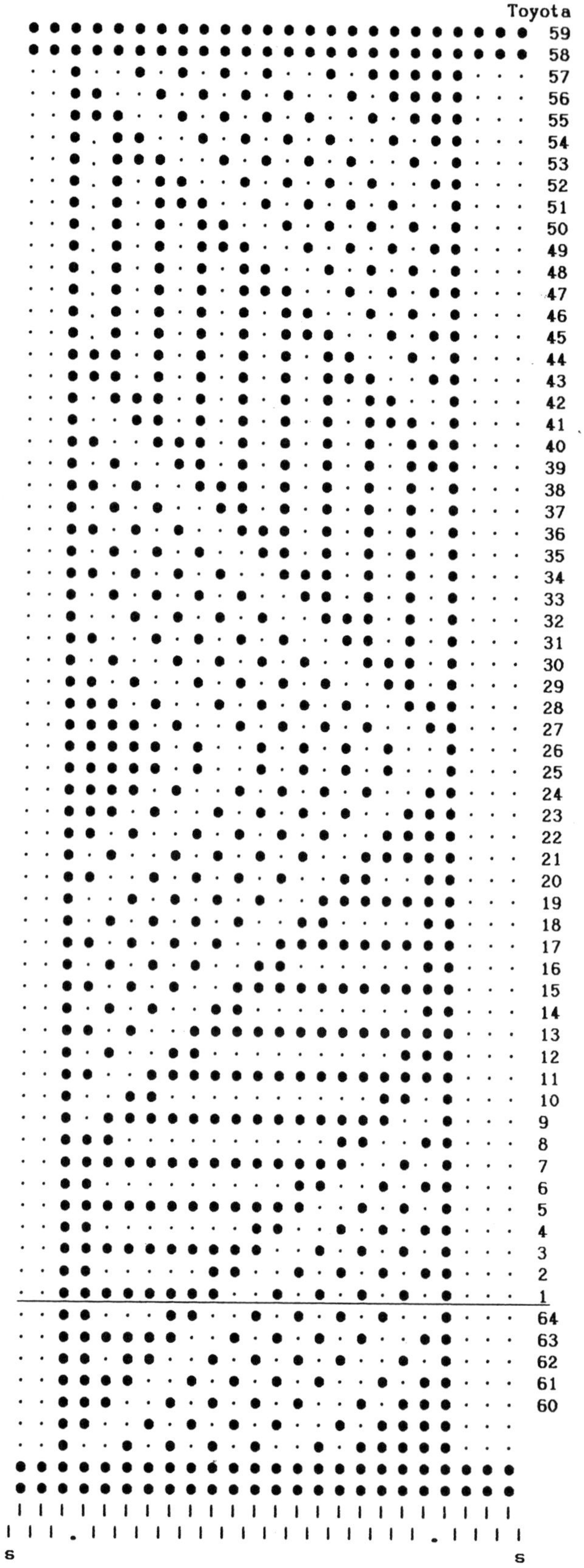

Fig. 73 *The punch card for Simulknit; an adaptation of the Brother/Knitmaster design.*

Patterns for Electronic Machines

There is not the same restriction with electronic machines. Wider patterns can be used with any width of purl section on the rib bed which the style of garment suggests. When there are more than 10 or 12 purl stitches it may help to pick up single main bed stitches, knit them for a few rows, then transfer them to the rib bed and pick up others. If this is not done there is a tendency for the wide stretches of rib bed stitches to tuck. Careful weighting is needed.

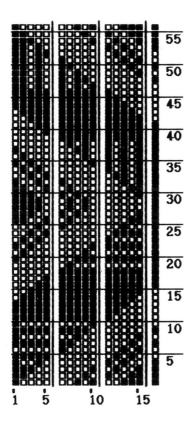

Fig. 74 *The electronic chart copied from the Brother/Knitmaster punch card.*

Making the Punch Cards

Many Fair Isle patterns can be adapted. Notice that the pattern has been placed in the centre of the punch card. This is usually the most convenient position. This is not printed as a single bed punch card because the wide sections in both colours make it unsuitable for Simulknit. The fabric was knitted, but the rib sections and the purl at the sides distorted it.

Plenty of extra blank squares should be left at both sides, then you can use the same chart for alternate plain and patterned vertical stripes, making the plain stripes as wide as you like.

Notice the two rib bed needles in non-working position just under the edge of the embossed section. This is the same idea as in mock pleats. The main bed stitches either side of the empty needles curl slightly, accentuating the embossed effect.

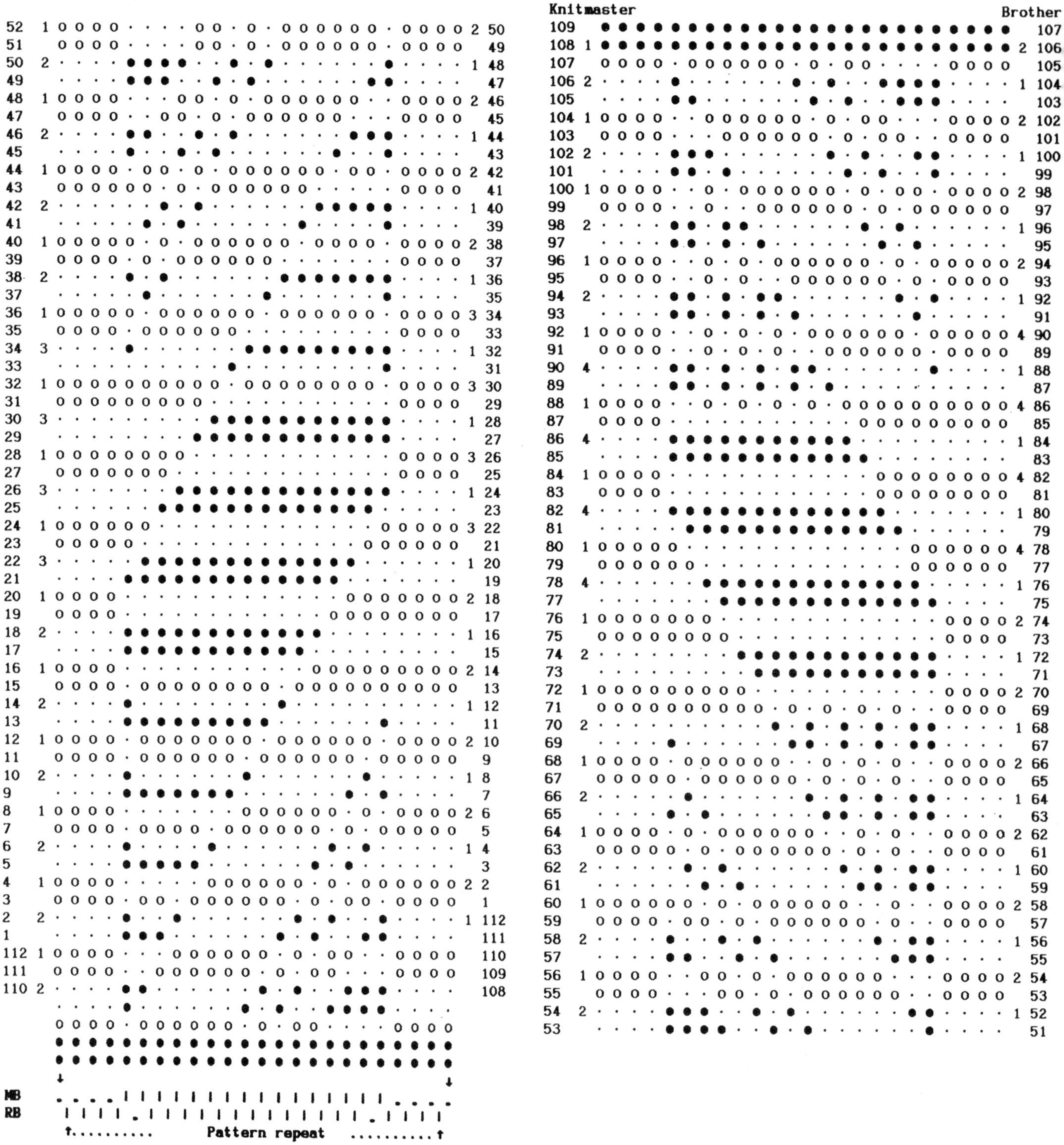
Knitmaster
Brother
MB
RB
Pattern repeat

Fig. 75 *The Double Jacquard punch card and needle diagram.*

Knitting Patterned Embossed Double Jacquard

Rib Bed Settings

Brother 830, 850, Knitmaster SRP 50, Knitmaster SRP 60 Without Auto Drive The rib bed knits 2-row stripes as in Fabric 1.

Brother and Knitmaster SRP 60N, 1 × 1 Slip Setting This is also suitable, but will need more rows.

Method for Toyota Simulknit The stitch cannot be knitted in the same way with this machine. First, the purl background will be in contrast yarn, not in stripes. Second, there will be main yarn floats across the non-working sections of the main bed. There is an interesting variation, which, although it is a little slow, is well worth the effort and has been used for the Toyota outfit.

15. ABOVE LEFT
The Brother/Knitmaster outfit in embossed Double Jacquard.

16. ABOVE RIGHT
The Toyota outfit knitted in embossed Simulknit with weaving, another new development for Simulknit.

Floats left by the main yarn, as it knits from block to block, are hooked up every 3 rows and placed on the middle rib bed needle (marked * in the needle diagram, Figure 73). This can be done without lowering the rib bed, taking care to pick up all the threads. Receiving rib bed needles should be pushed to upper working position or holding position to make it easier to knit them. There is not much room between beds, and it is easier to be sure all threads are picked up if single thickness yarn is used. Stranded 2/30s is definitely not recommended.

Knitmaster SRP 60 Using Auto Drive and Other Machines Altering Ribber Setting Manually The same effect as the Toyota 'special' can be knitted on these machines. They should be set to give contrast yarn backing (see page 99). The row count will be twice as great as on Toyota machines. Knitmaster SRP 60 uses the same needle arrangement as Toyota, while other machines require end needles on main bed.

Knitting Tension Swatches for the Outfit

Skirt and Waistcoat

The pattern uses Fabrics 1 or 4a, but you are recommended to test-knit all fabrics suitable for your machine.

1. Arrange needles for full needle rib as follows:

    Brother 830, 850, Knitmaster SRP 50, SRP 60N without using Auto Drive – 74 MB 73 RB
    Brother 850, Knitmaster SRP 60N, 1 × 1 slip setting – 73 MB 72 RB
    Toyota Simulknit, Knitmaster SRP 60 using Auto Drive – 72 MB 73 RB

2. Cast on. Knit 1st and 2nd rows of selvedge; the 1st and 3rd rows are knitted on the bed which is to keep all its stitches, in this case the rib bed. Transfer main bed stitches not required to rib bed, following the needle diagram in Figure 75 carefully. Bring rib bed needles to holding position to assist knitting. Knit 3rd selvedge row, programming pattern.

3. Change to main yarn only. Tension 4·/4·. Knit 28 rows in pattern, self-coloured
    (Toyota 14 rows). Toyota knitters pick up floats every 3 rows, and place in the hook of centre rib bed needle in each group. SRP 60 knitters do this every 6 rows, noting that there will be three threads to pick up in each case.

4. Change to main yarn and contrast yarn. Knit 60 rows in pattern.

5. Change to main yarn only. Continue to knit in pattern for 28 more rows (Toyota 14 rows).

6. Transfer all stitches to main bed. Cast off.

Swatch for Jumper

Knit in stocking stitch in whichever colour you choose. Alternatively, 2-row purl-side stripes can be used. Use the correct tension for your machine. (The jumper is not illustrated.)

Calculating the Skirt Pattern

Measure the hips and add approximately 5cm for ease. One pattern width, consisting of 8 purl stitches and an embossed panel, measures 7cm. The skirt will need two or three lengths of fabric according to size. Select the size required from the following table and knit the given number of fabric lengths in the widths indicated.

Width of fabric at hip-line		91	98	105	112	119	126
Waist measurement		66	73	80	87	94	101
Brother/Knitmaster Number of pattern widths		13	14	15	16	17	18
Number of fabric lengths		2	2	3	3	3	3
Number of pattern widths in panels	1	6	7	5	5	6	6
	2	7	7	5	5	6	6
	3	—	—	5	6	5	6
Toyota Number of pattern widths		15	16	17	18	20	21
Number of fabric lengths		3	3	3	3	3	3
Number of pattern widths in panels	1	5	5	6	6	7	7
	2	5	5	6	6	7	7
	3	5	6	5	6	6	7

For unobtrusive seaming, joins on the skirt should be underneath the edge of an embossed panel. For this reason, none of the lengths is wider than seven patterns. Ends of each fabric length must be arranged as shown.

Fig. 76   Needle diagram for Brother/Knitmaster plain Jacquard mock-pleated skirt.

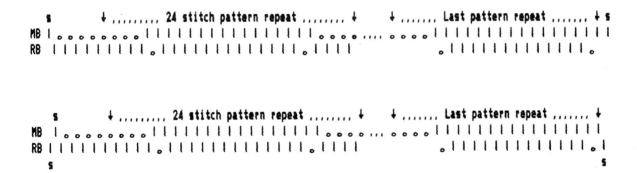

The Toyota skirt was knitted in long stitch. This gave a better effect in the yarn used than did plain Double Jacquard. The proportion of main bed to rib bed rows is 1:2 in both fabrics. Long stitch is knitted as follows: Main bed ← Knit Slip → Rib Bed ← Knit Knit →.

Fig. 77   Needle diagram for Toyota long-stitch mock-pleated skirt.

Shaping the Skirt

The only shaping in the width of the skirt is in the last 20 per cent of the rows, from hip-line to waist. Rib bed stitches are gradually removed from the back of embossed panels, which then taper in towards the waist. Follow the needle diagrams given in the pattern, and the instructions for decreasing into waistband.

Lengthening the skirt at the back, which is an advantage for larger sizes, is by short

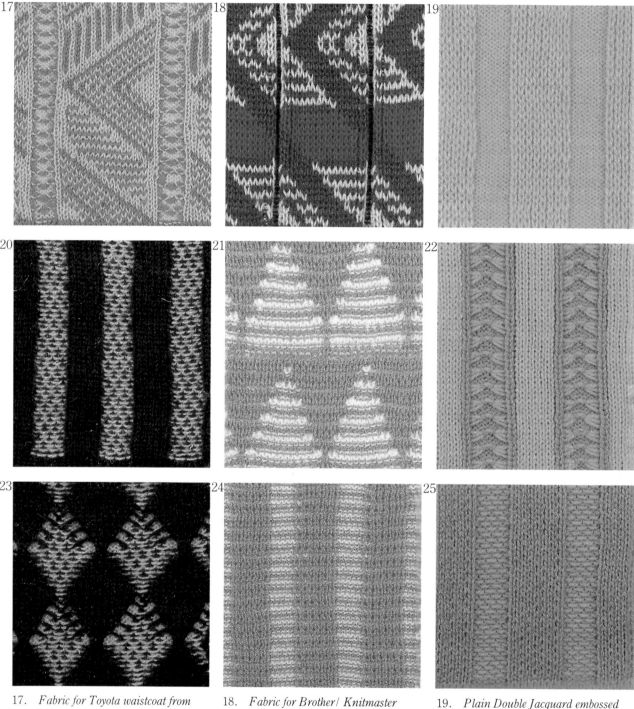

17.   Fabric for Toyota waistcoat from Chapter 7.

18.   Fabric for Brother/ Knitmaster waistcoat from Chapter 7.

19.   Plain Double Jacquard embossed stripes.

20.   The Toyota sleeve fabric shown in colour photograph 27.

21.   The Brother/Knitmaster main fabric shown in colour photograph 26.

22.   Embossed stripes using Simulknit showing picked up floats – a combination of weaving and Simulknit.

23.   The Toyota main fabric. The navy diamonds are in tubular knitting because the main bed is knitting in blue.

24.   The Brother/Knitmaster sleeve fabric.

25.   Embossed stripes using 1 × 1 slip background knitted on a Brother 850 ribber. Knitmaster and Toyota knitters reverse beds and use card 1, Figure 24, for slip on main bed.

row knitting. This is easy in mock-pleated skirts because the turning places can be arranged to coincide with the line of the pleat. Since short row knitting causes problems with weighting in ribbed fabrics, in the skirt shown in colour photograph 16 I spread the shaping rows evenly throughout the first four sections. Each skirt must be worked out individually. This is just an example.

The skirt needed to be 2.5cm longer at the centre back – that is, 10 rows, which is five shapings of 2 rows each. I knitted the second length to 71cm. The first four sections totalled 364 rows. A shaping was knitted every 70 rows from the beginning. Shaping on one fabric length started at the right, and on one at the left. The two longer edges are at the centre back, and the waistband was marked to indicate this. The method is as follows.

Knit 70 rows (69 on 2nd piece). Carriages to holding position. Push needles of left (right) panel to holding position. Knit 2 rows. There is no need to wrap because the pleat fold hides the minute hole. *Knit 68 rows right across. Shape again, this time pushing needles of 2 patterns to holding position.* Repeat from * to * 3 more times, each time putting 1 more pattern into holding position. Knit to RC 364, and then shape the fifth section of skirt. Some slight adjustment of weight positions may be necessary as the shaping progresses.

Working Out the Waistcoat Pattern

It is important to work out the pattern carefully to give maximum effect to the design of the stitch. The edge of a complete embossed panel looks better at the centre front than does either part of a panel or a purl section. Because both fronts are alike, the two embossed panels need to overlap. This means there can be extra stitches on the fronts, and they are eased into the shoulder seam at the purl sections, giving fullness to the fronts of the waistcoat. Four sizes are given, six, seven, eight and nine panels wide. The extra stitches on the second and fourth sizes are placed as half-panels at the ends of the rows. This makes the needle arrangement for the front neck the same in all sizes. Needle arrangements have been worked out in detail for both machines and all sizes, and they are given in the pattern.

To Knit the Skirt, Waistcoat and Jumper

To fit bust sizes in centimetres	81	86	91	96	102	107
in inches	32	34	36	38	40	42
hip sizes in centimetres	86	91	96	102	107	112
in inches	34	36	38	40	42	44

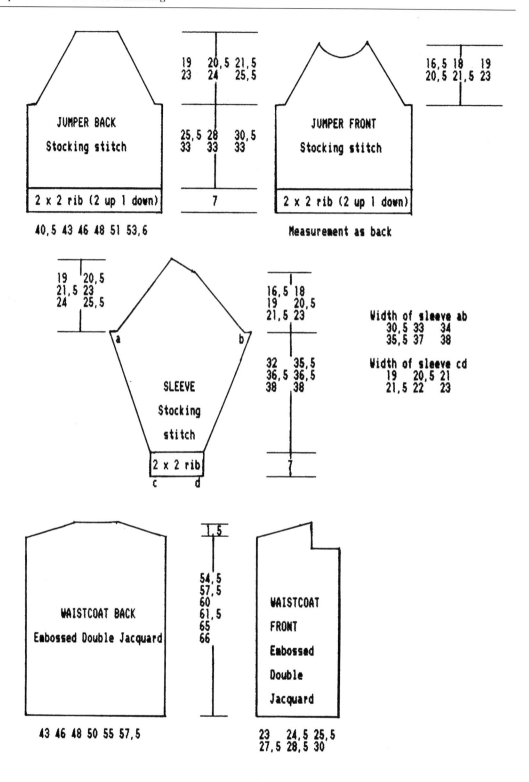

Fig. 78 *Garment blocks for jumper and waistcoat.*

Skirt

Cast on and knit required number of panels, arranging needles across
width as shown in Figures 76 and 77. Knit selvedge, arranging needles for
pattern as in tension swatch.

	5	6	7
All machines Number of patterns in panel	5	6	7
Number of main bed needles	122	146	170
Length in centimetres	66	71	76
Brother/Knitmaster Total rows	372	400	424
Section 5 – for shaping see Figure 79	72	80	80
Toyota Total rows	422	454	486
Section 5 – for shaping see Figure 79	84	90	98

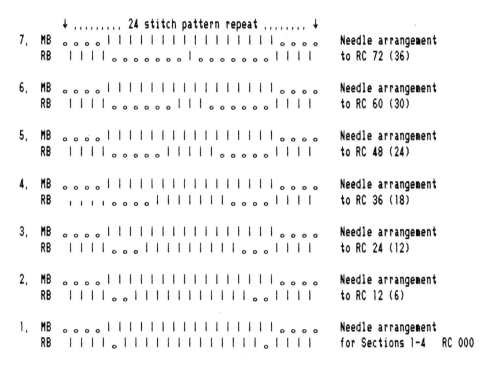

Fig. 79 *Rib bed needle
diagrams to show the shaping of
Section 5 by transferring rib bed
stitches in embossed patterns to
adjacent rib bed needles. The
Toyota row count is given in
brackets.*

Brother/Knitmaster Knit panels as follows

5 pattern panels	—	—	3	2	1	—
6 pattern panels	1	—	—	1	2	3
7 pattern panels	1	2	—	—	—	—
Total number of pieces	2	2	3	3	3	3

Toyota Knit panels as follows

5 pattern panels	3	2	1	—	—	—
6 pattern panels	—	1	2	3	1	—
7 pattern panels	—	—	—	—	2	3
Total number of pieces	3	3	3	3	3	3

After knitting to RC 72 (36), proceed as shown in Figure 80. Where there are 2 stitches on a needle latch back stitch off over front leaving 1 stitch. After stage 9 there are 16 stitches to each pattern. Tension 8. Knit 1 row. Cast off with latch tool.

Fig. 80   Needle diagram to show preparation for waistband by transferring stitches to main bed to decrease width.

```
9, MB . I 2 . 2 I . 2 I 2 . I 2 . 2 I 2 . I 2 . 2 I .    Main bed working needles reduced by one third,

8, MB . I 2 . 2 I I I I I I I I 2 I I I I I I 2 . 2 I .    '2' indicates 2 stitches on I needle,

       I 2  3              4            5  6 7
7, MB  o o o o I I I I I I I I I I I I I I I I I o o o o    After RC 72 (36) transfer all RB stitches
   RB  I I I I o o o o o o o o I o o o o o o o I I I I    to MB to numbered positions shown,
       I 2 2 3              4            5 6 6 7
```

Waistband

Brother/Knitmaster Stitches are calculated at the rate of 16 to each panel. 80 stitches = 5 patterns, 96 = 6, 112 = 7, 160 = 2 × 5, 176 = 5 + 6, 192 = 2 × 6.

| Number of stitches: piece 1 | 96 | 112 | 160 | 160 | 176 | 192 |
| piece 2 | 112 | 112 | 80 | 96 | 96 | 96 |

Toyota Stitches are calculated at the rate of 14 to each panel. 70 stitches = 5 patterns, 84 = 6, 98 = 7, 140 = 2 × 5, 154 = 5 + 6, 168 = 2 × 6, 194 = 2 × 7. When placing cast-off loops of panels on to waistband reduce each panel from 16 to 14 stitches.

| Number of stitches: piece 1 | 70 | 84 | 70 | 84 | 84 | 98 |
| piece 2 | 140 | 140 | 168 | 168 | 196 | 196 |

Seam fabric lengths together. Cast on for stocking stitch using waste yarn. Knit several rows finishing with one nylon cord row. Change to main yarn, stocking stitch tension. Knit 20 rows. Turn up hem. With wrong side facing, place stitches of correct fabric length(s) on needles. Take care to attach waistband pieces to correct length(s). Tension 10. Knit 1 row. When all waistband sections are attached, sew joins on right side, leaving opening inside waistband for threading elastic.

Waistcoat

Arrange needles as follows:
Brother/Knitmaster

Size	←		Back		→		←		Left Front		→ ←		Right Front		→
1	1		6 × 24		1 = 146		1		3 × 24 20	1 =	94 = 1	20	3 × 24		1
2	1	12	6 × 24	12	1 = 170		1	12	3 × 24 20	1 =	106 = 1	20	3 × 24	12	1
3	1		8 × 24		1 = 194		1		4 × 24 20	1 =	118 = 1	20	4 × 24		1
3L	1		3 × 24	20	1 = 94										
3R	1	4	4 × 24		1 = 102										
4	1	12	8 × 24	12	1 = 218		1	12	4 × 24 *20*	*1* =	130 = *1*	*20*	4 × 24	12	1
4L	1	12	3 × 24	20	1 = 106										
4R	1	4	4 × 24	12	1 = 114										

N.B. In sizes 3 and 4 it is necessary, with punch card machines, to knit the back in 2 pieces because more than 7 patterns are needed across the width. The pieces are not the same size. This is so that the seam is under an embossed section rather than in the centre of 8 purl stitches. This attention to detail shows the importance of very careful planning. With electronic machines it is possible to knit the back in one piece.

Toyota

Size	←		Back		→	←		Right Front			→	←		Left Front			→
1	1		6 × 24		1 = 146	1		3 × 24	21	1 =	95	1	22	3 × 24		1 =	96
2	1	12	6 × 24	12	1 = 170	1	12	3 × 24	21	1 =	107	1	22	3 × 24	12	1 =	108
3	1		8 × 24		1 = 194	1		4 × 24	21	1 =	119	1	22	4 × 24		1 =	120
4	1	12	8 × 24	12	1 = 218	1	12	4 × 24	21	1 =	131	1	22	4 × 24	12	1 =	132

Back

Arrange needles for full needle rib: all punch card machines	146	170	L94	R102	L106 R114
electronic machines	146	170	194		L106 R114

Knit zigzag row and 2 circular rows. Arrange stitches as shown in chart. Knit 3rd circular row on rib bed. Carriage right. Tension 1/1. Knit 2 rows full needle rib programming pattern. Knit in pattern. Brother/Knitmaster to RC

Brother/Knitmaster to RC	288	308	328	348
Toyota to RC	260	276	296	312

N.B. Two ways are given for shaping shoulders and front neckline and for finishing edges. Toyota is by cut-and-sew, working to dimensions on blocks. Brother/Knitmaster is by decreasing.

Toyota Transfer stitches to main bed. Knit 1 row Tension 10. Cast off.

Shoulder shaping

Brother/Knitmaster Shape both ends on complete backs, left on left backs, right on right backs. Shape by transferring RB stitches to MB and putting groups to holding position on main bed only, wrapping inside needles. Shape at shoulder ends on alternate rows in groups as follows:

6 stitches ×	7	—	—		—	
7 stitches ×	1	4	—		—	
8 stitches ×	—	4	1		—	
9 stitches ×	—	—	7		—	
10 stitches ×	—	—	—		6	
11 stitches ×	—	—	—		2	
Total stitches decreased for each shoulder	49	60	71		82	
Stitches remaining for back neck: whole backs	48	50	52		54	
left and right backs			23	31	24	32
RC	304	324	344		364	

Transfer stitches to main bed. Cast off shoulders and back neck separately.

Left front

Cast on over width following main bed needles: Brother/Knitmaster	94	106	118	130
Toyota Left front	95	107	119	131
Right front	97	108	120	132

N.B. Arrange needles correctly for punch card position.

Knit selvedge as for back. Knit in pattern to: Brother/Knitmaster	236	256	268	284
Toyota	260	276	296	316

Toyota Cast off as for back.

Brother/Knitmaster Shape neck by casting off stitches at right.	35	36	37	38
Knit to RC	288	308	328	348

Shape shoulder by casting off in groups at left on alternate rows.

Group of stitches as follows:					
7 stitches ×	5	—	—	—
8 stitches ×	3	2	—	—
9 stitches ×	—	6	—	—
10 stitches ×	—	—	7	—
11 stitches ×	—	—	1	4
12 stitches ×	—	—	—	4
Total stitches for shoulder	59	70	81	92
Knit to RC	304	324	344	364

Trims

Toyota Colour 1. Cast on 10 stitches for stocking stitch trims. Tension 0. Knit 3 lengths for neckline and armholes. (Armholes optional.)

To make up

Brother/Knitmaster Join all seams, easing fullness on front shoulders into width of back shoulders. Using colour 1, work 2 rows double crochet on front edges and neckline, and round armholes.

Toyota Mark out and secure shoulder and front neckline by zigzag machining. Seam together and press seams flat. Join side seams. With right sides facing, backstitch trims to neckline (and armholes). Turn to wrong side and hem down.

All machines Make 3 button loops at 3cm intervals at top of right front. Sew on buttons to match, overlapping the embossed panels. Sew press stud inside other corner.

Jumper

Back

Welt

Cast on for 2 × 2 ribbing (2 up 1 down) over width of following main bed needles	152	161	170	179	188	197
Tension 1·/1·. Knit to RC	36	36	36	36	36	36
Transfer stitches for stocking stitch. Increase 1 or 2 stitches if required to	152	162	172	180	188	198

RC 000. Tension 4. Knit in stocking stitch to RC	168	176	182	182	196	196

Adjust length to individual requirements.

Armhole and raglan shaping

RC 000. At beginning next 2 rows cast off following stitches	8	8	9	9	9	10
Using 3-stitch transfer tool decrease 1 stitch fully fashioned at both ends of next and every following 3rd row following number of times	10	8	6	8	8	6
Stitches remaining	116	130	142	146	154	166
Knit 2 rows. RC	32	26	20	26	26	20
Decrease 1 stitch at both ends of next and every following alternate row following number of times	36	42	48	49	52	58
RC	104	110	116	124	130	136
Stitches remaining for back neck	44	46	46	48	50	50

Release on waste knitting.

Front

Knit as back to armhole and raglan shaping.

Armhole and raglan shaping

RC 000. Decrease as for back dividing for neck at RC*	68	74	80	88	94	100
Stitches remaining	80	82	82	84	86	86

Neck shaping

Put stitches for centre neck together with all stitches left of centre to holding position. Centre neck stitches	14	16	16	18	20	20

All sizes Continue to shape raglan at right 12 more times. Put stitches at neck edge to holding position wrapping inside needle, as follows.
Alternate rows: 3 stitches twice, 2 stitches 3 times. Every row: 1 stitch 7 times.
Stitches in neck curve: 19. Extra stitches decreased on raglan: 12. Put remaining 2 stitches to holding position.*
Bring needles at left of centre neck stitches to upper working position.
Repeat from * to *, reversing shapings.

Stitches in holding position	56	58	58	60	62	62

Knit 1 row right across. Release on waste knitting.

Sleeves

Knit 2 alike.

Welt

Cast on and knit as before over width of following main bed needles.	71	74	74	80	80	86
Transfer stitches for stocking stitch. Increase 1 or 2 stitches if necessary to	72	74	76	80	82	86
All sizes Tension 4. RC 000. Using 2-stitch transfer tool increase 1 stitch fully fashioned at both ends at following row intervals:	8	7	7	7	7	7
Number of decreases both sides	21	24	25	25	26	27

Number of stitches	116	122	126	130	134	140
Knit straight to RC	182	188	188	194	194	202

Shape raglan

RC 000. At beginning of next 2 rows cast off following stitches	8	8	9	9	9	10
Using 3-stitch transfer tool decrease 1 stitch fully fashioned at both ends of next and every following 3rd row. Number of decreases both sides	18	18	22	26	28	30
Number of stitches remaining	64	70	64	60	60	60
Knit 2 rows RC	56	56	68	80	86	92

Decrease 1 stitch at both ends of next row and every following alternate row

Number of decreases	18	21	18	16	16	16
Number of stitches	28	all sizes				
Knit 1 row. RC	92	98	104	112	118	124

All sizes Put 10 stitches at left into holding position. Set carriage to hold. Continue to decrease 1 stitch on raglan at right on alternate rows 6 more times *at same time* starting on 3rd row put stitches to holding position on alternate rows as follows: 4 2 2 2. Wrap inside needles. RC

	104	110	116	124	130	136

Put remaining 2 stitches into holding position. Knit 1 row right across. There are 22 stitches. Release on waste knitting.

Collar

Before knitting collar sew three raglan seams. Knit collar in rib as for welts over width of following main bed needles

	101	104	104	110	113	113

Knit 20 rows at each of following tensions: 2·/2·, 2/2, 1··/1··. Knit 30 rows at tension 1·1·. Arrange needles for circular knitting by picking up heels to fill gaps. Increase rib bed stitches to same number as main bed. Tension 4/4. Knit 4 rows on main bed. Pull down length of yarn beween beds. Knit 4 rows on rib bed. Transfer rib bed stitches to main bed. Tension 6. Knit 1 row. Wrong side facing, put stitches of neckline on same needles. Wrong side is purl for one-colour jumper, knit for striped jumper. Tension 10. Knit 1 row. Release on waste knitting.

To make up

Backstitch through the loops of tension 10 row of collar. Unravel waste knitting. This gives more stretch to the neckline than a latch tool cast off. Block and press as necessary. Seam collar and fourth raglan. Take care to seam collar on correct side. Sew up long seams.

– 8 –
Embossed Double Jacquard: Plain, Spotted and Striped

– TWO JUMPERS TO KNIT –

The yarns for the garments in this chapter are Tamm yarns from The House of Corbiere. The Brother/Knitmaster garment in colour photograph 26 was knitted in Estilo 3135 pastel random (1) and 3165 blue (2). The Toyota garment in colour photograph 27 was knitted in Suavi 2360 pale blue (1) and 2370 navy (2). The tension swatch measurements for the triangle and striped patterns for the Brother/Knitmaster garment, which is illustrated in colour photographs 21 and 24 are:

28 stitches and 54 rows = 10cm   Tension 4/4
Stocking stitch   33 stitches and 48 rows = 10cm   Tension 4

The tension measurements for the diamond and striped patterns for the Toyota garment, which are illustrated in colour photographs 20 and 23 are

30 stitches and 36 rows = 10cm Tension 5/6
Stocking stitch 33 stitches and 46 rows = 10cm Tension 3
Racked 1 × 1 rib frills both yarns 60 rows = 13cm, 50 rows = 10.5cm, 40 rows = 8.5cm, 30 rows = 6.5cm Tension 4/4; tubular 3/3

The fabrics in this chapter are based on the knitting sequence of plain Double Jacquard. They consist of vertical stripes or geometric shapes knitted on a purl background, either plain or striped. The background can also be a small slip or tuck pattern. Frequently the stripes and shapes are knitted in plain Double Jacquard, but they can be knitted in small Fair Isle patterns.

Self-coloured fabrics can be knitted on any machine. Striped backgrounds can be knitted on Brother or Knitmaster machines. Small slip-patterned backgrounds, knitted with the punch card either moving or locked on one row, can be worked on Toyota machines using Simulknit. An alternative for Simulknit is plain knitting on the main bed with floats picked up and knitted in. Brother and Knitmaster machines can also knit slip backgrounds, using a punch card and knitting twice the number rows as the Toyota. The Brother and Knitmaster SRP 60N with RJ1 ribber can also knit 1 × 1 slip and tuck.

Knitting the Samples

First Needle Arrangement

In the following samples all the needles are in work on the rib bed and selected needles on the main bed. Plain Double Jacquard setting is used on the main bed.

Embossed Vertical Stripes and Self-coloured Stripes and Background
All Machines

1. Cast on for full needle rib. Knit selvedge so that the last row is on rib bed. Before the last selvedge row, rearrange the stitches as in Figure 81. (Any main bed needle arrangement can be used. Always have half a group of non-working needles and a seaming stitch at both ends. If the non-working group is an odd number of needles, divide it and arrange needle with the smaller group on the left. Do the same for all garment pieces to ensure correct matching of the pattern when seaming.)

Fig. 81 *Needle diagram for embossed stripes: the sample shown in colour photograph 19 is self-coloured, while the sample in colour photograph 25 has a 1 × 1 purl background.*

2. Complete the selvedge, programming for plain Double Jacquard on the last row that is knitted right to left. Lock the punch card so that first 2 rows are punched rows. Start knitting with the colour that is to be used for stripes.
3. Change to main tension in graduated steps to give good edge. Knit in pattern for approximately 60 rows, finishing carriage right. Leave on machine to continue with next sample.

Plain Stripes with 2-row Striped Background
Any Machine Using Double Bed Colour Changer (or Manual Colour Change)

1. Knit 60 rows using the following colour sequence.

Rows	Colour	MB	RB
3 4	2	Slip	Knit
1 2	1	Knit	Knit Repeat 4-row sequence

   Main bed knits colour 1.
2. Knit 60 rows using the following colour sequence.

Rows	Colour	MB	RB
11 12	2	Knit	Knit
9 10	4	Slip	Knit
7 8	2	Knit	Knit
5 6	3	Slip	Knit
3 4	2	Knit	Knit
1 2	1	Slip	Knit Repeat 12-row sequence

   Main bed knits colour 2. Any of the colours can be selected to knit on the main bed by changing the chosen colour with colour 2.

Pattern Variations
Knit a sample if you have the type of machine below.

Brother 850 and Knitmaster SRP 60N 1 × 1 slip background can be used for plain or striped fabric. Set the ribber for Double Jacquard with 1 × 1 backing.

Fig. 82 *Embossed stripes with
1 × 1 slip background for
Brother/Knitmaster machines.
Use card 1, Figure 24, for any
machine. If you have a Brother
850 ribber, reverse the beds and
use a plain Double Jacquard
card to knit one colour only on
main bed and 1 × 1 slip
background.*

Fig. 83 *Needle diagram for
Toyota embossed stripes with
woven-in floats.*

Toyota Using Simulknit Set change-over slots to vertical position. All end needles will be selected when cam is on C. ('End' means any main bed needle next to a non-working needle.) When Simulknit is used with the needle setting for this section, all the needles marked * in the needle diagram will knit in contrast yarn, and the rest of the main bed needles will knit in main yarn. Pick up main yarn strands every 3 rows as before (see page 100).

Second Needle Arrangement

This is a reversal of the previous arrangement. All needles are in working position on the main bed, and selected needles on the rib bed. An extra needle must be used at both ends of the rib bed to assist correct knitting of the last group of main bed needles (see the needle diagram in Figure 84 on page 114). Knit all the samples relevant to your machine.

All Brother and Knitmaster Machines and Ribbers
The main bed knits continuously, and the rib bed knits as follows either in main or in contrast yarn, being set to slip for the other colour. The knitting sequence, which starts at the left, is one of the following (main yarn = 1, contrast yarn = 2):

Contrast Yarn Embossed Vertical Stripes

Row	Colour	RB	
3 4	2	Knit	Main yarn = 1
1 2	1	Slip	Contrast yarn = 2

Main Yarn Embossed Vertical Stripes

Row	Colour	RB
3 4	2	Slip
1 2	1	Knit

This method is a little slower because of altering the rib bed setting every 2 rows. Even so, it is sometimes easier to use this arrangement, particularly when there are wide stripes of purl stitches. Notice how the ends of the work should be arranged.

26.   *The Brother/Knitmaster jumper with embossed triangles and racked fisherman's rib frills.*

Fig. 84   *Needle diagram for vertical stripes. All machines. Dots show position of sellotape strips on punch card for Toyota sleeves.*

Dotted lines above needle positions 5–9, 17–21 apply to the Toyota variation on page 116 (Sample 2).

Knitmaster SRP 60 Using Auto Drive

This gives the same effect as Brother and other Knitmaster machines, but without the need to change rib bed settings manually. Omit the stitches marked * in the needle diagram so that the end stitches at both ends are on the rib bed.

The action of the rib bed is exactly the same as in the other machines – that is, it knits 2 rows in one colour and slips 2 rows in the other. The colour used for the stripe

27.   *The Toyota diamond jumper showing a Simulknit method of knitting embossed shapes – another new method for Simulknit.*

is decided by the position of the selection lever before knitting the 1st row. Start the pattern at the left using main yarn. Use this facility to knit these two variations.

1. Contrast yarn embossed vertical stripes – selection lever to 0 before 1st row.
2. Main yarn embossed vertical stripes – selection lever to 1 before knitting 1st row.

Pattern Variations
Knit a sample if you have the type of machine below.

Toyota Using Simulknit
Sample 1 Arrange needles as in needle diagram for Knitmaster SRP 60 in Figure 84. Use basic card 1, Figure 24, for the main bed. The purl-side of slip pattern forms background to vertical stripes knitted in contrast colour on the bed. Remember that there should be an extra needle at both ends of rib bed.

Sample 2 Modify a double-length version of Figure 24 (see Figure 141), by sticking strips of sellotape the whole pattern length on one side of the card to cover needle positions 5–9 and 17–21 (counting from left). The needle diagram is the same as for Sample 1 – that is, Figure 84. This stitch is the sleeve stitch of the jumper shown in colour photograph 27.

Tuck/Knit Background – Brother and Knitmaster Machines Only Use basic card 1, Figure 24, with the main bed set to tuck in one direction and knit in the other. Change colour every 2 rows. The same main bed needles will tuck each time, while the rib bed is changed manually to knit 2 rows and slip 2 rows as in the samples just knitted.

A tucking needle on the main bed will cause the rib bed needles on either side of it to part slightly. It is, therefore, important to consider the effect of tucking when selecting the rib bed needles. Figures 85 and 86 give two needle arrangements. Try them out. You will see that the first is badly arranged, the second has an attractive appearance.

Fig. 85 *Needle diagram showing a poor arrangement for tuck/knit embossed stripes.*

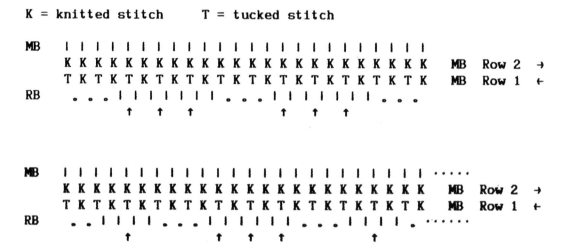

Fig. 86 *Needle diagram showing a good arrangement for tuck/knit embossed stripes.*

Tuck/Tuck Background – All Brother and Knitmaster Machines Knit a similar sample with main bed set to tuck in both directions. Take care over the arrangement of rib bed needles.

When you knit garments in all these types of stitch do make sure that ends of pieces match up where they will be seamed together. I find it helpful to plan my knitting while I am sitting at the machine. I put the needles of both beds into formation and make sure that the ends work out properly before I start knitting. Next, I check the stitches for the ribbing. That must fit in with the main pattern. Sometimes, too, it is necessary to adjust the number of stitches after knitting the welts. In the patterns in this book and in my previous ribber book, *The Machine Knitter's Guide to the Ribber*, I have told you when to do this. If a pattern does not give this information, you must check carefully before you start. When all that has been done write it down so that you get the same layout for the front as for the back. Sleeves will not necessarily be the same, and you must work them out too before starting.

☐   represents 1 stitch knitted for 1 row in main yarn on main bed

■   represents 1 stitch knitted for 1 row in contrast yarn on main bed

·   represents 1 stitch knitted for 1 row in contrast yarn on rib bed

‡   place floats on these needles

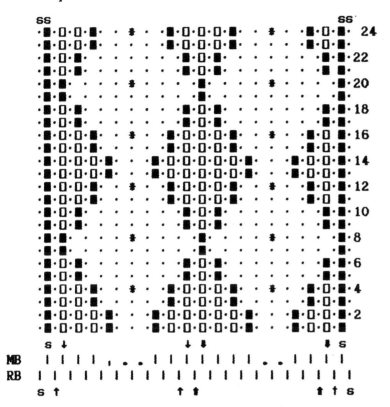

Fig. 87   *The design chart for embossed shapes knitted in Simulknit.*

Embossed Double Jacquard in Geometric Patterns

First Needle Arrangement

Two Colours, One on Each Bed – Toyota Simulknit

1. Set change-over slots to vertical position so that end needles select. Cast on. Use an unpunched line of punch card and leave it locked throughout. Programme card on last row from left to right.

2. Set the machine for Simulknit and thread contrast yarn. Transfer stitches according to the diagram below the pattern chart. Note the extra rib bed stitch required at †. Main bed needles, except for end ones, will be unselected and will knit in main yarn. End main bed needles and rib bed needles will knit in contrast yarn. Throughout knitting, pick up floats except on end groups every 4th row and place on centre rib bed needles, bringing those needles to upper working position.

3. *Knit 2 rows. Transfer end stitches of each main bed group to adjacent main bed needles.* Repeat from * to * 3 times in all. RC 6. There are now only single stitches on main bed.

28. *Simulknit diamonds outlined in main yarn.*

30. *Embossed triangles with 1 × 1 slip background.*

31. *Simulknit Fair Isle stripes with woven-in floats.*

33. *Simulknit Fair Isle diamonds with woven-in floats.*

29. *Fabrics for the Toyota garment from Chapter 9 showing how to crochet the stripes.*

32. *Fabrics for the Brother/Knitmaster jumper shown in colour photograph 35.*

4. **Knit 2 rows. Push one needle each side of main bed stitches to working position except at ends of knitting.** Repeat from ** to ** 3 times in all. RC 12. This completes one pattern.

5. Repeat steps 3 and 4 for required length, remembering to pick up floats every 4th row.

This pattern, which is illustrated in colour photograph 28, is just one idea. Take care that you do not get lost on the way. You cannot see what is happening and it is very easy to decrease the groups when you should be increasing them, or the other way round! If you make your own designs, do work to a chart, or unplug the phone! This stitch is not really suitable for the other machines.

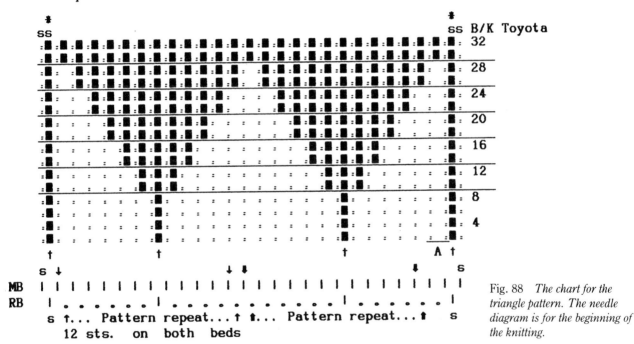

■ represents 1 stitch on rib bed (all machines)

: represents 1 stitch knitted for 2 rows on main bed

Fig. 88 *The chart for the triangle pattern. The needle diagram is for the beginning of the knitting.*

Second Needle Arrangement

Self-colour Triangles – All Machines

1. Bring 64 main bed needles to working position and arrange the needles of both beds for full needle rib. A sample five triangles wide needs stitches as follows:

    5 × 12 for backing for triangles = 60 main bed
    2 main bed, 1 rib bed at A to complete pattern = 2 main bed
    1 seaming stitch both beds left and right = 2 main bed

It is necessary to have seaming stitches at *both ends on both beds* to assist with weighting work and knitting the large groups of main bed needles when only a few rib bed needles are in working position.

2. Cast on and knit 2 selvedge rows, 1st row on main bed. Transfer to main bed all rib bed stitches except those marked †. Knit 3rd selvedge row.

3. Set main bed to knit throughout. Set rib bed as follows:

   Rows 3 4 Slip
        1 2 Knit

   Make triangles by bringing extra rib bed needles into working position after every 4th row. There are two ways of doing this. You can pick up heels from the nearest main bed stitches and leave the extra rib bed needles in working position for the first of each group of 4 rows so that they slip in that row. Alternatively, you can put extra rib bed needles into upper working position for the first of each group of 4 rows so that they pick up a loop in that row. Work the first set of triangles by one method and the second set by the other so that you can see the difference. After that the choice is yours in all stitches of this type.

4. After knitting row 28, transfer all rib bed stitches except those marked * to main bed. (In all these patterns stitches can be transferred to the main bed either by using the double-ended bodkin or the transfer carriage. Brother and Toyota knitters should be careful to rack back to the knitting position after each transfer. Knitmaster knitters should be careful to move the pitch lever back to half-pitch before knitting. In practice I have found it quicker to use the double-ended bodkin when there are only a few stitches to be transferred, and the transfer carriage if there are a lot of stitches, such as the end of the triangles.)

5. Knit 4 rows to complete the pattern. RC 32. Push up the rib bed stitches which start the next set of triangles. Use the same method as the one used during the knitting. Are you sure you have pushed up the correct needles?

6. Knit two sets of triangles – that is, 64 rows – and transfer the 2 remaining rib bed stitches. Cast off.

The pattern can be altered by omitting rows 29–32 and going straight on with another set of triangles. If that is done, the middle stitch of each triangle is left on the rib bed and the rest are transferred. The pattern is then in multiples of 28 rows.

Diamonds or Triangles with 2-row Striped Background
Any Machine Using Double Bed Colour Changer Stitch and row symbols are the same as for the triangles.

1. Bring 64 main bed needles to working position and arrange needles of both beds for full needle rib. For this sample, five diamonds wide, stitches are the same as for triangles just knitted. Remember, 2 extra rib bed stitches are needed if you are using an SRP 60N.

2. Cast on and knit the selvedge using the colour which will be used for diamonds. Transfer stitches as before. The pattern is knitted from left: 2 rows main colour on both beds, 2 rows contrast colour on main bed only.

3. Knit to row 32, increasing shapes as before. Shaping is then reversed. Before knitting row 33, and every following 4th row, transfer the rib bed stitches to adjacent needles on the same bed to shape the second part of diamond. Follow the pattern diagram carefully. The diamonds are continuous, so no rib bed stitches are transferred to the main bed until knitting is complete. At the end of work, knit rows 1–8 and then transfer the remaining rib bed stitches to the main bed.

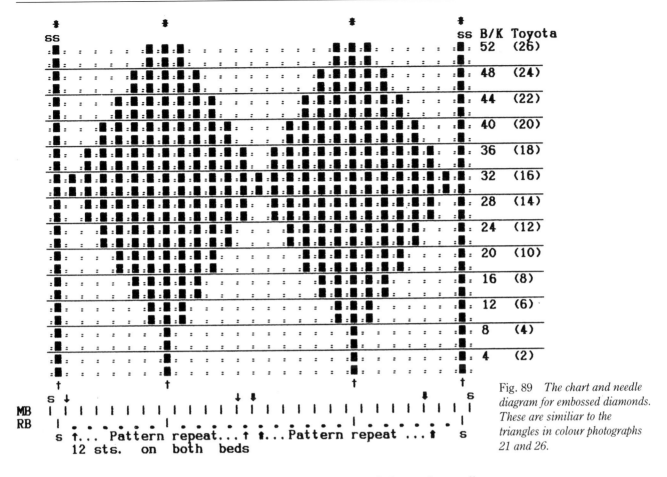

Fig. 89 *The chart and needle diagram for embossed diamonds. These are similiar to the triangles in colour photographs 21 and 26.*

4. Knit another pattern and the extra 8 rows. Transfer rib bed stitches and cast off.

Figure 88 can be used to knit triangles with a 2-row striped background. After knitting row 32, transfer all stitches except those marked * to the main bed and start again.

Pattern Variations

Knit a sample if you have the type of machine below.

Purl-side Slip Backing
Diamonds or triangles can be knitted, using the same charts, on a background of the purl side of any small Fair Isle pattern. Try basic card 1, Figure 24, either moving or locked on row 1.

Brother/Knitmaster Use the slip setting with a small punch card pattern, changing colour and working the shapes as for the striped background.

Toyota Set the machine for Simulknit. The row numbers are those given in brackets at the right of the diagram. No adjustment of rib bed controls is needed during knitting because of Simulknit setting. Knit 2 sets of diamonds, transferring the remaining stitches to main bed after 2 patterns and 2 extra rows – that is, 50 rows. Cast off.

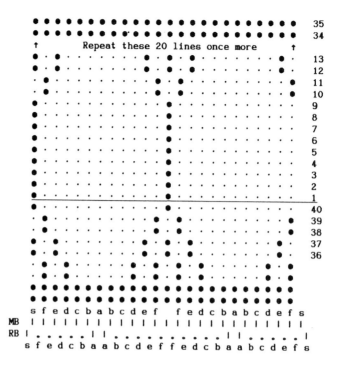

Fig. 90 *The punch card for the Toyota embossed diamonds shown in colour photographs 23 and 27.*

An interesting pattern, which was used for the back and front of the jumper shown in colour photograph 27 on page 115, can be made using a special punch card made from the one in Figure 141 for the background, and circular knitting for the diamonds. This pattern is used in the garment. Try designing similar patterns using different shapes.

1. Cast on. Knit ribbed welt or chosen edging using contrast yarn. (If you are using 2 × 2 (2 up 1 down) rib, as in the jumper in colour photograph 27, select rib bed needles starting with those either side of 0. This ensures that the correct needles are in working position for the needle arrangement for the pattern.) Finish carriage left. Transfer the stitches for the pattern, arranging the rib bed so that groups of 2 stitches and seaming stitches are continuous with edging. Tension 5/5. Knit 1 row to programme card. Change contrast yarn to S feed. Thread main yarn in O feed. Set machine for Simulknit. Tension 5/6.

2. Knit the following row sequence, increasing or decreasing on rib bed then knitting 2 rows. Transfer stitches towards the middle of the diamond as shown below.

	RB needles		*RC*
Knit 2 rows on	b a a b	then transfer bb to bb on MB	20
Knit 2 rows on	c b a a b c	then transfer cc to cc on MB	18
Knit 2 rows on	d c b a a b c d	then transfer dd to dd on MB	16
Knit 2 rows on	e d c b a a b c d e	then transfer ee to ee on MB	14
Knit 2 rows on	f e d c b a a b c d e f	then transfer ff to ff on MB	12
Knit 2 rows on	e d c b a a b c d e	then bring ff to UWP	10
Knit 2 rows on	d c b a a b c d	then bring ee to UWP	8
Knit 2 rows on	c b a a b c	then bring dd to UWP	6
Knit 2 rows on	b a a b	then bring cc to UWP	4
Knit 2 rows on	a a	then bring bb to UWP	2

34.   *The Simulknit version of three colours in a row, the third colour being added as crochet stripes. This method of decorating ladders is discussed on the next page and the garment pattern is in Chapter 9.*

Tuck/Knit and Tuck/Tuck Backgrounds – All Brother and Knitmaster Machines
Use card 1, Figure 24, on the main bed, setting the carriage to tuck in one or both directions. Make shapes on the rib bed as before.

Patterned Stripes and Shapes

The stripes and shapes are on the main bed, so the first needle arrangement is used – that is, all needles are in work on the rib bed. The shapes are knitted in small Fair Isle patterns, which are arranged for Double Jacquard according to the machine being used. The background on the rib bed can be knitted in Fabrics 1, 3, 4a and 4b (see Chapter 3) depending on the machine used.

Toyota knitters will by now be aware that the main yarn will form floats across the gaps. These can be picked up every 3 or 4 rows and put on a rib bed needle as before. In that case, the number of non-working main bed needles in each group should, if possible, be even so that there is a central needle opposite. This is so in the striped sample shown in colour photograph 31. When there is an even group on the rib bed the pick-ups are either side of the two central needles, and this can be seen in colour photograph 33. Smaller groups, three or four needles wide, can be left as ladders. Ribbons and cords can be threaded through the ladders for decoration, or crochet can be used as in the fabrics shown in colour photographs 29 and 34. This also applies to Fabric 4b, knitted by Knitmaster Auto Drive.

It is sometimes difficult to make all the rib bed stitches knit when there are empty needles on the main bed. The following precautions can be taken:

1. Use end stitch presser plates if you are knitting on a Brother machine.
2. Have a rib bed needle in working position next to the end main bed needle. Use side weights.
3. If the exposed piece of main bed knitting is very wide it may be necessary to hang claw weights high on the knitting between the beds.

Embossed Stripes Using 1 × 1 Fair Isle – All Machines

Knit these two samples of embossed Fair Isle fabric.

Fig. 91   *Toyota knitters should use Simulknit and basic card 1, Figure 24.*

Fig. 92   *The electronic chart for 1 × 1 Fair Isle.*

Fig. 93   *Brother/Knitmaster punch card machines can knit Double Jacquard from card 1, Figure 24, without punching a special card. Each set of 4 rows fits the Double Jacquard row sequence used in Chapter 3.*

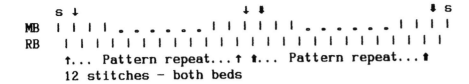

Fig. 94 *Needle diagram for Sample A: embossed Fair Isle stripes.*

Sample A Cast on for full needle rib, main bed needles divisible by 12 plus 2. End needles on rib bed for Knitmaster Auto Drive and Toyota Simulknit, so omit extra seaming stitches on main bed. Knit selvedge so that last row is on rib bed. Before knitting that row, arrange stitches according to the needle diagram, Figure 94. Programme pattern during last selvedge row.

Sample B Arrange rib backing as follows:
Fabric 1 – any machine with colour changer; no floats.
Fabric 2 – any machine with colour changer. There will be alternate colour floats between the groups of main bed needles. Pick them up every 3rd or 4th row and place on centre rib bed needle, pushing that needle to upper working position.
Fabric 3 – Brother 850, Knitmaster SRP 60N. No floats. The rib bed background will be purl-side 1 × 1 Fair Isle.
Fabric 4a – Toyota Simulknit. Floats of main yarn must be picked up.
Fabric 4b – Knitmaster SRP 60 automatically, other machines with colour changers by altering ribber settings. Since only one colour will be knitted on ribber, floats of the other must be picked up as in Fabric 2.

Sample B is knitted in the same way as Sample A, but there will be no floats to pick up because the stripes of main bed knitting are wider. The knitting is therefore much quicker. Narrow ladders will be formed when knitting all fabrics except numbers 1 and 3, in which both colours knit continuously on the rib bed.

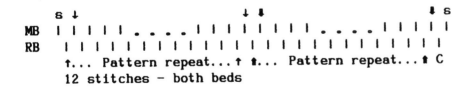

Fig. 95 *Needle diagram for Sample B: another layout for embossed Fair Isle stripes.*

More Spots and Stripes for Decoration

Here are a few ideas for you to try out. The punch cards are not printed in full; a pattern repeat across the width of the card is given in each case, and a chart is given for electronic machines. Make complete punch cards, if they are not in your basic set, and use them as you have just used card 1, Figure 24. There are many other simple, basic cards which could be used in the same way.

2 × 2 Spots

Fig. 96   *2 × 2 spots for Toyota Simulknit.*

Fig. 97   *2 × 2 spots for electronic machines. Start at right and use the Jacquard switch/button. Change colour after row 1 and then on alternate rows. Brother machines need only one of each pair of lines in all double row charts.*

Fig. 98   *2 × 2 spots for Brother/Knitmaster punch card machines.*

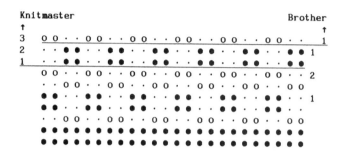

1 × 1 Stripes

Toyota Use basic card 1, Figure 91, locked on row 1 for Simulknit. Main and contrast yarn will each knit on the same needles in every row.

Fig. 99   *The electronic chart for 1 × 1 stripes.*

Fig. 100   *The punch card for Brother/Knitmaster machines. Do you recognize this card? It is a standard one; there are two in Brother and Toyota sets, and seven in Knitmaster. By starting on row 2, you can be use it for Double Jacquard. Begin knitting at the right, working the 4-row sequence: main, contrast, contrast, main.*

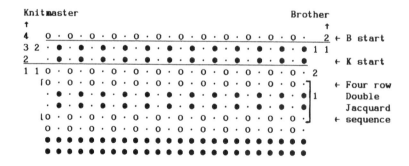

2 × 2 Stripes

Toyota For Simulknit use the card given for 2 × 2 spots, Figure 96. Lock on any row. This method can be used for any width of stripe you wish to knit in Simulknit. Just punch a single-row card, remembering that the stitches to be knitted in contrast yarn must correspond to the punched holes.

Electronic Machines Use one line from the 2 × 2 spot chart, Figure 97.

Brother/Knitmaster Punch Card Machines Use the card for 2 × 2 spots, Figure 96, and start as for 1 × 1 stripes.

Diagonal Stripes
Toyota For Simulknit use card, Figure 101.
Electronic Machines Use chart, Figure 102.
Brother/Knitmaster Punch Card Machines Use card, Figure 103.

Fig. 101 *2 × 2 diagonal stripes: the punch card for Toyota Simulknit.*

Fig. 102 *The electronic chart for 2 × 2 diagonal stripes.*

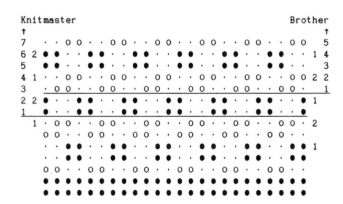

Fig. 103 *The punch card for Brother/Knitmaster machines.*

Balancing the Fabric

When you are designing garments using embossed shapes it is important to realize that the shapes need not be across the whole width of a garment piece as long as the fabric is balanced both widthwise and lengthwise. This is necessary because the Double Jacquard sections have larger tension measurements than the background knitting. The embossed areas must, therefore, be spread evenly so that the fabric is not distorted. For example, you cannot have a vertical row of diamonds at one side of a jumper, while all the rest is knitted in stocking stitch. You could have diamonds balanced by stripes. Remember always to have one stitch on both beds at the ends of the work so that you can keep the edges tensioned by using side weights.

To Knit the Jumpers

To fit bust sizes in centimetres	76	81	86	91	96	101	106	111	116	122
in inches	30	32	34	36	38	40	42	44	46	48

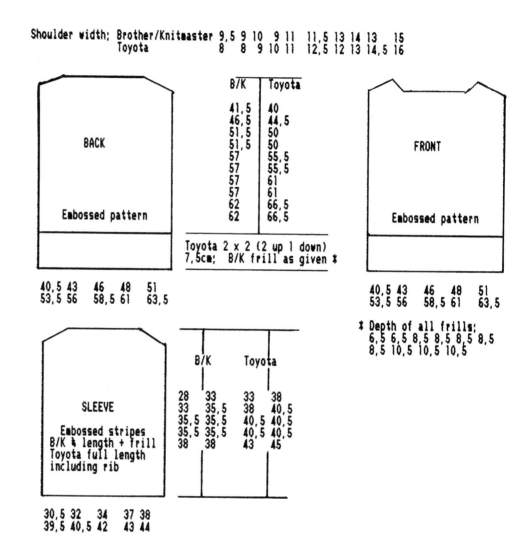

Fig. 104   *Garment blocks for jumpers.*

Back

Brother/Knitmaster Arrange needles for full needle rib; same number on both beds
*Tension 4/4. Cast on by racking (see page 51) using contrast yarn. Knit in racked rib to make frill to RC
Tension 3/3. Knit 5 rows separately on both beds. Knit 1 row full needle rib.* Arrange stitches for pattern, allowing for complete triangles, 12 rib bed needles maximum width. Extra stitches are placed at both ends on main bed only with 1 stitch on rib bed to

114	122	128	136	146	150	158	164	170	182
30	30	40	40	40	40	40	60	60	60

	1	2	3	4	5	6	7	8	9	10
provide tension. Number of triangles	9	10	10	11	12	12	13	13	14	15

Knit 2 rows main colour, 2 rows contrast colour. Tension 4/4.

Knit in pattern to RC	138	162	180	174	194	192	184	178	198	192

N.B. Alter length if required by 1 pattern, 32 rows = 5cm.

Mark armhole both ends. Knit to RC	208	240	272	272	304	304	304	304	336	336

Shoulder shaping

At beginning of next and following rows transfer stitches to main bed as necessary and cast off at both ends:

3 stitches ×	5	7	4	6	1	—	—	—	—	—
4 stitches ×	3	1	4	2	7	7	3	—	3	—
5 stitches ×	—	—	—	—	—	1	5	8	5	5
6 stitches ×	—	—	—	—	—	—	—	—	—	1
Number of stitches cast off both ends	27	25	28	26	31	33	37	40	37	43
Stitches for neck. Cast off	60	72	72	84	84	84	84	84	96	96
RC	224	256	288	288	320	320	320	320	352	352

Toyota Arrange needles for 2 × 2 (2 up 1 down) rib. Cast on. Knit selvedge. Knit 1 row rib at each of following tensions: 0/0, 0··/0··, 1·/1·, then 24 rows at tension 2/2. Over width of following main bed needles

	122	131	137	143	152	158	167	176	182	191
Increase if necessary to	122	132	138	144	152	160	168	176	184	192
Number of diamonds	10	11	11	12	12	13	14	14	15	16

Set machine for Simulknit. Contrast yarn in S feed, main yarn in O feed. Tension 5/6. Knit in pattern to RC

	82	100	114	110	124	122	138	134	148	144

N.B. Alter length if required by 1 pattern, 20 rows = 5.5cm.

Mark armhole both ends. Knit to RC	132	152	172	170	190	188	208	208	226	224

Shoulder shaping

At beginning of next and following rows transfer stitches to main bed as necessary and cast off at both ends:

10 stitches ×	4	—	—	—	—	—	—	—	—	—
11 stitches ×	—	4	3	1	—	—	—	—	—	—
12 stitches ×	—	—	1	3	2	—	—	—	—	—
13 stitches ×	—	—	—	—	2	3	—	—	—	—
14 stitches ×	—	—	—	—	—	1	4	1	—	—
15 stitches ×	—	—	—	—	—	—	—	3	2	—
16 stitches ×	—	—	—	—	—	—	—	—	2	3
17 stitches ×	—	—	—	—	—	—	—	—	—	1
Number of stitches cast off both ends	40	44	45	47	50	53	56	59	62	65
Stitches for neck. Cast off.	42	44	48	50	52	54	56	58	60	62
RC	140	160	180	180	200	200	220	220	240	240

Front

Brother/Knitmaster Knit as back to RC

Using separate lengths of yarn, cast off following stitches at centre
Divide for neck. Decrease 1 stitch at neck edge on alternate rows 12
times in all, then knit straight. *At same time* shape shoulder as for
back. Knit other side reversing shaping.

192	224	256	256	288	288	288	288	320	320
36	48	48	60	60	60	60	60	72	72

Toyota Knit as back to RC

Using separate length of yarn cast off following stitches at centre
Divide for neck. Decrease 1 stitch at neck every row 12 times in all,
then knit straight. *At same time* shape shoulder as for back. Knit other
side reversing shaping.

120	140	160	160	180	180	200	200	220	220
18	20	24	26	28	30	32	34	36	38

Sleeves

All machines Knit 2 alike. Arrange needles for full needle rib. Cast
on using waste yarn. Hang comb and release rib bed loops. Knit
several rows waste and 1 row with nylon cord on main bed, finishing
carriage right. Change to main yarn. Knit 1 row. Starting at centre,
arrange stitches for stripes, picking up heels to place on rib bed
where required.

Brother/Knitmaster Cast on

Knit in pattern to RC

Cast off 4 stitches at beginning of next row and following rows.
Number of times

Cast off 6 stitches at beginning of next row and following rows 8 times
in all. Number of stitches decreased at both sides

Cast off remaining stitches. Number to cast off

RC

86	90	98	104	106	110	114	118	120	124
152	184	186	192	192	192	194	194	206	206
4	4	6	8	8	8	10	10	10	10
32	32	36	40	40	40	44	44	44	44
22	26	26	24	26	30	26	30	32	36
164	176	200	208	208	208	212	212	224	224

Frill

Arrange needles for full needle rib. Knit as back from * to *. Transfer
to main bed. Place loops of 1st sleeve row on same needles,
2 stitches to each needle. Tension 10.
Knit 1 row. Knit several rows waste yarn. Release. Backstitch
through loops of tension 10 row.

43	45	49	51	53	55	57	59	60	62

Toyota Cast on

Knit in pattern to RC

Cast off 5 stitches beginning of next row and following rows.
Number of times

Cast off 8 stitches beginning of next row and following rows 6 times in
all. Number of stitches decreased at both sides

Cast off remaining stitches. Number to cast off

RC

92	96	102	110	114	118	122	126	130	134
100	118	118	128	128	128	128	128	136	136
4	4	6	8	8	6	10	10	10	10
34	34	39	44	44	49	49	49	49	49
24	28	24	22	26	30	24	28	32	36
118	136	136	146	146	146	146	146	154	154

Cuffs
Cast on and knit in rib as welt over width of following main bed
needs

62 65 68 68 71 74 77 77 80 80

Release both beds separately on waste knitting. Replace on main bed
needles, 1 stitch to a needle. This spreads out rib and makes a looser
join. With wrong side facing, place stitches from beginning of sleeve
evenly on same needles. Tension 10. Knit 1 row. Release on waste
knitting. Backstitch through loops of last row.

Collar

Collar required for Brother/Knitmaster garment. For Toyota either
knit collar or rib neckband. Before knitting, seam 1 shoulder.
Arrange needles for full needle rib. Brother/Knitmaster
                                   Toyota

122 156 156 170 170 170 170 170 194 194
156 170 170 170 170 170 194 194 194 194

Knit as back frill from * to *. Transfer to main bed. Wrong side
facing, place stitches or edge loops of garment evenly on same
needles. Tension 10. Knit 1 row. Cast off with latch tool.

Neckband

Before knitting neckband, seam 1 shoulder. Hang comb on following
main bed needles.

125 128 137 148 149 158 161 164 173 182

Tension 6. Knit 4 rows. Transfer for rib as welts picking up heels to
to complete layout. Tension 2/2. Knit 4 rows. Tension 1··/1··.
Knit 4 rows. Tension 1·/1·. Knit 4 rows.
Knit 12 more rows reversing tensions. Transfer to main bed, putting
pairs of rib bed stitches on to empty needles. Pick up heels of main
bed stitches of 1st rib row and place on same needles. Tension 6.
Knit 4 rows. Pick up stitches of 1st row of stocking stitch and place
on same needles. Tension 8. Knit 1 row. With wrong side facing,
attach garment to neckband in same way as sleeves to cuffs.

To make up

Seam shoulder. Join ends of collar or neckband. Make 2 holes 2.5cm apart in tubular
band at centre front by stretching the stitches apart in chosen position, taking care not
to break a thread. Make and thread cord tie. Trim ends of cord with pompons. Pin
sleeve heads into position. Tack and sew. Seam sleeve, cuff or frill and underarm
seams, leaving opening inside frills for threading elastic. This is threaded into cuff and
waist frills.

– 9 –
Multicoloured Double Jacquard
– A SQUARE-YOKED SWEATER TO KNIT –

The yarn for the Brother/Knitmaster garment in colour photograph 35 is Sara Machine from Celandine (70 per cent acrylic, 20 per cent wool, 10 per cent alpaca). The main yarn is Shade Card Number 1 beige (1), and the contrast colours are Shade Card Number 6 green (2) and Shade Card Number 2 maroon (3). The yarn for the Toyota garment in colour photograph 34 is 4 ply Concorde (100 per cent acrylic) by Water Wheel. The main yarn is 4274 platinum (1), and the contrast colours are 157 maroon (2) and 437 blue (3). The tension swatch measurements for the Brother/Knitmaster garments shown on page 118 in colour photograph 32 are:

Fabric 1 variation   30 stitches and 86 rows = 10cm   Tension 5·/2·
Fabric 3 variation   30 stitches and 100 rows = 10cm   Tension 6/6
Stocking stitch   30 stitches and 40 rows = 10cm   Tension 6

The tension for the fabrics used in the Toyota garments, which are shown in colour photograph 29 on page 118, are:

24 stitches and 36 rows = 10cm Tension 6··/7··
Stocking stitch 30 stitches and 40 rows = 10cm Tension 6

Multicoloured Double Jacquard means knitting a pattern with three or more colours in a row on the main bed while the rib bed knits a backing. As with all Double Jacquard patterns for Brother and Knitmaster machines, a special punch card must be made in order to separate the colours so that they are knitted in different pairs of rows. In these machines the total number of carriage rows – that is, lines on the punch card – for 2 complete pattern rows depends upon the number of colours. All two-colour patterns need 4 lines, three colours need 6, and four colours need 8.

Working this type of pattern would be very slow for knitters without a double bed colour changer, but the method of making the punch card is also used for single bed multicoloured Fair Isle. Toyota knitters with a single bed colour changer can, therefore, make the cards given here and use them to knit a similar garment on the single bed, remembering, of course, to allow for different tension swatch measurements and to tidy up all the floats. However, it is possible to use Simulknit and some handwork to produce fabric with three colours in a row, as in the garment for which the pattern has been given.

Designing a Multicoloured Pattern

Big, bold patterns are very effective. This garment requires a 24-stitch pattern and a smaller one. The first one is the main pattern, the second is for the yoke. In the diagram of the designs, colours are represented by the following symbols:

Colour 1   ϴ

Colour 2   ◆

Colour 3   ✳

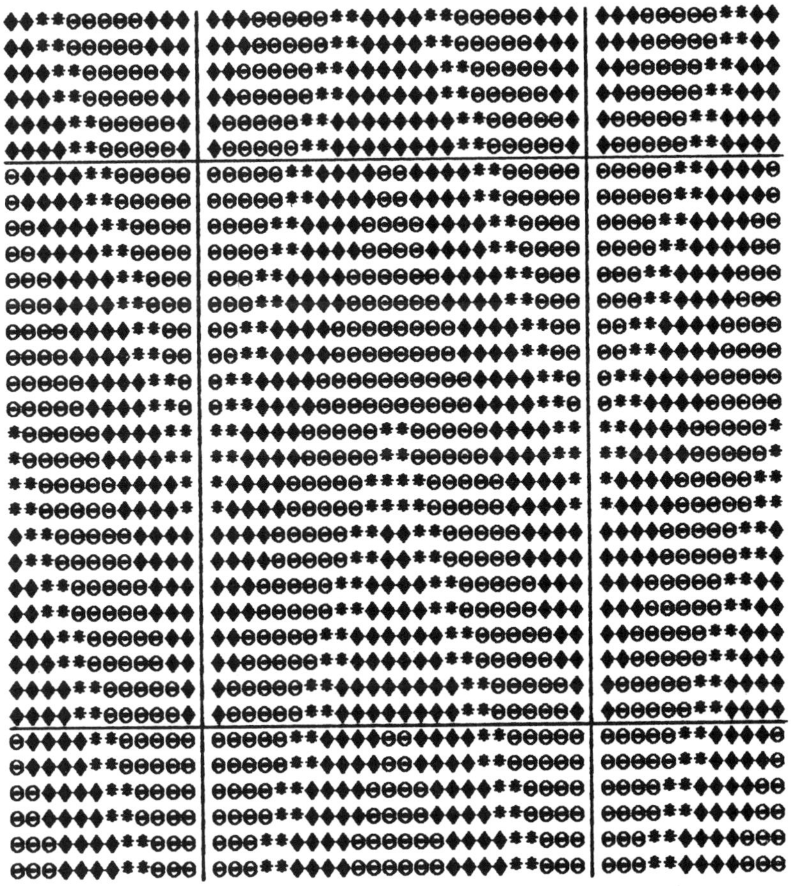

Fig. 105   *The pattern chart for the multicoloured Double Jacquard main pattern.*

Fig. 106   *The pattern chart for the multicoloured Double Jacquard yoke pattern.*

35.   *A pullover with two Double Jacquard patterns with three colours in a row. This was knitted on Brother punch card machine with an 850 ribber using the reduced backing technique.*

The pattern repeats are between two horizontal lines and two vertical lines. Notice how the diagrams have been extended at the top, bottom and both sides. This is always advisable when designing. It ensures that patterns continue correctly in all directions.

Brother and Knitmaster Punch Card Machines

The designs use three colours in a row, as they are intended for a sweater to be knitted in 4 ply yarn. Four colours make for a thicker backing, which is better suited to lighter weight yarns. The knitting sequence for this type of pattern is like that in Chapter 4 because the pattern consists of pairs of identical rows. It is, therefore, programmed from right to left, and knitted as follows:

Row 6 Colour 3 ←
Row 5 Colour 3 → Rows 5 and 6 complete 2 pattern rows in colour 3
Row 4 Colour 2 ←
Row 3 Colour 2 → Rows 2 and 3 fill in colour 2
Row 2 Colour 1 ←
Row 1 Colour 1 → Rows 1 and 2 lay the foundation in colour 1

Making the Punch Card

When one makes a design for multicolour Fair Isle, it often requires several cards to accommodate the pattern when it has been rewritten with the colours separated out. In this case there are 22 rows in the large pattern repeat, but only one of each pair needs to be marked out because the double length setting will be used. One pattern repeat therefore requires 33 rows when the colours have been separated. The 33 rows must be repeated in order to link the card correctly, making 66 rows in all.

I always mark my card using a different colour felt tip pen for each of the colours. It helps when you check that every one of the 24 spaces in each set of 3 rows has been punched once and only once. In the first punch card diagram, Figure 107, the colours are shown using the same symbols as in the pattern diagram. All the spaces marked by these symbols must be punched.

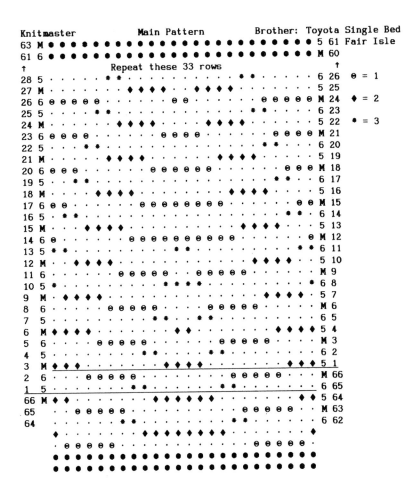

Fig. 107 *The punch card for Brother/Knitmaster main pattern.*

```
Knitmaster              Yoke Pattern         Brother: Toyota Single Bed
33 M • • • • • • • • • • • • • • • • • • • • • 5 31 Fair Isle
32 6 • • • • • • • • • • • • • • • • • • • • • M 30
↑              Repeat these 12 rows twice more          ↑
 7 5 · · · · · · • • • · · · • • • · · · · · · 6  5 Main yarn      = o
 6 M · · • • • · · · · · · · · · • • • · · 5  4
 5 6 0 0 · · · 0 0 · · · 0 0 0 0 · · · 0 0 · · · 0 0 M 3 Contrast yarns = •
 4 5 · · · · · · • • • · · · • • • · · · · · · 6  2
 3 M · • • • · · · · · · · · · · · • • • · 5  1
 2 6 0 · · · 0 0 0 0 · · · 0 0 · · · 0 0 0 0 · · · 0 M 36
 1 5 · · · · · • • • · · · • • • · · · · · · 6 35
36 M · · • • • · · · · · · · · · • • • · 5 34
35 6 0 0 · · · 0 0 · · · 0 0 0 0 · · · 0 0 · · · 0 0 M 33
34 5 · · · · · · • • • · · · • • • · · · · · · 6 32
        · • • • · · · · · · · · · • • • ·
     0 · · · 0 0 0 0 · · · 0 0 · · · 0 0 0 0 · · · 0
     • • • • • • • • • • • • • • • • • • • • •
     • • • • • • • • • • • • • • • • • • • • •
```

Fig. 108　*The punch card for Brother/Knitmaster yoke pattern.*

Electronic Machines

Making the Pattern Chart

At the time of writing, the pattern for most of the electronic machines must be broken down into colour rows, just as for punch card machines. It is a copy of the punch card in Figure 107. The exception is the Knitmaster 580, which has a special method of entering multicoloured patterns which knitters will find in the manual. All knitters should use as much of the chart as is necessary for their particular machine.

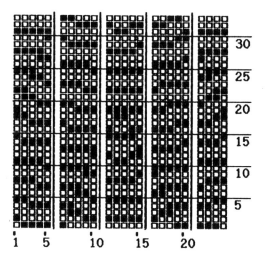

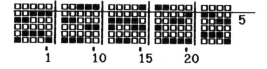

Fig. 109　*The electronic chart for Brother/Knitmaster main pattern.*

Fig. 110　*The electronic chart for Brother/Knitmaster yoke pattern.*

Reduced Stitch Rib Bed Backing and Needle Arrangement

On all Brother and Knitmaster machines the backing consists of leaving some of the rib bed needles in non-working position, so reducing the bulk. This is advisable because of the extra rows knitted on the rib bed. The following variations on Fabrics 1 and 3 are suitable and have been used for the pattern calculations, where they are shown as 1V and 3V.

Fabric 1V

Arrange the rib bed so that some needles are in non-working position. In the pattern one in every three is empty, so the rib bed arrangement can continue from the welts if you make certain that you arrange the rib suitably. The rib bed knits 2 rows in each colour, so the tension must be much lower than the main bed – approximately three whole numbers. Other rib bed arrangements are possible. Note that the fewer stitches there are on the rib bed, the narrower and longer will be the tension swatch.

This type of backing is suitable for geometric designs. Whenever possible it should be arranged symmetrically because the rib shows through on to the right side. It is not suitable for animals and single motifs.

Fabric 3V

Arrange the rib bed in the same way (2 up 1 down). If any other arrangement is chosen, always have an even number of needles in each group. When that is done, the needles will knit a slip stitch backing as before, but this time there will be ladders in between on the wrong side, although they do not show through to the pattern. The tension on both beds is the same.

Arrange the needles so that a rib bed needle is in working position at both ends immediately inside the end main bed needles. It does not matter if this alters the needle arrangement slightly, but it is necessary to keep the work tensioned at the ends. Side weights should be used. Rib bed needles must be in even-numbered groups when knitting in Fabric 3V. To see why, select needles in groups of three and push the rib carriage across, set for 1 × 1 slip backing. When increasing, do not increase by 1 stitch on the rib bed. Increase on the main bed only and leave the rib bed until you have room for 2 extra stitches. The same applies when you decrease.

Knitting the Tension Swatches

Brother and Knitmaster Machines

1. Arrange needles for 2 × 2 (2 up 1 down) ribbing. Using waste yarn, knit the selvedge and several rows of rib. Select needles and transfer stitches as above.
2. Knit several rows with waste yarn. On the last row, right to left, programme the pattern. Change to main colour and tension for stitch. Knit tension swatches. Transfer stitches to main bed. Cast off.

Toyota Machines

Single Bed Fair Isle

Cast on on main bed using waste yarn. Use the punch cards, Figures 107 and 108, to knit the patterns, using a single bed colour changer. Latch up longer floats as knitting progresses.

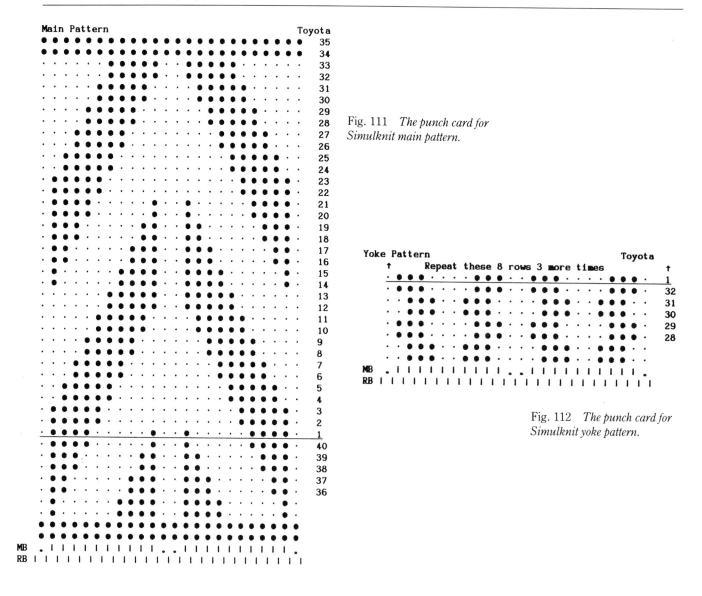

Fig. 111 *The punch card for Simulknit main pattern.*

Fig. 112 *The punch card for Simulknit yoke pattern.*

Simulknit and Handwork to Give Three Colours in a Row
Use these special punch cards and needle arrangements in Figures 111 and 112.

1. Before knitting main pattern, set left change-over slot in vertical position so that the end needles and those next to ladders select to upper working position, and knit in contrast yarn on all rows knitted left to right. Before knitting yoke pattern, set both change-over slots in vertical position so that these needles knit in contrast yarn throughout. Cast on for full needle rib using waste yarn. Knit several rows. Rearrange needles according to diagram below punch card. Knit several more rows, ending carriage right, programming punch card on last row.

2. Thread colour 1 into feeder 0. Set carriages for Simulknit. Thread colour 2 into feeder S. Knit 60 rows in pattern. Change to waste yarn and full needle rib. Take care to reset carriages correctly. All Simulknit controls must be cancelled.

3. When the piece is released from the machine use the second contrast yarn, number 3 (blue), to cover the ladders. Use one of following methods. Make 2

rows of crochet on ladders using latch tool or crochet hook and double yarn. Row 1 from bottom: make 1 chain loop over each pair of main yarn floats. Row 2 from top: make 1 single crochet stitch into each chain loop. Alternatively, make circular cords using both beds and sew to ladders or attach using latch tool. Cords can be round (3 + 2 stitches) or flat (3 + 3 stitches).

To Knit the Sweater

To fit chest sizes in centimetres	76	81	86	91	96	101	107	112	117	122
in inches	30	32	34	36	38	40	42	44	46	48

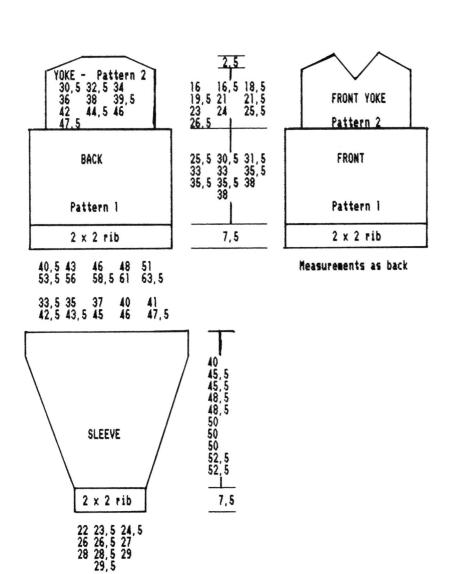

Fig. 113 *Garment blocks for sweater.*

Back and front main part

Fabrics 1V and 3V Over width of following main bed needles
arrange needles of both beds for 2 × 2 rib (2 up 1 down).
Tension 3/3. Knit 30 rows. Finish carriage right.

| 122 | 128 | 137 | 143 | 152 | 161 | 167 | 173 | 182 | 191 |

Fabric 4a Over width of following main bed needles arrange needles
of both beds for 2 × 2 rib (2 up 1 down).
Tension 3/3. Knit 30 rows. Finish carriage left.

| 95 | 101 | 107 | 113 | 119 | 125 | 131 | 137 | 143 | 149 |

Increase 1 or 2 stitches as necessary to give following stitches:

Fabrics 1V and 3V

| 124 | 130 | 138 | 144 | 152 | 162 | 168 | 174 | 184 | 193 |

Fabric 4a

| 96 | 102 | 108 | 114 | 120 | 126 | 132 | 138 | 144 | 150 |

Arrange needles for pattern. Knit 1 row programming pattern.
Knit in pattern

Fabric 1V to RC

| 222 | 264 | 270 | 282 | 282 | 306 | 306 | 306 | 324 | 324 |

Fabric 3V to RC

| 258 | 306 | 318 | 330 | 330 | 354 | 354 | 354 | 378 | 378 |

Fabric 4a to RC

| 92 | 110 | 114 | 118 | 118 | 128 | 128 | 128 | 136 | 136 |

All machines Transfer stitches to main bed. Tension 10. Knit 1
row. Cast off.

Back yoke

Over width of both beds arrange needles for circular knitting.

Fabrics 1V and 3V Carriage left.

Fabric 4a Carriage right.

| 116 | 120 | 126 | 132 | 138 | 144 | 150 | 156 | 162 | 168 |
| 94 | 102 | 102 | 108 | 112 | 116 | 124 | 128 | 132 | 136 |

All machines Tension 0/0. Colour 2. Knit zigzag row. RC 000.
Tension 1/1. Knit 2 rows. Tension 2/2. Knit 2 rows.
Fabrics 1V and 3V Tension 3/3. Fabric 4a Tension 4/4. *Decrease 1
stitch both ends both beds. Knit 4 rows.* Repeat from * to * 3 more
times. RC 20. Transfer stitches to main bed. Wrong side facing, place
stitches of main piece on rib bed needles. Knit 1 row full needle rib
programming pattern. Fabric 4a Arrange rib bed needles for pattern.

Stitches remaining Fabrics 1V and 3V

| 108 | 112 | 118 | 124 | 130 | 136 | 142 | 148 | 154 | 160 |

Fabric 4a

| 86 | 94 | 94 | 100 | 104 | 108 | 116 | 120 | 124 | 128 |

RC 000. Knit in pattern 2 Fabric 1V to RC

| 138 | 144 | 162 | 168 | 180 | 186 | 198 | 204 | 222 | 228 |

Fabric 3V to RC

| 162 | 168 | 186 | 198 | 210 | 216 | 228 | 240 | 258 | 258 |

Fabric 4a to RC

| 58 | 60 | 66 | 70 | 76 | 78 | 82 | 86 | 92 | 96 |

Shape shoulders

Casting off is permissible. Use of holding position gives smoother line.
Fabrics 1V and 3V on left, Fabric 4a on right. Drop length of 4 ply
acrylic (not nylon cord, which slips) between beds and fasten end.
Use this to knit back groups of stitches below to non-working position
first transferring rib bed stitches to main bed. At opposite end
transfer stitches from each group to main bed. Use holding position
on main bed. Be careful with weighting.

Fabric 1V 3 stitches. Number of times both ends

| 11 | 9 | 9 | 7 | 5 | 3 | 1 | — | — | — |

4 stitches. Number of times both ends

| — | 2 | 2 | 4 | 6 | 8 | 10 | 9 | 8 | 6 |

5 stitches. Number of times both ends

| — | — | — | — | — | — | — | 2 | 3 | 5 |

RC

| 160 | 166 | 184 | 190 | 202 | 208 | 220 | 226 | 244 | 250 |

Fabric 3V 2 stitches. Number of times both ends | 12 | 10 | 10 | 8 | 6 | 4 | 2 | — | — | —
3 stitches. Number of times both ends | 3 | 5 | 5 | 7 | 9 | 11 | 13 | 14 | 13 | 11
4 stitches. Number of times both ends | — | — | — | — | — | — | — | 1 | 2 | 4
RC | 192 | 198 | 216 | 228 | 240 | 246 | 258 | 270 | 288 | 288
Stitches cast off both shoulders | 33 | 35 | 35 | 37 | 39 | 41 | 43 | 46 | 47 | 49
Fabric 4a 5 stitches. Number of times both ends | 4 | 2 | 2 | — | — | — | — | — | — | —
6 stitches. Number of times both ends | 1 | 3 | 3 | 4 | 2 | 2 | 1 | — | — | —
7 stitches. Number of times both ends | — | — | — | 1 | 3 | 3 | 4 | 4 | 3 | 1
8 stitches. Number of times both ends | — | — | — | — | — | — | — | 1 | 2 | 4
Stitches cast off both shoulders | 26 | 28 | 26 | 30 | 32 | 33 | 34 | 36 | 37 | 39
RC | 68 | 70 | 76 | 80 | 86 | 88 | 92 | 96 | 102 | 106

All machines Transfer remaining stitches to main bed. Release on waste yarn for back neck Fabrics 1V and 3V

Fabrics 1V and 3V | 42 | 42 | 48 | 50 | 52 | 54 | 56 | 56 | 60 | 62
Fabric 4a | 34 | 38 | 38 | 40 | 40 | 42 | 48 | 48 | 50 | 52

Front Yoke

Cast on and knit as back until following rows of pattern have been knitted:

Fabric 1V | 18 | 18 | 18 | 18 | 24 | 24 | 30 | 30 | 36 | 36
Fabric 3V | 40 | 40 | 40 | 40 | 50 | 50 | 50 | 50 | 60 | 60
Fabric 4a | 12 | 12 | 12 | 12 | 18 | 18 | 18 | 18 | 22 | 22

Either divide for neck, or finish as back and use cut-and-sew method. N.B. When dividing for neck in patterns requiring colour changer it is easier to put work at right of machine into HP and knit left side first. Toyota machines knit right side first. Remember to note pattern row number in order to knit right side correctly.
Decrease 1 stitch at neck edge as follows:
Fabric 1V Sizes 1 and 2: every 3/4 rows alternately. Sizes 3–10: every 6 rows. Fabric 3V: every 6 rows. Number of times

Number of times | 21 | 21 | 24 | 25 | 26 | 27 | 28 | 28 | 30 | 31
Fabric 4a: every 2/3 rows alternately. Number of times | 17 | 19 | 19 | 20 | 20 | 21 | 24 | 24 | 25 | 26

At same time shape shoulder as on back. Knit other side reversing shaping.

Neckband

Before knitting and attaching neckband, join both shoulders. Make rib band to match welts. Cast on over width of following main bed needles. Knit selvedge.

Fabrics 1V and 3V | 113 | 122 | 134 | 146 | 155 | 155 | 164 | 170 | 176 | 188
Fabric 4a | 104 | 107 | 112 | 122 | 128 | 131 | 140 | 146 | 152 | 158

All machines Tension 2·/2·. Knit 1 row. Make mitres at both ends by increasing fully fashioned at both ends alternate rows. *At same time* increase tensions to 2··/2·· after 4 rows and 3/3 after 8 rows.
Fabrics 1V and 3V Increase 6 times both ends both beds.
Fabric 4a Increase 5 times both ends both beds.

Stitches after increase Fabrics 1V and 3V

125 134 146 158 167 167 176 182 188 200

Fabric 4a

114 117 122 132 128 141 150 156 162 168

Knit 1 row. Fill empty needles from heels of stitches to give same number on both beds. Tension 6. Knit 3 or 4 rows separately on both beds. Transfer stitches to main bed. Tension 8. Knit 1 row. Wrong side facing, place neckline of garment on same needles. Left side front goes to right end of band. Do this in sections, knitting 1 row at tension 10 and casting off.

Sleeves

Knit 2 alike.

Fabrics 1V and 3V Cast on over following main bed needles

68 71 74 77 80 83 83 83 86 86

Tension 2/2. Knit 48 rows rib. Increase 1 stitch sizes shown to

68 72 74 78 80 84 84 84 86 86

Fabric 4a Cast on over following main bed needles

53 56 59 65 68 68 68 68 68 71

Tension 2/2. Knit 48 rows rib. Increase sizes shown to

54 58 60 66 68 70 70 70 70 72

Knit in pattern to RC Fabric 1V

21 24 17 18 15 16 14 14 12 10

Fabric 3V

24 28 20 21 18 18 16 16 14 12

Fabric 4a

8 8 8 8 6 6 6 6 6 6

Increase 1 main bed stitch and rib bed stitches as required at both ends of next row and at same row intervals following number of times

Fabrics 1V and 3V

14 14 19 20 23 23 27 30 34 37

Fabrics 4a

12 12 14 16 19 19 21 24 27 28

Stitches after increase Fabrics 1V and 3V

96 100 112 118 126 130 138 144 154 160

Fabric 4a

78 82 88 98 106 108 112 118 124 128

Knit to RC Fabric 1V

342 390 390 414 414 432 432 432 450 450

Fabric 3V

402 456 456 486 486 504 504 504 528 528

Fabric 4a

144 164 164 174 174 180 180 180 190 190

All machines Knit 1 row full needle rib. Transfer stitches to main bed. Tension 8. Knit 1 row. Release on waste knitting.

Yoke trims

Follow instructions for trim on back yoke. Knit 2 alike.

Fabrics 1V and 3V Stitches on both beds

104 108 120 126 134 138 146 152 162 168

Decrease at both ends to

96 100 112 118 126 130 138 144 154 160

Fabric 4a Stitches on both beds

86 88 96 102 108 112 118 124 130 136

Decrease at both ends to

78 80 88 94 100 104 110 116 122 128

After knitting final row in full needle rib, transfer stitches to main bed. With wrong side facing, place side loops of yokes evenly on same needles. Knit 1 row on tension 10. Cast off.

To make up

Hem sleeves to yokes under trim. Sew sleeves to cast off stitches of main pieces. Mattress stitch long seams. Sew mitred corners of trims.

– 10 –
Half-Milano Jacquard
– THREE JUMPERS TO KNIT –

The yarns used for the Brother/Knitmaster rose design were 1 end each 2/30s high-bulk acrylic, cream and fuchsia (Fabric A); for the Brother/Knitmaster embossed design garment, 2 ends each 2/30s high-bulk acrylic navy and emerald green were used (Fabric E). The Toyota Half-Milano block design was worked with 1 end each Fantasia F6 and Denfine DF1 from Denys Brunton Designer Yarns (Fabric C). The Brother/Knitmaster garments are shown in colour photographs 36 and 37, and the Toyota jumper can be seen in colour photograph 38. The fabrics can be seen in colour photographs 43, 40 and 46.

Tension swatch measurements are given on page 157. It should be noted that Fabrics A, B, D and E can all be knitted in 1 or 2 ends of high-bulk acrylic. When 1 end is used, 38 stitches are required to 10cm; when 2 ends are used, 30 stitches are required. Of the Toyota fabrics, C requires 38, and F, 30. Length measurements vary a great deal. In the instructions I show you a simple calculation which enables you to knit all the variations.

Half-Milano Jacquard is a double bed fabric; there is no single bed version, so it is not necessary to use the word 'double' in its title. This stitch is particularly useful for fine yarns. It can be worked with one strand of 2/30s industrial yarn, knitted at a low tension, and it can be knitted as plain fabric, using either side as the right side, or as patterned fabric, either self-coloured or two-coloured, when the main bed side is normally the right side.

The method of working is to increase the proportion of rib bed rows to main bed rows so that there are 4 rib bed rows to 1 main bed row. This is the same for all Brother and Knitmaster machines. The special facilities on Brother 850 and Knitmaster SRP 60N ribbers are not used. Plain fabric can be knitted in one colour only or, perhaps, in wide stripes of contrasting colours on all machines, as can self-coloured embossed patterns. Two-coloured patterned fabric can be knitted by anyone with a double bed colour changer – and by those without, given endless time and patience!

Toyota knitters can also knit attractive geometric patterns, but irregular designs such as the rose used in this chapter are not suitable. In addition, the rose is not suitable for conversion to a Simulknit card because it is not long enough for that type of fabric. It would need at least 30 lines. In Chapter 5 we saw how different rib backings affect length of fabric.

Brother and Knitmaster Machines

The row sequence for patterned Half-Milano is as follows:

Row 4 MB Slip all stitches	RB Knit main yarn	→
Row 3 MB Knit pattern stitches contrast yarn	RB Knit contrast yarn	←
Row 2 MB Slip all stitches	RB Knit contrast yarn	→
Row 1 MB Knit background stitches main yarn	RB Knit main yarn	←

Working 2 rows in main colour and 2 rows in contrast colour is also possible, but the sequence given above is the one used in this chapter. I tried both methods for the rose, but the first one gave the pattern better definition.

The row sequence for the patterned version shows that the main bed knits one complete pattern row in rows 1 and 3 and slips the other 2 rows, while the rib bed knits all 4 rows. This balance of 1 to 4 between main bed and rib bed is the essential feature of Half-Milano Jacquard.

You may come across a row sequence in which rows 1 and 2 and rows 3 and 4 are reversed. This makes no difference as long as the colour changing is 2 rows main colour, 2 rows contrast colour. Can you see why the other colour change sequence will not give the same effect as in the jumper? (The answer is given at end of chapter.)

Design for Half-Milano Jacquard: Fabric A

This design is asymmetrical, so if you wish your pattern to face the same way as the design chart remember to mark the punch card on the back and turn it to the right side to knit. In this instance, however, it probably does not matter.

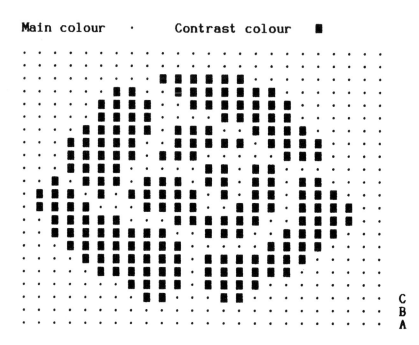

Fig. 114 *The design chart for Half-Milano rose, which is illustrated in colour photographs 36 and 44.*

Marking the Punch Card for Brother and Knitmaster Machines

1. Start at the bottom of the card and rule a line across the 2nd row above joining rows, then across alternate rows to the top. The rows ruled out are ones in which the main bed will be slipping while the rib bed knits. They will, therefore, remain unpunched. Ruling them out in this way ensures that they are not marked for punching.

2. Each pattern row takes 4 punch card rows. The first 2 pattern rows, A and B, are knitted entirely in main yarn. Punch out the 1st row to make all stitches knit on the main bed as well as on the rib bed.

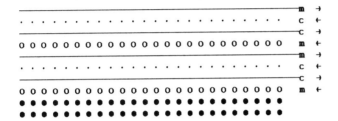

Fig. 115 *Making the rose punch card – Step 1, lines 1–8.*

3. Look back at the row sequence for the stitch, and then at the rose diagram, Figure 114. The 3rd line, C, is a mixed one. The symbol for the main yarn is ·, and these symbols must be marked for punching on the 9th line, at the start of the next group of rows. Notice that contrast yarn symbols, ▮, are not central. Two groups of two holes for contrast yarn must be marked in the 11th line. Does yours match this?

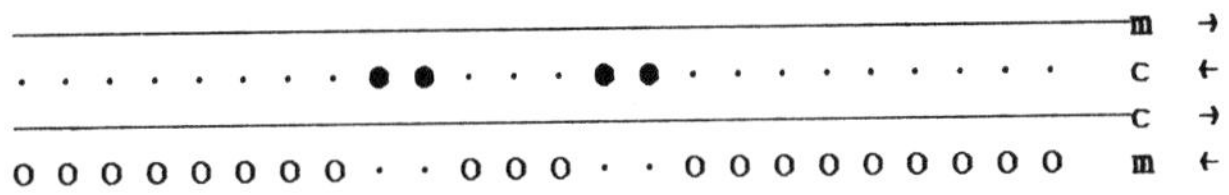

```
                                                        m   →
. . . . . . . .   ● ● · ·   ● ● · · . . · . . .         c   ←
────────────────────────────────────────────────────    c   →
o o o o o o o · · o o o · · · o o o o o o o o           m   ←
```

Fig. 116 *Making the rose punch card – Step 2, lines 9–12.*

4. Continue marking alternate rows of the card in this way. Use the diagram of the complete card (Figure 117) to check yours before you punch it. When punching is complete, mark in colour change numbers. When colour changing alternates between two colours at 2-row intervals this may seem unnecessary. However it can be helpful if any work has to be unravelled, and for less experienced knitters it is definitely advisable.

Have you noticed that the ruled lines are on all the odd-numbered rows?

At the present stage of development knitters with electronic machines will not be able to take a short cut in marking out the pattern. The whole pattern as seen in the punch card is required. Use skip or slip setting, not Double Jacquard. The knitting sequence is the same as in punch card machines:

Row   4   Main yarn
Rows 2 3 Contrast yarn
Row   1   Main yarn starting at right

Decide which way you wish to view your roses. Knitmaster roses will look like the diagram, but knitters using Brother machines should use the reversing switch if they wish theirs to do the same. See Figure 118.

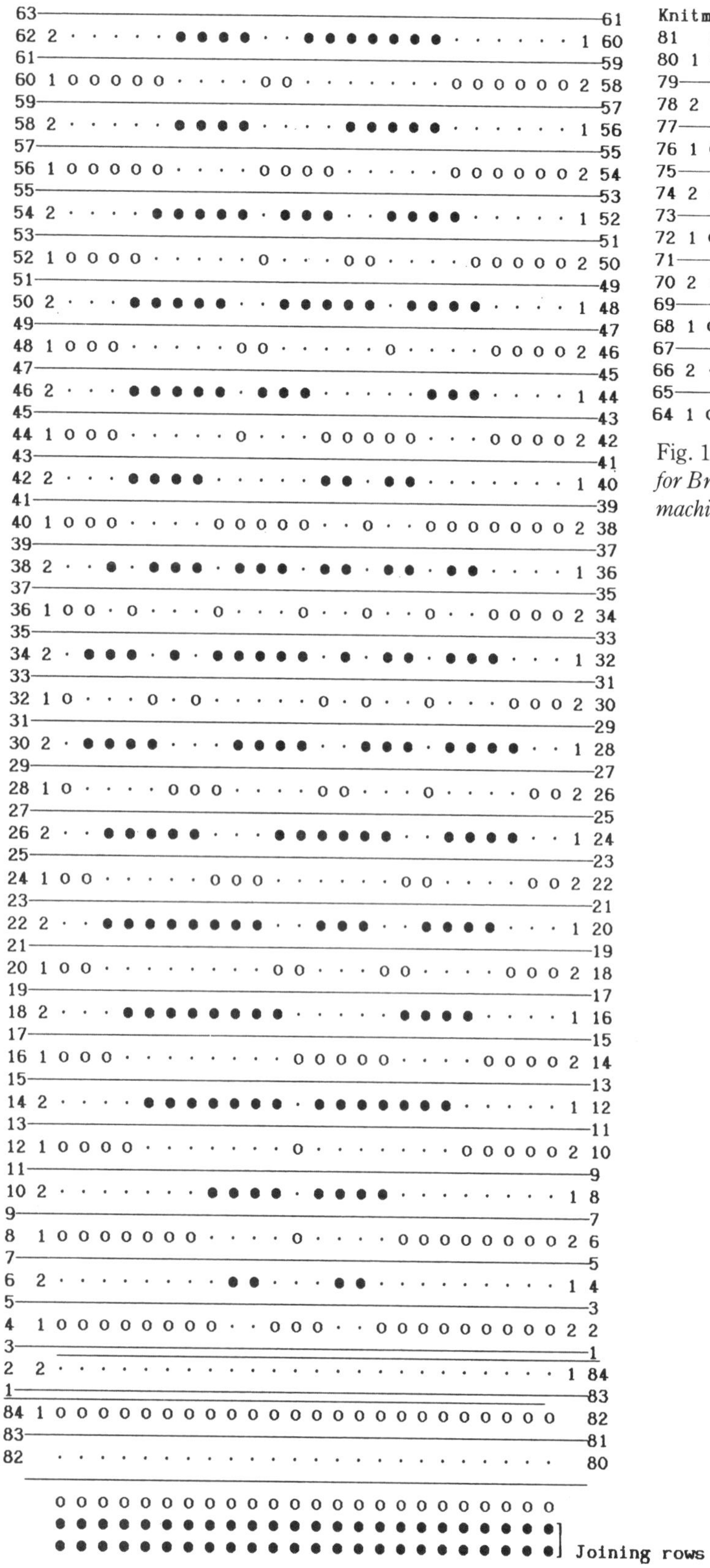

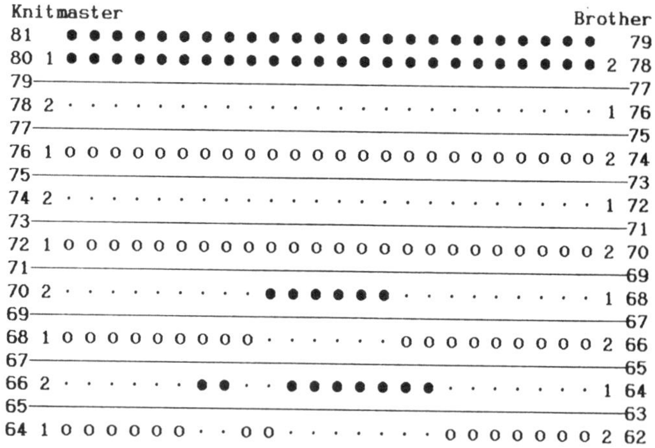

Knitmaster   Brother

Fig. 117 *The rose punch card for Brother/Knitmaster machines only.*

Fig. 118 *The rose electronic chart.*

Joining rows

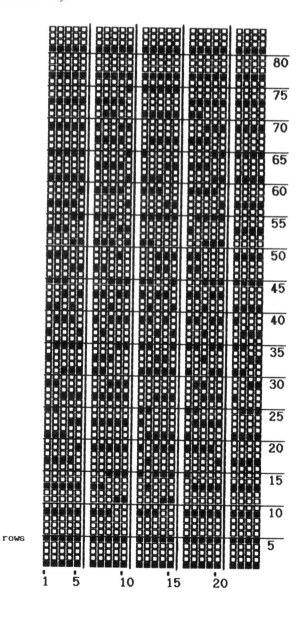

Plain Half-Milano Jacquard: Fabric B

Plain Half-Milano has already been shown at the beginning and end of punch card and mylar sheet. If you look again at the original design in Figure 114 you will see 2 plain rows, A and B, knitted in main colour on the main bed. Each row is represented by 4 rows on the marked pattern, as follows:

Row 4	MB Slip	RB Knit main
Row 3	MB Slip – no contrast stitches to be knitted	RB Knit contrast
Row 2	MB Slip	RB Knit contrast
Row 1	MB Knit all stitches	RB Knit main

36.   ABOVE LEFT
The Brother/ Knitmaster Half-Milano rose up with English rib sleeves. This was knitted mainly in one strand of 2/30s.

37.   ABOVE RIGHT
The Brother/Knitmaster embossed Half-Milano jumper, which was knitted in two strands of 2/30s.

Fig. 119 *The punch card for plain Half-Milano Jacquard; this can be used with any punch card machine.*

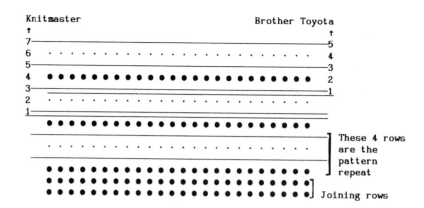

These 4 rows are the pattern repeat

Fig. 120 *The electronic chart for plain Half-Milano Jacquard.*

Geometric Design for Simulknit Half-Milano Jacquard: Fabric C

Consider again the row sequence used by the other machines:

Row 4	MB Slip all stitches	RB Knit main yarn	→
Row 3	MB Knit pattern stitches contrast yarn	RB Knit contrast yarn	←
Row 2	MB Slip all stitches	RB Knit contrast yarn	→
Row 1	MB Knit background stitches main yarn	RB Knit main yarn	←

In Simulknit, rows 1 and 3 must be combined, knitting a complete pattern row using both colours. This leaves 2 rows when the main bed slips and the rib bed knits. Simulknit Half-Milano cards need rows that are divisible by three.

In the other machines, rib bed knitting is striped. In Simulknit it is in contrast yarn only. This is why irregular patterns are not suitable – there are peculiar bulges in the finished fabric! Trying out the rose, and discarding it, led me to make a very simple block pattern.

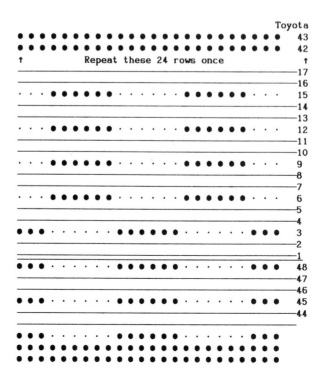

Fig. 121 *Toyota block design.*

To Knit Simulknit Half-Milano Jacquard

1. Set change-over slots to vertical position so that end needles are selected. Cast on for full needle rib using main yarn. Knit several rows, ending right, programming punch card on last row.
2. Simulknit Half-Milano row sequence and knitting method is this:

Row 6 → MB Leave setting as Row 5   Main yarn slips   Rib bed and
Row 5 ← MB Cam lever to E♦   Main yarn slips   coupling are set
Row 4 → MB Reset cam lever to C   Both yarns knit pattern to S throughout
Row 3 ← MB Leave setting as row 2   Main yarn slips   the knitting and
Row 2 → MB Cam lever to E♦   Main yarn slips   knit in contrast
Row 1 ← MB Set cam lever on C   Both yarns knit pattern yarn continuously

In pattern rows 1 and 4 the contrast and main yarns knit alternate blocks on the main bed. In the other rows, when the main bed slips, the main yarn is laid along between the beds and held down by the end stitches which knit in contrast yarn, which also knits continuously on the rib bed. Laid main yarn combined with extra rib bed rows causes a ridged effect in the contrast blocks, while the main yarn blocks remain smooth.

3. Thread contrast yarn and set carriages. Knit in pattern following directions above.

Getting into rhythm when knitting this stitch is easy. Whenever groups of main bed needles are selected to upper working position, move the cam lever to C. When end main bed needles only are selected, move it to E♦. Use side weights as knitting grows. There is a build up of rib bed knitting towards the end of each block, so use end weights and move them up frequently.

Hours of experimenting goes into developing new stitches, and sometimes there is a bonus. The first time I tried the stitch I used Fantasia and two ends of 2/30s high-bulk acrylic; this is shown in colour photograph 45. The wrong side was towards me when I removed this sample from the machine, and it is a beautiful stitch. The contrasting texture of raised tubular squares alternating with ridged ones combined with the random hues of Fantasia yarn to reward my efforts. Using one strand of Denfine with the Fantasia, as I have done in the jumper shown in colour photographs 38 and 46 gives even greater depth to the ripples, but it is not suitable on the block side. When this fabric comes off the machine the buried floats stick out of the blocks. Pull it hard, horizontally and vertically, and they will go underneath the blocks of Fantasia.

Knitting Tension Swatches

All machines can be used for plain and striped Half-Milano. Those with colour changers should start knitting at the left. The rows in each stripe must be divisible by four so that the first row in the new colour is a rib row. This gives a good effect on both sides. Knit one striped, one plain and one patterned swatch.

39.   *Toyota embossed Half-Milano pattern. Fabric F.*

40.   *The main fabric E in embossed Half-Milano for the Brother/Knitmaster jumper shown in colour photograph 37. This is knitted in 2/30s, two strands of each colour.*

41.   *The sleeve fabric E for the Brother/Knitmaster jumper in colour photograph 37.*

42.   *Toyota embossed Half-Milano stripes. Fabric F.*

43.   *The Half-Milano rose design. Fabric A.*

44.   *The same pattern as shown in colour photograph 40 but this time knitted in one strand only of each colour. Fabric E.*

45.   *Toyota block design, Fabric C, knitted in two strands of 2/30s high-bulk acrylic and Fantasia.*

46.   *The Toyota block design as used in the jumper shown in colour photograph 38. The ripple effect is caused by the combination of Fantasia (2 or 3 ply) and one strand of bright acrylic. Fabric C.*

38.   *A jumper knitted in the Toyota block design for Half-Milano. This shows the rippled effect obtained by using a very fine yarn with a thicker one.*

Embossed Half-Milano Jacquard

The embossed form of this stitch is knitted in a similar way to embossed Double Jacquard (see Figure 122). Simple geometric shapes make the best patterns.

Self-colour: Fabric D – All Machines

Method 1
The main bed knits continuously. The rib bed knits 1 row, slips 3 rows, and the controls are changed manually. The triangles are knitted on the rib bed. The advantage of this arrangement is that the ribber transfer carriage can be used to transfer stitches to the main bed when a group of stitches is to be transferred, although it must be done slowly to avoid breaking the fine yarn. In this design that is not necessary. The disadvantage is that it is slower because manual controls are used.

To Knit the Sample

1. Knit welt or hem using contrast yarn. Transfer stitches according to needle diagram.

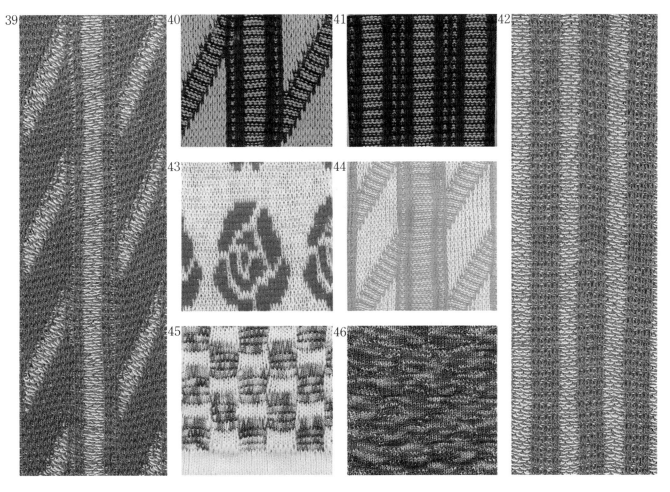

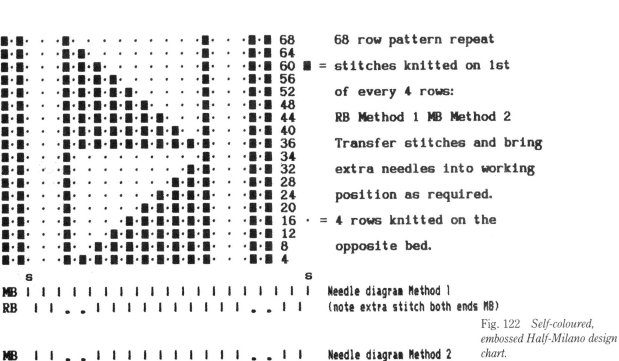

68 row pattern repeat

■ = stitches knitted on 1st

of every 4 rows:

RB Method 1 MB Method 2

Transfer stitches and bring

extra needles into working

position as required.

· = 4 rows knitted on the

opposite bed.

Needle diagram Method 1

(note extra stitch both ends MB)

Needle diagram Method 2

Fig. 122 *Self-coloured, embossed Half-Milano design chart.*

2. Knit 4 rows. Carriage right. First design row now complete. Decrease 1 stitch of triangle according to diagram.
3. Repeat step 2 until 1 stitch of triangle remains. Carriage right. RC 36.
4. Bring 8 needles into upper working position and pick up heels for next triangle. Repeat steps 2, 3 and 4 for required length.

Method 2

Use the plain Half-Milano punch card or chart (Figures 119 and 120) and set the main bed to slip. The rib bed knits continuously on all needles within width of knitting. Needles on main bed are brought to working position as required, following the pattern chart carefully. They will knit according to the sequence of plain Half-Milano. When stitches are finished with, they are transferred to the rib bed and needles returned to non-working position. As with the embossed shapes in Chapter 8, the two methods of bringing new needles into work give a different effect.

The advantage of this arrangement is that knitting on both beds is controlled automatically. The disadvantage is that finished knitting is the reverse of the pattern diagram. In some cases this does not matter. The design given here is one of them, as the two triangles face opposite ways. When it does matter, the pattern can be traced and the tracing turned over.

Two-colour Embossed Half-Milano Jacquard

Fabric E – Brother and Knitmaster Machines

This stitch must be knitted by the first method using pattern selection by punch card or electronic means. The pattern looks better facing the way it does in colour photograph 37 rather than reversed, and the punch card diagram is, therefore, the pattern diagram in reverse.

The electronic chart, Figure 125, is not reversed. Knitters using Brother machines will have to use the reversing switch, although this is not necessary with Knitmaster machines. The needle arrangement is the same as for punch card machines.

Try designing your own patterns, avoiding too much detail. The most striking results come from outlined shapes.

Fig. 123 *The design chart for 2-row striped, embossed Half-Milano.*

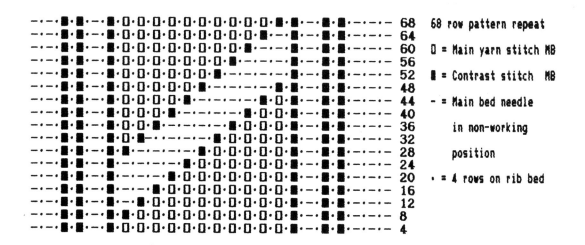

Chart	Row
`-·--·■-■--·■-0-0-0-0-0-0-0-0-0-0-■-■--·■-■---·-`	68
`-·--·■-■--·■-0-0-0-0-0-0-0-0-■--·■-■--·■-■---·-`	64
`-·--·■-■--·■-0-0-0-0-0-0-0-■--·--·■--·■-■---·-`	60
`-·--·■-■--·■-0-0-0-0-0-0-■--·--·--·■--·■-■---·-`	56
`-·--·■-■--·■-0-0-0-0-0-■--·--·--·--■--·■-■---·-`	52
`-·--·■-■--·■-0-0-0-0-■--·--·--·--·■-■--·■-■---·-`	48
`-·--·■-■--·■-0-0-0-■--·--·--·--■-0-■--·■-■---·-`	44
`-·--·■-■--·■-0-0-■--·--·--·--■-0-0-■--·■-■---·-`	40
`-·--·■-■--·■-0-■--·--·--·--■-0-0-0-■--·■-■---·-`	36
`-·--·■-■--·■-■--·--·--·--■-0-0-0-0-■--·■-■---·-`	32
`-·--·■-■--·■--·--·--·--■-0-0-0-0-0-■--·■-■---·-`	28
`-·--·■-■--·--·--·--·--■-0-0-0-0-0-0-■--·■-■---·-`	24
`-·--·■-■--·■--·--·--■-0-0-0-0-0-0-0-■--·■-■---·-`	20
`-·--·■-■--·■-■--·--■-0-0-0-0-0-0-0-0-■--·■-■---·-`	16
`-·--·■-■--·■-■--·■-0-0-0-0-0-0-0-0-0-■--·■-■---·-`	12
`-·--·■-■--·■-■-■-0-0-0-0-0-0-0-0-0-0-■--·■-■---·-`	8
`-·--·■-■--·■-■-0-0-0-0-0-0-0-0-0-0-■-■--·■-■---·-`	4

68 row pattern repeat

0 = Main yarn stitch MB

■ = Contrast stitch   MB

- = Main bed needle

   in non-working

   position

· = 4 rows on rib bed

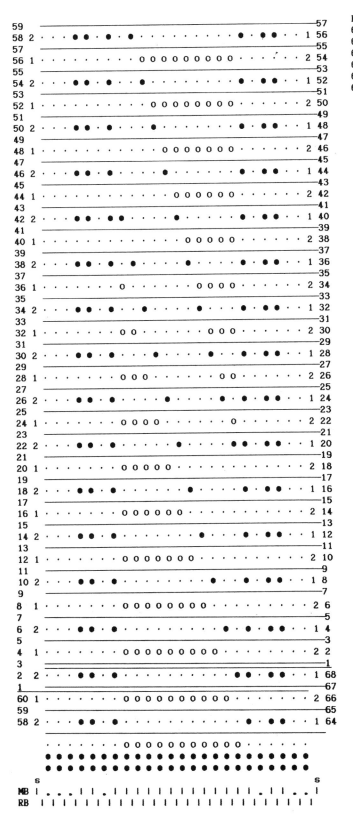

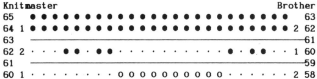

Fig. 124 *The punch card for two-colour embossed Half-Milano.*

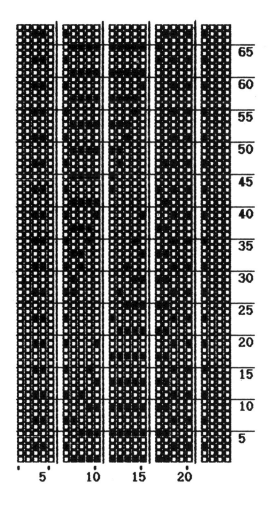

Fig. 125 *The electronic chart for two-colour embossed Half-Milano.*

To Knit a Sample

1. Cast on and knit welt or hem using contrast yarn. Programme pattern. Carriage right. Arrange stitches according to needle diagram, noting that, in this design, needles selected remain in working position throughout, except for the diagonals across the centre of each panel. When arranging stitches, use those from the welt on main bed, picking up heels to fill rib bed as necessary. Arrange for end needle selection on main bed unless end needles are any of the following: 3, 4, 6, 18, 20 or 21 (those are needles which form vertical stripes in contrast yarn). If necessary, end needles must be pushed to upper working position at the beginning of every row.

2. Knit 10 rows. Carriage right. Contrast yarn. Decrease contrast stitch at right of 10 main yarn stitches. Needle to non-working position.

3. Knit 4 rows. Decrease as before. Decrease every 4th row to RC 26.

4. There is now a group of 7 needles at left and 4 needles in non-working position. Continue to decrease at left every 4th row. *At same time*, push needle at right of 5 non-working needles to working position to cast on in next row. Continue in this way every 4th row to RC 50, when last stitch is decreased at the left.

5. Continue increasing every 4th row to RC 68. End of one pattern. Needle arrangement is now the same as at the beginning.

6. Knit to RC 120 for tension swatch and halve length for row calculation.

Fabric F – Toyota Machines

The only method I would recommend for Toyota machines is the use of the purl-side of Figure 24 or Figure 141 on the main bed, and the embossed shape, which will be in contrast colour only, on the rib bed. Experiment showed that the other method used in embossed Double Jacquard – that of picking up floats – is not satisfactory. There are too many floats for the restricted length of the knitting.

In the course of working out this stitch I came to the conclusion that, for this machine, the contrast yarn needs to be thicker than the main yarn. Using single ends of 2/30s for both yarns is not satisfactory. The tension needed was 2/2··, otherwise main bed stitches occasionally dropped off, and this tension did not give a good texture to the knitting. The contrast yarn used in the garment is, therefore, approximately 3 ply, and the main yarn is two ends of bright acrylic. The tension for those yarns was 3··/4.

Fig. 126 *The design chart for Toyota embossed Half-Milano.*

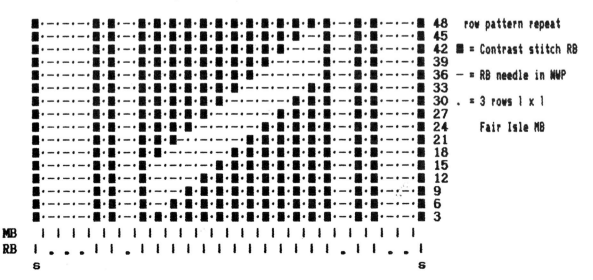

Tension swatch measurements for this fabric are very different from the knitting done by the other machines. This is an advantage, because this is not a quick piece of knitting; rather it is a challenge for Toyota knitters to exploit their machines to the full. The aim is continuous Fair Isle on the main bed, with 1 of every 3 rows knitted on the rib bed. The normal Simulknit setting is used for the main bed and coupling. That is: cam lever C, main yarn O, contrast yarn S. But what about the rib bed? Do you know how to make it knit 1 row, slip 2 rows when the machine is knitting Simulknit? Do you know which direction of the rib carriage is affected by which Simulknit lever? See if you can find out without any knitting on the machine. The answers to both these questions are in the instructions for the stitch.

1. Knit welt or hem using contrast colour. In this pattern the contrast yarn is the more predominant colour, and it is thicker. Finish carriage left. Arrange needles according to Figure 126, using the same embossed pattern as the other machines but knitting the embossed part on the rib bed in one colour only. Knit 1 more row at rib tension *at same time* programming card 1, Figure 24. RC 000.
2. Replace contrast yarn with fine yarn in feeder O. Set coupling to S and thread contrast yarn. Leave side levers on O. Set cam lever to C. Release punch card. Knit row 1. Both beds knit. Put rib bed front levers to empty.
3. Start at row 2 of the following row sequence and knit the 6-row sequence throughout.

Row	RB needle position	Before knitting row set Simulknit levers		Effect of Simulknit levers on rib bed	Direction of knitting
6	WP	S	O	Slip; needles to UWP	→
5	WP	O	O	Slip; needles in WP	←
4	UWP	O	O	Knit; needles to WP	→
3	WP	O	S	Slip; needles to UWP	←
2	WP	O	O	Slip; needles in WP	→
1	UWP	Left O Right O		Knit; needles to WP	←

4. Knit 3 rows. Shaping begins. Follow the pattern diagram in Figure 126. Note that all shaping is on the 11 centre stitches of the 13-stitch block every 3 rows. End stitches remain working throughout as do pairs of stitches either side. Rows 3 and 6 are preparation rows. A Simulknit lever prepares the next row for knitting, and 1 stitch is increased and/or decreased on central shape, which is, of course, a diamond. Decrease by transferring rib bed stitch to right. Increase by picking up heel of main bed stitch. Rib bed needles are left in working position and so do not knit until following row. Take care to keep 1 × 1 knit/slip formation on main bed if needles have to be pushed back to aid shaping.
5. Continue knitting in sequence and shaping diamonds.

To Knit the Jumpers

Three jumpers have been knitted, two, in Fabrics A and E, for Brother/Knitmaster machines, and one, in Fabric C, for Toyota machines. You are recommended to knit all the samples for your machine as listed in the tension swatch measurements on page 157 and at least two of the jumpers.

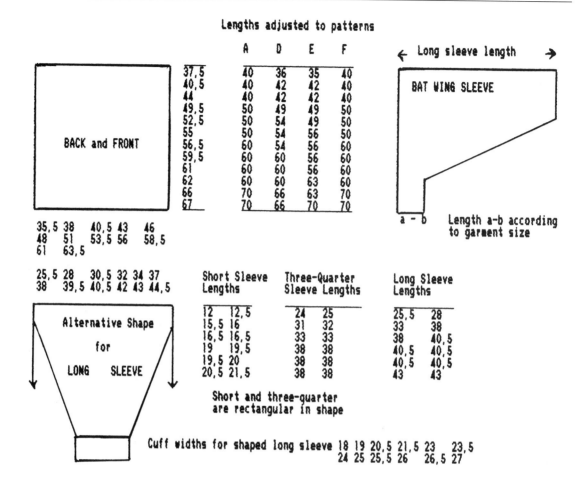

Lengths adjusted to patterns

	A	D	E	F
37,5	40	36	35	40
40,5	40	42	42	40
44	40	42	42	40
49,5	50	49	49	50
52,5	50	54	49	50
55	50	54	56	50
56,5	60	54	56	60
59,5	60	60	56	60
61	60	60	56	60
62	60	60	63	60
66	70	66	63	70
67	70	66	70	70

BACK and FRONT

35,5 38 40,5 43 46
48 51 53,5 56 58,5
61 63,5

Long sleeve length

BAT WING SLEEVE

a – b   Length a–b according to garment size

25,5 28 30,5 32 34 37
38 39,5 40,5 42 43 44,5

Alternative Shape
for
LONG   SLEEVE

Short Sleeve Lengths		Three-Quarter Sleeve Lengths		Long Sleeve Lengths	
12	12,5	24	25	25,5	28
15,5	16	31	32	33	38
16,5	16,5	33	33	38	40,5
19	19,5	38	38	40,5	40,5
19,5	20	38	38	40,5	40,5
20,5	21,5	38	38	43	43

Short and three-quarter
are rectangular in shape

Cuff widths for shaped long sleeve 18 19 20,5 21,5 23   23,5
24 25 25,5 26   26,5 27

Fig. 127   Garment blocks for jumpers.

It is not always possible to knit complete patterns in either the width or length of a garment. Sit at the machine and select the given number of needles. Check how many complete patterns there are, and arrange to knit the remainder, divided evenly both sides, as follows:

Fabric A – plain Half-Milano
Fabric C – part blocks
Fabrics D, E and F – as background with a stitch at both ends on the rib bed

Long patterns always present problems. If possible, it is better to knit complete patterns from the end of the welt to the back and front necklines. This has been done in the pattern. It is an easy matter to adjust the length by knitting a different number of patterns.

Many of these fabrics are very fine. I have therefore used the cut-and-sew method for all the necklines except for the garment in Fabric C, which has ribbed yokes and a round neck because I think it would be a very difficult fabric to machine. The pattern pieces given below are rectangular and can be used for any of the styles illustrated.

I have given three sleeve blocks. The rectangular sleeve in Fabric B goes with garments sizes 66–96cm knitted in Fabric B1 in one end of high-bulk acrylic and knitted in stocking stitch for the Toyota garment in Fabric C.

The high-bulk acrylic fabrics and Fantasia do not produce sufficient width for sizes

102–122cm. The batwing design of the rose jumper takes care of that problem. English rib, knitted in full needle rib formation using 1 end and tension 0/0, is wide enough when knitted sideways to extend the main pieces as much as necessary for larger sizes. The same is true of Fantasia knitting at tension ··/··. When the required amount has been knitted, about a quarter of the stitches are cast off for the underarm seam. Stitches are then decreased evenly for the length of the sleeve, leaving sufficient to gather into the welt. The batwing pattern without front extensions has been given for all Group 1 patterns.

The jumper in Fabric E2, which is knitted in two ends of high-bulk acrylic, does not need a full sleeve. It has a standard sleeve in embossed striped fabric. This type of sleeve should be used for any garment knitted in two ends or in Neon.

Fabric	Machine	Pattern	Yarn	Tension	St.	10cm	1 pattern
A1	Brother/Knitmaster	Rose	1 end HB acrylic	1/0	38	84R	10cm
B1	All machines	Plain Half-Milano	1 end HB acrylic	1/0	38	84	—
D1	All machines	Self-colour embossed	1 end HB acrylic	1/0	38	112	11
E1	Brother/Knitmaster	Two-colour embossed	1 end HB acrylic	1/0	38	96	7
C	Toyota	Block pattern	1 end Denfine DF1 &				
			1 end Fantasia T2	4/2	38	76	1.5
A2	Brother/Knitmaster	Rose	2 ends HB acrylic	4/2	30	64	13
B2	All machines	Plain Half-Milano	2 ends HB acrylic	4/2	30	64	—
F	Toyota	Two-colour embossed patterned or striped	2 ends Neon N10 & Denfine DF1	3·/4	30	64	10
D2	All machines	Self-colour embossed	2 ends HB acrylic	4/2	30	84	8
E2	Brother/Knitmaster	Two-colour embossed patterned or striped	2 ends HB acrylic	4/2	30	72	9.5
Stocking stitch			1 end Fantasia	2	32	48	

To fit chest/bust size in centimetres	66	71	76	81	88	91	96	102	107	112	117	122
in inches	26	28	30	32	34	36	38	40	42	44	46	48

Throughout the pattern all garments knitted with 1 end of high-bulk acrylic or with Fantasia will be Group 1. Those knitted with 2 ends or with Neon will be Group 2. This will apply to all stitch information but not to rows.

Back and front

For all fabrics Welts 2 × 2 rib (2 up 1 down) tensions: knitting with 1 end: as fine and as firm a rib as possible. Tension 0/0 with extra tension on yarn; slide lever 2 for Brother machines. Knitting with 2 ends or with Fantasia: tension 1/1. Knitting with Neon: tension 1··/1··. Knit tension swatches. All welts knitted in 1 strand HB acrylic are double length and elasticated with wide elastic net used for shirring. Calculate lengths for welts.

Cast on for welts over following main bed needles: Group 1	134	143	155	164	173	182	194	200	200	200	200	200
Group 2	107	113	122	128	137	143	152	161	167	176	182	191

N.B. Sizes with stitches in bold type in Group 1 require batwing sleeves and extension of front and back.

All sizes Knit welt to required length. Arrange stitches for chosen fabric. Knit straight in pattern at tensions given above. Notice details of method of calculation. Knit in pattern to RC

A1 Multiply length by	8.4 Adjust rows to be	÷ 84	336	336	336	420	420	420	504	504	504	504	588	588
B1	× 8.4	÷ 4	316	340	372	416	440	460	472	472	500	520	552	560

Fabric C. Rows to yoke. Follow on at †.

C	× 7.6	÷ 12	204	228	252	276	300	312	324	324	348	360	384	384
D1	× 11.2	÷ 68	408	476	476	544	612	612	612	680	680	680	748	748
E1	× 9.6	÷ 68	340	408	408	476	476	544	544	544	612	612	670	670
A2	× 6.4	÷ 84	252	252	252	336	336	336	336	336	420	420	420	420
B2	× 6.4	÷ 4	240	260	284	316	336	352	364	364	380	396	420	428
F	× 6.4	÷ 64	256	256	256	320	320	320	384	384	384	384	448	448
D2	× 8.4	÷ 68	340	340	340	408	408	476	476	476	476	544	544	544
E2	× 7.2	÷ 68	272	272	272	340	340	408	408	408	408	408	476	476

All fabrics except C transfer stitches to main bed. Cast off.

† Fabric C

Yoke, shoulders, neckline Rearrange stitches for rib as welts. Tension 1/1. Knit in rib to RC

56	56	56	94	94	106	106	**106**	**106**	**106**	**106**	**106**

Cast off in groups for shoulder on alternate rows over following main bed needles: 5 stitches ×

2	—	—	—	—	—	—	—	—	—	—	—
6	7	2	—	—	—	—	—	—	—	—	—
—	1	6	7	5	3	—	—	—	2	4	6
—	—	—	1	3	5	6	5	6	6	4	2
—	—	—	—	—	—	2	3	2	—	—	—

(6 stitches × / 7 stitches × / 8 stitches × / 9 stitches ×)

Stitches for shoulder	46	49	54	57	59	61	66	**67**	**66**	**62**	**60**	**58**
Stitches remaining for back neck	42	45	47	50	55	60	62	**66**	**68**	**76**	**80**	**84**
RC	72	72	72	110	110	122	122	**122**	**122**	**122**	**122**	**122**

Front

Knit in rib to RC	30	30	30	60	60	66	66	66	66	66	66	66
Transfer stitches at centre to main bed over width of following main bed needles	22	23	23	24	27	30	30	**32**	**34**	**38**	**40**	**42**

Put stitches of front neck and all at left of work to holding position. Continue right side, putting 1 main bed needle to holding position on alternate rows. Remember that 2 rib bed stitches count as 1 main bed stitch.

Number of main bed needles put to holding position	10	11	12	13	14	15	16	**17**	**17**	**18**	**20**	**21**
Knit in rib to RC	56	56	56	94	94	106	106	**110**	**110**	**114**	**114**	**118**

Shape shoulder as for back. Knit left side to match. Release stitches of neck curve on waste knitting.

Neckband

Join 1 shoulder seam. Make double-ribbed band, 4 rows stocking stitch, 24 rows rib, 4 rows stocking stitch.

Transfer to main bed. Wrong side facing. Place stitches of back neck, front curve and side loops of straight edges of front neck on same needles. Tension 10. Knit 1 row. Release on waste knitting. Backstitch through loops.

Stitches for neckband											
110	116	128	134	146	158	164	**164**	**170**	**170**	**176**	**176**

Neckline

All fabrics except C Cut and sew neckline on both pieces. Seam cast-off edges for shoulders taking measurements from garment blocks. Measure opening. Make and attach ribbed neckband, working out size from rib tension piece.

Rectangular sleeve

For Fabrics A, B, D and E in Group 1, sizes 66–96cm, knit sleeves in Fabric B1. For Fabric C, knit sleeves in stocking stitch.

Fabric B1 Cast on. Main bed needles	96	106	116	122	130	140	144	—	—	—	—	—
Short sleeve Knit to RC	100	104	132	136	140	140	160	—	—	—	—	—
Three-quarter sleeve Knit to RC	200	212	260	268	276	276	320	—	—	—	—	—
Long sleeve Knit to RC	216	236	276	320	320	340	340	—	—	—	—	—

Transfer stitches to main bed. Knit 1 row stocking stitch tension and release on waste knitting.

Stocking stitch. Cast on. Main bed needles	82	90	98	102	108	118	122	—	—	—	—	—
Short sleeve Knit to RC	58	60	74	76	80	80	92	—	—	—	—	—
Three-quarter sleeve Knit to RC	116	120	148	154	158	158	182	—	—	—	—	—
Long sleeve Knit to RC	122	134	158	182	182	194	194	—	—	—	—	—

Release on waste knitting.

Cuffs

Calculate width of rib required. Knit as welts, increasing tension by 1 number for last row. Transfer to main bed. Stocking stitch tension. Knit 1 row. Wrong side facing, gather stitches of sleeve evenly on to needles. Tension 10. Knit 1 row. Release on waste knitting and backstitch through loops.

Long sleeve (alternative shape for Group 2 garments)

Knit in Fabrics B2 or E2 embossed stripes.

Cast on at top. Main bed needles												
76	84	92	96	102	111	114	118	122	126	129	134

Knit selvedge and 1 row full needle rib. Programme for Half-Milano. Fabric E2: arrange rib bed needles for embossed rib.

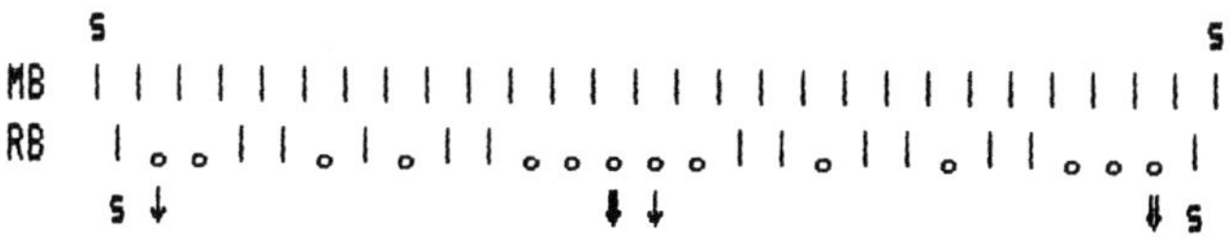

Fig. 128 *Needle diagram for the sleeves of the Brother/Knitmaster embossed garment, which can be seen in colour photographs 37 and 41.*

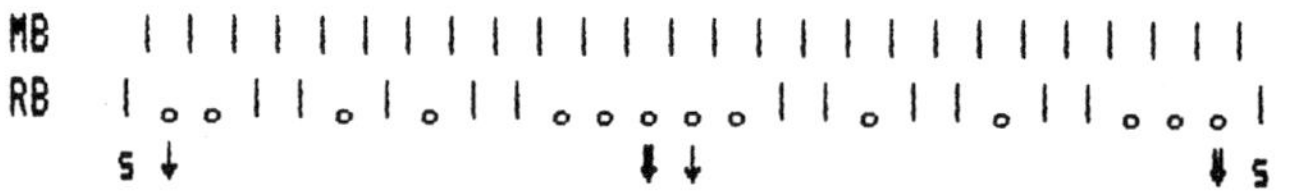

```
                 S                                                    S
MB   | | | | | | | | | | | | | | | | | | | | | | | | | | | | | | | | |
RB   | o o | | o | o | | o o o o o | | o | | o | | o o o |
     S ↓                        ↓ ↓                      ↓ S
```

Fig. 129 *Needle diagram for the sleeves of the Toyota jumper, worked in Fabric F.*

```
MB   | | | | | | | | | | | | | | | | | | | | | | | | | | | | |
RB   | o o | | o | o | | o o o o o | | o | | o | | o o o |
     S ↓                      ↓ ↓                      ↓ S
```

Knit to RC: Fabric B2	*14	12	14	16	14	13	12	11	11	10	11	10
Fabric E2	**16	14	15	18	16	14	13	13	12	12	12	11
Decrease following stitches at both sides	11	14	15	15	17	20	21	22	23	24	24	26
Rows between decreasings as above at * and **												
Stitches at cuff	54	56	62	66	68	71	72	74	76	78	81	82
Total rows: Fabric B2	164	180	212	244	244	260	260	260	260	260	276	276
Fabric E2	184	200	236	272	272	292	292	292	292	292	308	308

Transfer stitches to main bed. Knit 1 row. Release on waste knitting.

Calculate size of welt from rib sample. Knit welt. Transfer stitches to main bed. Wrong side facing, put stitches of main piece of sleeve evenly on same needles. Tension 10. Knit 1 row. Release on waste knitting. Backstitch through loops.

Batwing sleeve and extension for sizes 102–122cm

Batwing sleeve on ¾ length of side for other sizes.
Tack shoulder seam line.

Main bed needles required: Fabric A1	84	84	84	105	105	105	126	**126**	**126**	**126**	**147**	**147**
Fabric B1	80	84	92	104	112	116	120	**124**	**128**	**132**	**136**	**140**
Fabric D1	76	88	88	100	112	112	112	**126**	**126**	**126**	**138**	**138**
Fabric E1	76	88	88	104	104	118	118	**118**	**132**	**132**	**148**	**148**

Right side facing. Pick up front bed side loops and place on main bed needles as above. Use 4 ends contrast yarn. Tension 5. Knit 1 row. Tension 8. Knit 2 rows. Tension 5. Knit 1 row.

Sizes 66–96cm Cast off at opposite end to shoulder.

Number of stitches: Fabric A1	21	21	21	27	27	27	32	—	—	—	—	—
Fabric B1	20	21	23	26	28	29	30	—	—	—	—	—
Fabric D1	19	22	22	28	28	28	28	—	—	—	—	—
Fabric E1	19	22	22	26	26	29	29	—	—	—	—	—

Change to main yarn and ribber. Bring rib bed needles to working position for full needle rib formation. Tension 2/0. Knit 1 row. Tension 0/0. Change to English rib.

Sizes 102–122cm Knit straight to RC	—	—	—	—	—	—	—	10	20	36	46	60
Transfer stitches at waist edge to main bed: Fabric A1	—	—	—	—	—	—	—	32	32	32	37	37
Fabric B1	—	—	—	—	—	—	—	31	32	33	34	35
Fabric D1	—	—	—	—	—	—	—	30	30	30	34	34
Fabric E1	—	—	—	—	—	—	—	29	33	33	37	37

Put needles of both beds at waist end to upper working
position. Knit 1 row. Cast off stitches at waist end by
winding method, working from bed to bed to avoid tight
edge. Number of stitches remaining:

	Fabric A1	63	63	63	78	78	78	94	94	94	94	110	110
	Fabric B1	60	63	69	78	84	87	90	93	96	99	102	103
	Fabric D1	57	66	66	72	84	84	84	96	96	96	104	104
	Fabric E1	57	66	66	78	78	89	89	89	99	99	111	111

Main bed stitches to be decreased:

	Fabric A1	26	24	21	34	32	29	44	42	41	40	53	53
	Fabric B1	23	24	27	34	38	38	40	41	43	45	48	48
	Fabric D1	20	27	24	28	38	35	34	44	43	42	50	49
	Fabric E1	20	27	24	34	32	40	39	37	46	45	57	56

Decrease 1 stitch on both beds at armhole edge of sleeve at
following row intervals until only stitches for wrist remain.

	Fabric A1	8	10	13	9	10	12	8	8	8	9	7	7
	Fabric B1	9	10	10	9	8	9	8	8	8	8	7	7
	Fabric D1	11	9	12	11	8	10	10	8	8	8	7	7
	Fabric E1	11	9	12	9	10	8	9	9	7	8	6	6

Main bed stitches remaining for wrist: all fabrics

37	39	42	44	46	49	50	52	53	54	54	55
224	246	290	334	334	356	356	356	356	364	378	378

Knit to RC
N.B. Decrease when carriage is at decreasing end. Knit
main bed stitch manually; transfer to rib bed. Knit 2 stitches
together then transfer to main bed. Knit 2 stitches together.
This prevents a tight edge to slope. Transfer stitches to
main bed. Tension 4. Using 2 ends, knit 1 row. Cast off
using winding method.
Knit 3 more sleeve pieces reversing shaping on 2 pieces.

Welts
Measure wrists. Calculate stitches and rows from tension
swatch. Knit double length welts. Tension 7/7. Cast off
from bed to bed.

To make up

Where not already attached, sew sleeves to armholes. Sew all long seams. Hem up
double length welts using wide elastic net used for shirring inside hems.

Answer to question on page 144

	Colour change 1	Colour change 2
Row 4 MB Knit pattern stitches	RB Knit main yarn	RB Knit contrast yarn
Row 3 MB Slip	RB Knit contrast yarn	RB Knit contrast yarn
Row 2 MB Knit background stitches	RB Knit contrast yarn	RB Knit main yarn
Row 1 MB Slip	RB Knit main yarn	RB Knit main yarn

Using Colour change order 1 the background would be knitted in contrast yarn and the
pattern in main yarn; with Colour change order 2 the knitting would be correct.

– 11 –
Combining Tuck with Double Jacquard

– A BATWING JUMPER IN 2/30s
AND A SIMULKNIT JUMPER IN 4 PLY TO KNIT –

The yarns used for the Brother/Knitmaster garment shown in colour photograph 47 are from Studley Yarns; they are: Suki and Suki Smooth, 1 strand each of 13 jade (1), 06 lemon (2), 02 peach (3) and 013 turquoise (4). The yarns used for the Toyota garment in colour photograph 48 are from Amber Yarns; they are: Academy 18 navy (1), Heather Mix 48 blue (2), 36 light blue (3) and 45 pale pink (4). The tension swatch measurements for the Brother/Knitmaster fabrics, which can be seen in colour photograph 49 are:

Tuck Jacquard   19 stitches and 74 rows = 10cm   Tension 4·/4·
Stocking stitch   32 stitches and 48 rows = 10cm   Tension 5

The tension swatch measurements for the Toyota fabrics, which can be seen in colour photograph 54, are:

Simulknit   28 stitches and 36 rows = 10cm   Tension 5/6
Stocking stitch   28 stitches and 40 rows = 10cm   Tension 6

Some interesting variations can be knitted in patterned Double Jacquard on Brother and Knitmaster machines by using tuck stitch in both directions on the main bed instead of slip. The fabric, which has been used for the garment for these machines, is considerably widened and thickened, so fine yarns can be used very successfully, even for large sizes. This type of knitting needs trying out with various designs, as some are more effective than others. Two variations on Tuck Double Jacquard can be knitted using any pattern made from pairs of like rows. To work the first variation, set the main bed to tuck the main colour and slip the contrast colour. In the second variation tuck the main colour and knit the contrast colour.

Tuck Double Jacquard is not a stitch for Toyota machines because tuck cannot be combined with Simulknit. However, a punch card has been given which can be knitted in Simulknit. A different style has been chosen for the Toyota garment because of the weight of the Simulknit fabric. It is possible to lessen the thickness by knitting on alternate rib bed needles; tension 6/6 would then be used.

Tuck on the Main Bed

This simple geometric design is suitable for basic Double Jacquard, Simulknit or Tuck Jacquard. The three colours are represented as follows:

⊙ = main colour (1)

◆ = Contrast colour(s), C = 2, 3 or 4, or 2 only

In both garments the contrast colour is changed every pattern repeat – that is, 16 rows in Simulknit and 32 rows in Tuck Jacquard. You could choose a different colour sequence for the Toyota garment if you wish. The length could be divided into three, approximately equal sections, and the contrast yarns knitted in order. Either method can be used for the given pattern. The remainder of the fabric samples use one contrast yarn only. It is entirely a matter of choice.

Make a colour change row list as follows: rows 1–32 1/2; rows 33–64 1/3; rows 65–96 1/4; rows 97–128 1/2; rows 129–60 1/3 and so on. Use the double length mechanism and start at the left.

47.   ABOVE LEFT
The Brother/Knitmaster garment knitted in Tuck Double Jacquard, from Chapter 11.

48.   ABOVE RIGHT
The Simulknit version of the pattern from Chapter 11.

Fig. 130   *Design chart for fabrics and garments shown in colour photographs 47 and 49. The design has been shown single length but is knitted or punched as a double length pattern.*

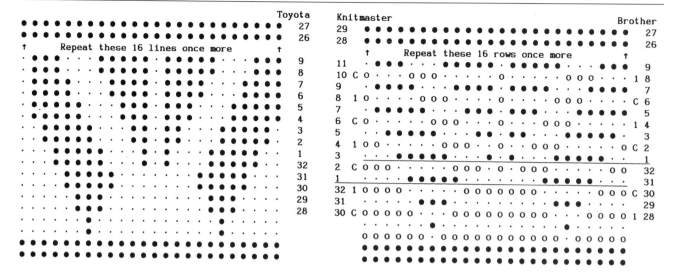

Fig. 131 *The punch card for the Toyota garment shown in colour photographs 48 and 54.*

Fig. 131 *The punch card for the Toyota garment shown in colour photographs 48 and 54.*

Fig. 132 *The punch card for Tuck Jacquard on Brother/ Knitmaster machines.*

Electronic Machines

Brother machines and Knitmaster 580 use Jacquard and double length controls. For Knitmaster 500 and 560 mark each line twice and use the Jacquard button. Change contrast colour as for punch card machines.

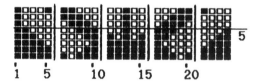

Fig. 133 *The electronic Tuck Jacquard chart.*

To Knit Tuck Jacquard Tension Swatch

Use fine or very fine yarn. One strand of bright acrylic and one strand of bright ripple yarn were used for the Brother/Knitmaster garment and the tension was 4·/4·. Knit as follows: main bed ← → tuck, rib bed ← → knit.

After knitting the welt or hem, increase 1 stitch on both ends of the rib bed, so breaking the end needle rule. This ensures that the end main bed stitches are tucked or knitted according to the pattern. It is a better method for all the stitches in this chapter than setting the end main bed needles to knit. If that is done the edges of the knitting are too long. Use side weights.

Watch the way the stitch is formed as you knit. Those main bed needles which have not knitted in any particular row will have tucked. If you look at the Toyota punch card diagram, Figure 131, you will see that there are many unpunched spaces. Those are the needles which tuck or slip in Brother and Knitmaster machines according to the setting of the carriage. At first sight it might seem impossible to tuck all those adjacent needles, and so it would be on the single bed. In this stitch, however, there are rib bed needles between the main bed ones, so making tucking possible.

When you have finished a swatch knitted in this way look at the wrong side. This is the side shown in colour photograph 49; it is used as the right side in the garment. Some very attractive shadow fabrics can be knitted in this way. Why not try out some standard Double Jacquard punch cards or those in this book? Those with electronic machines could try some of their basic Fair Isle patterns.

Variations Using the Same Pattern

Toyota Simulknit
As mentioned on pages 162 and 163, there are two variations on the Simulknit pattern. The first is the frequency of colour changing. When changing yarns in these machines, always take great care to thread the contrast yarn correctly. The other alternative is to reduce the number of stitches on the rib bed, so making a less bulky fabric. Knit on alternate rib bed needles and set both beds to the same tension.

Brother and Knitmaster Punch Card and Electronic Machines
Use patterns with pairs of like rows, or single row patterns knitted or marked out double length. Start at the left. Change colours every 2 rows.

1. Tuck/Slip: Tension 3··/3·· (see colour photograph 51)
   Rows 3 4 MB Slip or tuck RB Knit colour 2
   Rows 1 2 MB Tuck or slip RB Knit colour 1
2. Tuck/Knit: Tension 3··/3·· (see colour photograph 53)
   Rows 3 4 MB Knit or tuck RB Knit colour 2
   Rows 1 2 MB Tuck or knit RB Knit colour 1

Notice that changes in main bed cam settings coincide with colour changes.

Tuck on the Rib Bed

Brother 850 and Knitmaster SRP 60N Ribbers
It is possible to knit 1 × 1 tuck bird's eye automatically using these ribbers. The fabric is shown in colour photographs 50, 51 and 52.

1. Use an even number of needles on the rib bed. The method is the same as for 1 × 1 slip except that, in addition to the normal Double Jacquard setting, the ribber carriage is set for tuck. In each row the second needle from the carriage and following alternate needles will knit, and the others will tuck. Set the rib bed tension one whole number higher than the main bed tension. In this case 3/4. This is the rib bed row sequence:

Row 4 Contrast colour	K T K T K T K T K T←
Row 3	T K T K T K T K T K→
Row 2 Main colour	K T K T K T K T K T←
Row 1	T K T K T K T K T K→

2. Repeated tuck rows make another very interesting fabric (seen in colour photograph 52). The number of repeats depends upon the thickness of the yarn. In the sample, two ends of 2/30s were used, and there were four tucks on alternate

49.   *A close-up of the Brother/Knitmaster fabric, used for the jumper shown in colour photograph 47, worked by tucking in both directions on the main bed.*

50.   *1 × 1 tuck backing knitted on a Brother 850 ribber.*

51.   *1 × 1 tuck backing with main bed tucking the main colour and slipping the contrast colour.*

52.   *Repeated tucks in 1 × 1 backing knitted on a Brother 850 ribber.*

53.   *Another variation – main bed tucking the main colour and knitting the contrast colour.*

54.   *A close-up of the Simulknit pattern used for the jumper illustrated in colour photograph 48.*

needles before they were knitted off. The tension was 3/4. This variation requires an odd number of needles on the rib bed. Here is the rib bed row sequence:

Row 8 Contrast colour   K T K T K T K T K ←
Row 7 Contrast colour   K T K T K T K T K →
Row 6 Main colour   K T K T K T K T K ←
Row 5 Main colour   K T K T K T K T K → Before knitting push end
                                                 needle carriage end to UWP to
                                                 reverse action of 1 × 1 setting.
                                                   Do this for 4 rows

Row 4 Contrast colour   T K T K T K T K T ←
Row 3 Contrast colour   T K T K T K T K T →
Row 2 Main colour   T K T K T K T K T ←
Row 1 Main colour   T K T K T K T K T →
Repeat these 8 rows.

Other Brother and Knitmaster Ribbers

Set the rib carriage to tuck. Follow the row sequences given above, using a 1 × 1 needle pusher to push the needles which are to knit to upper working position before each row. Even if you do not wish to knit a whole garment this way, you may like to use the method for knitting trims such as collars, cuffs and pockets. Try the samples and keep them for reference.

This type of knitting gives scope for experiment. Different tuck backings on the rib bed can be knitted on any Brother or Knitmaster machine by using other needle pushers to select needles to knit.

Plain Double Jacquard with Tuck Rib Backing

The main bed is set to slip and uses plain Double Jacquard patterning. The rib bed setting is changed manually. This stitch can be knitted by all machines with ribbers. The row sequence is as follows:

Row 4   MB   Slip   RB   Knit
Row 3   Knit   Knit
Row 2   Knit   Tuck
Row 1   Slip   Knit

Knit a sample using one colour only. It is a very suitable fabric for a skirt. An A-line skirt can be shaped in the way described in Chapter 3 (see page 47). The tension piece for a skirt consists of 100 rows, shaped and measured as described.

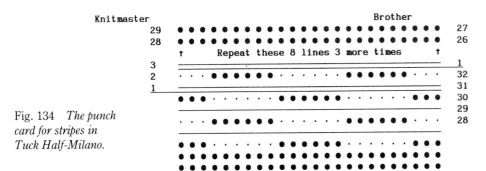

Fig. 134 *The punch card for stripes in Tuck Half-Milano.*

Fig. 135 *The electronic chart for Tuck Half-Milano.*

Tucked Half-Milano Jacquard

Use one strand of 2/30s and tension 0/0. A simple pattern was used to try out all the variations given.

Variations on Tucked Half-Milano

In all cases start at the left. Knit 2 rows main yarn, 2 rows contrast yarn.

Stripes
1. MB   Tuck   ← → Tuck   RB   Knit   ← →
2. MB   Slip   ← → Tuck   RB   Knit   ← →
3. MB   Tuck   2 rows colour 1 RB   Knit   ← →
   Slip   2 rows colour 2

Knitting Squares on Punch Card Machines
Each square is 24 rows long. Changing over the colour effect in each column requires this arrangement of rows. Notice that rows 23/24 are repeated as rows 25/26.

Fig. 136   *This is how the card in Figure 36 is used to give squares in alternate colours. It all depends on turning the card back at the correct row.*

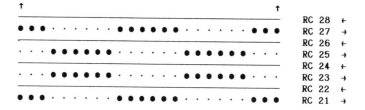

RC 28 ←
RC 27 →
RC 26 ←
RC 25 →
RC 24 ←
RC 23 ←
RC 22 ←
RC 21 →

It is not necessary to punch a second card. Make the change over as follows.

Brother Machines Knit to RC 23. Row 24 has already been selected. Turn the card back 2 rows. Continue knitting, changing colour every 2 rows. Do the same at RC 47, 71, 95 and so on.

Knitmaster Machines Knit to RC 24. Detach rib carriage. Main carriage is in slip. Move it to right. Turn punch card back 1 row. Lock it. Programme row. Carriage left. Link carriages. Turn row counter back to 24. Unlock card and continue knitting. Repeat at RC 48, 72, 96 and so on.

Fig. 137   *Electronic charts for patterns A and B for Tuck Half-Milano squares.*

Knitting Squares on Electronic Machines
Pattern A: rows 1–24, 49–72, etc. Pattern B: rows 25–48, 73–96, etc.

The method of entering the two patterns, A and B, depends on the machine in use. With the earlier Brother machines stop at RC 23 and enter pattern B, and with Knitmaster machines stop at RC 24. With later machines both patterns can be entered before the knitting is started.

Note that pattern B is not a reflection of pattern A, so the reverse control cannot be used.

Patterned Half-Milano Combined with Tuck

Try out the methods used for Tuck Double Jacquard by converting the Brother/Knitmaster card for Chapter 7, Figure 72, for Half-Milano. All needles are in working position.

To Knit the Jumpers

To fit chest/bust size in centimetres	71	76	81	86	91	96	102	107	112	117	122
in inches	28	30	32	34	36	38	40	42	44	46	48

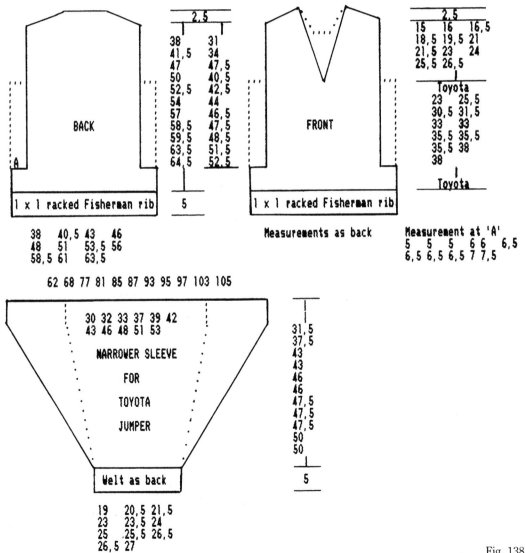

BACK

1 x 1 racked Fisherman rib

2.5

38	31
41,5	34
47	47,5
50	40,5
52,5	42,5
54	44
57	46,5
58,5	47,5
59,5	48,5
63,5	51,5
64,5	52,5

5

38   40,5 43   46
48   51   53,5 56
58,5 61   63,5

FRONT

1 x 1 racked Fisherman rib

Measurements as back

2.5

15   16   16,5
18,5 19,5 21
21,5 23   24
25,5 26,5

Toyota

23   25,5
30,5 31,5
33   33
35,5 35,5
35,5 38
38

Toyota

Measurement at 'A'
5   5   5   6   6   6,5
6,5 6,5 6,5 7   7,5

62 68 77 81 85 87 93 95 97 103 105

30 32 33 37 39 42
43 46 48 51 53

NARROWER SLEEVE

FOR

TOYOTA

JUMPER

Welt as back

31,5
37,5
43
43
46
46
47,5
47,5
47,5
50
50

5

19   20,5 21,5
23   23,5 24
25   25,5 26,5
26,5 27

NOTE All dotted lines and narrower sleeve apply to Toyota garment.

Fig. 138 Garment blocks for jumpers.

Back

Brother/Knitmaster Cast on with waste yarn over width of following main bed needles

72	78	82	88	92	98	102	108	112	118	122

Release rib bed stitches to hang comb on main bed. Knit several rows waste and 1 row nylon cord, finishing carriage left. Tension 8. Knit 2 rows in colour 1. Transfer heels of last row to rib bed to give full needle rib setting. Slip main carriage across and back to programme pattern. Tension 4·/4·. Knit in pattern to RC

52	56	72	72	76	76	80	84	84	88	88

N.B. On the row before casting off, push needles of stitches to be cast off to UWP so that they knit. All casting off must be very loose because of width of fabric. Cast off by winding method, transferring stitches from bed to bed. Before transferring stitch, knit it twice manually so making chain edge between stitches.

At beginning of next 2 rows cast off following stitches

10	10	10	12	12	13	13	13	13	14	15

Knit to RC

280	308	348	372	388	400	420	432	440	468	476

Stitches remaining

52	58	62	64	68	72	76	82	86	90	92

Shoulder shaping

Stitches to be cast off both ends

17	19	20	21	22	23	25	27	28	29	30

Cast off 1 stitch following number of times

3	1	1	—	—	—	—	—	—	—	—

Cast off 2 stitches ×

7	9	9	9	8	7	5	3	2	1	—

Cast off 3 stitches ×

—	—	—	1	2	3	5	7	8	9	10

RC

300	328	368	392	408	420	440	452	460	486	496

Cast off very loosely stitches which remain for back neck

18	20	22	22	24	26	26	28	30	32	32

Toyota Cast on for 2 × 2 rib (2 up 1 down) over width of following main bed needles

107	113	119	128	134	143	149	155	164	170	179

Tension 3··/3··. Knit 30 rows rib. Arrange for Simulknit, filling empty needles from heels of stitches. Knit 2 circular rows, programming pattern. Set machine for Simulknit, threading colour 2 into S feed. Tension 5/6. Knit in pattern to RC

80	96	112	112	112	112	128	128	128	136	136

At beginning of next 2 rows cast off following stitches

14	14	15	17	17	18	20	20	20	21	22

Knit to RC

136	150	170	180	190	194	206	210	214	228	232

Stitches remaining

79	85	89	94	100	107	109	115	124	128	135

Shoulder shaping

Stitches to be cast off both ends

22	25	26	26	28	30	31	34	37	37	39

Cast off 4 stitches following number of times

3	—	—	—	—	—	—	—	—	—	—

Cast off 5 stitches ×

2	5	4	4	2	—	—	—	—	—	—

Cast off 6 stitches ×

—	—	1	1	3	5	4	4	—	—	—

Cast off 7 stitches ×

—	—	—	—	—	—	1	1	3	3	1

Cast off 8 stitches ×

—	—	—	—	—	—	—	—	2	2	4

RC

146	160	180	190	200	204	216	220	224	238	242

Cast off stitches which remain for back neck

35	35	37	42	44	47	47	47	50	54	57

Front

Brother/Knitmaster Knit as back to RC

†180 203 238 246 256 256 272 272 275 291 292

Divide for neck, working left side first. *Decrease 1 stitch at neck edge at beginning of next row and following row intervals

12 11 10 10 12 12 12 12 11 11 12

Total number of stitches decreased

9 10 11 11 12 13 13 14 15 16 12

Knit to RC

280 308 348 372 388 400 420 432 440 468 476

Shape shoulder as back. Cast off. RC

300 328 368 392 408 420 440 452 460 486 496

Toyota Knit as back to RC

††108 118 138 148 154 158 170 174 174 188 196

Divide for neck. Right side first. *Put following stitches into HP in centre

17 17 17 20 22 25 25 25 26 28 31

**Decrease 1 stitch neck edge next row and following alternate rows. Number of times

9 9 10 11 11 11 11 11 12 13 13

Knit to RC

136 150 170 180 190 194 206 210 214 228 232

Shape shoulder as back. Cast Off. RC

146 160 180 190 200 204 216 220 224 238 242

All machines Bring needles of other side to WP. Reprogramme pattern. Reset row counter † or ††. Knit from * or ** reversing shaping.

Neckband (Toyota)

Arrange needles and cast on for rib as welts. Main bed needles Knit 4 rows at each following tension: 3/3, 3·/3·, 3··/3··. Pick up heels to fill empty needles; same number on both beds. Tension 6. Knit 4 rows stocking stitch separately on both beds. Transfer stitches to main bed. Tension 8. Knit 1 row. Place stitches of garment neck on same needles. Tension 10. Knit 1 row. Release on waste knitting.

98 107 107 110 113 119 122 125 134 137 143

Sleeves

Brother/Knitmaster N.B. Sleeves, which are very wide at top, must be knitted upwards from cuff. This stitch looks very different upside down. Care must be taken with weighting at sides because of increased width. Use side weights and claw weights. When work is long enough, rehang comb. Rows have been adjusted to give complete patterns. Total rows are less than might be expected from tension measurements to allow for 'drop factor' which is considerable due to weighting.

Cast on as before over width of following main bed needles

37 39 41 43 45 47 49 49 49 51 51

Increasing is 1 stitch at both ends of both beds as follows:
5th and every following 5th row following number of times

8 20 36 28 12 4 — 8 4 4 —

4th and every following 4th row ×

33 25 17 27 46 56 52 58 63 69 74

3rd and every following 3rd row ×

— — — — — — 12 — — — —

Number of stitches

119 129 147 153 161 167 177 181 183 197 199

Knit straight to RC

192 224 288 288 320 320 320 320 320 352 352

Set both carriages to knit. Tension 8. Knit 1 row. Transfer stitches to main bed. Tension 10. Knit 1 row. Release on waste knitting. Use thick 4-ply yarn and tension 8 to keep fabric wide.

Toyota Before knitting sleeves, seam shoulders.

Cast on as before over width of following main bed needles

53	56	59	62	65	68	71	71	74	74	77

Knit welt. Transfer for Simulknit as before. Increasing is 1 stitch at both ends of both beds as follows:

4th and every following 4th row following number of times	—	—	—	—	—	—	—	—	—	4	16
5th and every following 5th row ×	—	—	—	4	—	14	—	22	28	30	20
6th and every following 6th row ×	11	2	—	17	16	11	23	7	2	—	—
7th and every following 7th row ×	4	14	10	—	6	—	2	—	—	—	—
8th and every following 8th row ×	—	—	7	—	—	—	—	—	—	—	—
Total stitches	83	88	93	104	109	118	121	129	134	142	149
RC	94	110	126	122	138	136	152	152	152	166	164
Knit straight to RC	112	128	144	144	160	160	176	176	176	192	192

N.B. Lengths have been adjusted slightly to give complete patterns. Increase or decrease by 16 rows if required. There is no need to alter the increase rate.

Transfer stitches to main bed. Tension 8. Knit 1 row. Release on waste knitting.

Welts – back and front (Brother/Knitmaster)

Knit in colour 1. Arrange following needles for 1 × 1 rib.
Piece 1 – right and centre front: 1 point, 1 straight end
Piece 2 – back and left front: 2 straight ends

82	85	91	96	100	106	110	115	119	124	129
118	127	135	144	150	160	168	175	183	192	199

Cast on for racked fisherman's rib (page 51). Knit selvedge finishing carriage right. Tension 3/3. Knit 24 rows.

At same time shape as follows:
Piece 1 – increase 1 stitch at left on both beds every 4 rows. No shaping at right.
Piece 2 – increase 1 stitch at left at both ends on both beds, decreasing similarly at right.
All pieces – carriage left. Change direction of slope by changing direction of tucking after row 25. Reverse shaping for rows 26–48. Transfer stitches to main bed. Release on waste knitting.

Cuffs

1 straight and one pointed end. Knit 18 + 18 rows

64	68	70	74	76	78	80	82	84	84	86

Neck tie (optional)

2 pieces, 1 pointed end 1 straight. Knit 24 + 24 rows

118	127	135	144	150	160	168	175	183	192	199

Neck trim

Sizes 1–8 – seam both shoulders before knitting trim. Knit in one piece with mitres both ends.
Arrange following needles on both beds for circular knitting
Sizes 9–11 – seam right shoulder. Knit 2 pieces.
Piece 1 – right front and back neck. Mitre at left.
Piece 2 – left front. Mitre at right.
Tension 0/0. Knit zigzag row. Change to circular knitting. Knit 2 rows at tensions 0/0, 1/1, 2/2, 3/3. *Increase 1 stitch fully fashioned on both beds mitre end(s). Tension 4/4. Knit 4 rows.* Repeat from * to * twice more. Transfer stitches to main bed. Tension 7. Knit 1 row.

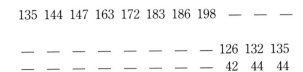

135 144 147 163 172 183 186 198 — — —

— — — — — — — — 126 132 135

— — — — — — — — 42 44 44

Attach garment
Sizes 1–8 – left half first at right end of trim. Set carriage to slip. Wrong side facing, place left neck edge on same needles starting with V at right, finishing centre back at centre of trim. Bring all these needles to UWP. They will knit, the remainder at left will not. Tension 8. Knit 1 row. Release on waste knitting. Attach remainder of neckline in same way. Backstitch through loops of tension 8 row.
Sizes 9–11 – knit longer piece first. Attach right side and back of neck. Knit shorter piece. Attach left side of neck. Seam left shoulder and trim.

Armhole trims

Knit 2 pieces for each armhole. Joins on shoulder and underarm.
Cast on, knit as neck trim. There are no mitres.
Wrong side facing, attach half armhole to each trim.

115 118 136 147 155 161 169 171 176 187 192

To make up

Hem loops of last row of sleeve under armhole trim. Join underarm and sleeve seams. Hem loops of sleeve stitches to underside of cuffs, overlapping points on outside of wrists. Seam waistband pieces into 1 length with point left of centre front. Sew down points with buttons for decoration. Seam neck tie into one length. Seam into tube sufficient for back neck and 5cm down front edges of neck. Flatten tube carefully with seam in centre of underside. Do not over press. Sew to neck inside trim. Sew on buttons for decoration at points on waistband and cuffs.

– 12 –
Reversible Double Jacquard
– TWO JACKETS TO KNIT –

The yarn used for the Brother/Knitmaster garment shown in colour photographs 64 and 65 is Atkinson 4 ply Easywash pure wool EW03 tobacco (1) and Poodle PO28 mahogany shadow (2). The yarn used for the Toyota garment in colour photographs 66 and 67 is James C. Brett's 4 ply Supersoft (80 per cent acrylic, 20 per cent wool) 78 grey (1) and Designer 4 ply D1 maroon (2).

The tension swatch measurements for the Brother/Knitmaster fabrics shown in colour photographs 55 and 57 are:

Pattern 1   30 stitches and 56 rows = 10cm   Tension 5/4
Pattern 2   30 stitches and 76 rows = 10cm   Tension 6/7

The tension swatch measurements for the Toyota fabrics shown in colour photographs 62 and 63 are:

Patterns 1 and 2   27 stitches and 38 rows   = 10cm   Tension 5/6

Stocking stitch knitted in the two plain yarns
    28 stitches and 40 rows   = 10cm   Tension 7

A reversible fabric is one in which either side is attractive enough to be used for the right side of a garment, or for part of the right side such as cuffs, revers and facings. Both sides may be identical, or they may be different but equally acceptable. Some of the fabrics already dealt with – Simulknit, Tuck Double Jacquard and the plain fabrics – are reversible.

In this chapter I have divided the types of fabric into categories, starting with identical patterns on both sides, and finishing with plain Tuck Jacquard knitted on both beds. In between there is great variety. I do not claim that this is the last word on the subject. No one will ever write the last word on any machine knitting subject. I have given you some ideas to experiment with and to expand.

Identical Patterning on Both Sides

This can be knitted only by manually selecting to upper working position on the rib bed the opposite needles to those selected on the main bed by the pattern selector. Since this has to be done every row, it is an exercise which few knitters, including the author, are likely to have time to attempt – not even a sample or two!

55. *Pattern 1 from Chapter 12. This is the pattern from Chapter 4 reversing to broken 1 × 1 stripes. This was knitted using a Brother 850 ribber and the author's method of reversing slip/knit mechanism on rib bed.*

58. *Horizontal stripes reversing to plain knitted using Simulknit.*

61. *Wide vertical stripes reversing to plain, knitted using Simulknit.*

56. *Nearly plain on both sides – a variation for Simulknit.*

59. *Pattern reversing to 1 × 1 vertical stripes.*

62. *Toyota Pattern 2 from the garment shown in colour photograph 66. The fabric was knitted in Simulknit, using grey as contrast colour. Note the rib effect on plain side.*

57. *Pattern 2 in the Brother/Knitmaster garment shown in colour photograph 55 – horizontal stripes of 2 rows, reversing to horizontal stripes of 4 rows.*

60. *1 × 1 vertical stripes both sides – double-sided slip pattern.*

63. *Toyota Pattern 1, which reverses to wide horizontal stripes.*

Pattern Reversing to Plain

This is Blister Jacquard, in which the pattern on the main bed reverses to one colour. It can be knitted automatically by Toyota knitters using Simulknit and on Knitmaster SRP 60 using Auto Drive and twice as many rows. Other knitters can also knit this stitch by altering the ribber settings manually (see page 22). Care needs to be taken in the choice of contrast yarn, as floats can show through.

Brother and Knitmaster machines can combine this with tuck stitch, setting the main bed in one of the ways suggested in Chapter 11. Experiment with some of the patterns in this book. Toyota machines cannot combine tuck and Simulknit.

Pattern Reversing to Horizontal Stripes

Any Double Jacquard pattern can be used for this fabric. The method is different for the two types of machine.

Brother/Knitmaster Machines

Because each colour is knitted separately, all that is required is to decide what sequence of striping is to be knitted on the reverse. The choice lies anywhere between 1 or 2 rows of both colours, Fabrics 2 and 1, and very wide stripes. Work out the stripes, remembering to change stripes on rows in which colour changes take place. Make a row chart and operate the slip levers accordingly. Again, be careful about your choice of contrast yarn.

Toyota Machines

The method used for these machines must take account of the fact that both yarns are knitted at the same time, the reverse automatically being knitted by whichever yarn is in the S feed. To make stripes on the back, it is therefore necessary to reverse the colours in the feeds. This will also reverse the colours in the pattern. Sometimes this would be acceptable, but, in the Toyota garment illustrated in colour photograph 66 I wished to have the textured maroon yarn forming the diamonds and triangles. To achieve this, I reversed the holes and blanks in the centre part of the card at the place where I wished to have a main colour stripe on the back of the fabric. The first three sizes need the yoke pattern, Figure 140, also in amended form.

To Knit Toyota Tension Swatch: Pattern 1 for Garment
1. Set change-over slots to vertical. Colour 1. Carriage right. Knit zigzag row. Tension 3/4. Knit 12 rows circular. Knit 1 row full needle rib, programming punch card.
2. Set for Simulknit. O feed colour 1, S feed colour 2 (1/2). Tension 4/5.

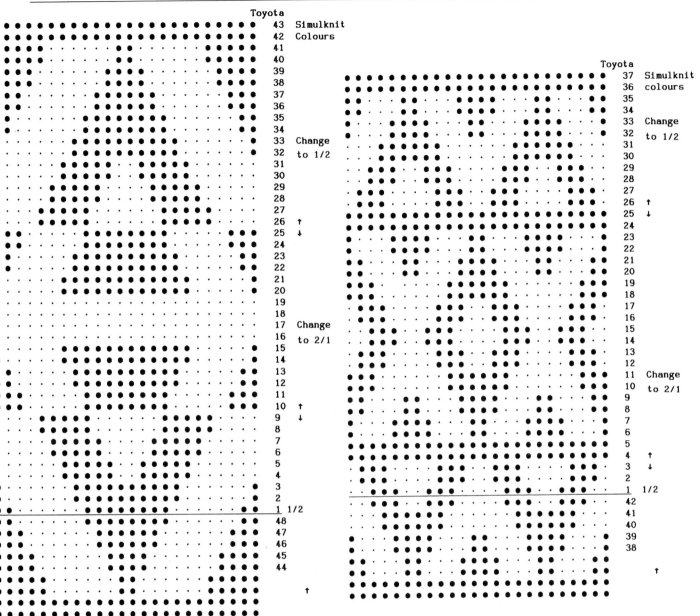

3.

	Large pattern	*Small pattern*
Yarns are 1/2		
Knit to RC	16 (16 rows)	10 (10 rows)
Change yarns to 2/1		
Knit to RC	32 (16 rows)	32 (22 rows)
Change yarns to 1/2		
Knit to RC	48 (16 rows)	42 (10 rows)
One pattern completed		
Make a colour table	49–64 (16 rows 1/2)	43–52 (10 rows)
	65–80 (16 rows 2/1)	53–74 (22 rows)
Two patterns completed	81–96 (16 rows 1/2)	75–84 (10 rows)

Fig. 139 *The punch card adapted from the design from Chapter 4 so that wide stripes can be knitted on the reverse in the Toyota garment; see colour photographs 63, 66 and 67.*

Fig. 140 *The punch card for adapting the small design from Chapter 4 in the same way. This is used for smaller sized garments.*

Notice that patterns begin and end with colours 1/2. Transfer stitches to main bed. Release on waste knitting.

Be careful not to cross the yarns when you re-thread.

64. *The Brother/Knitmaster reversible jacket, showing the pattern from Chapter 4. The stripes appear to be vertical because the garment is knitted sideways.*

65. *The reverse side of the Brother/Knitmaster jacket.*

Pattern Reversing to Vertical 1 × 1 Stripes

Main Bed Setting – All Machines

Use any Double Jacquard pattern of the paired-row type. Use the double length mechanism and slip setting on main carriage. Colour photograph 59 shows the small pattern from Chapter 4.

Rib Bed Settings

Brother 850 Ribber

With this ribber, the second and alternate needles from the carriage knit when all the needles are in working position, and the ╷╷╷ button setting is used. Work with an odd number of needles on the rib bed and start from the left, knitting 2 rows in colour 1, 2 rows in colour 2. Stripes are automatic when knitting in colour 1. When colour 2 is

66. *The Toyota reversible jacket showing the design from Chapter 4.*

67. *The reverse side of the Toyota jacket showing the wide stripes.*

68. *A close-up of the button and loop method of fastening both jackets.*

knitted, push the end needle at the carriage end to the upper working position to make the first and alternate needles knit, thus knitting stripes in the second colour. This is the knitting sequence:

Row 4	Colour 2	RB	K S K S K S K S K	Push end needle at right to UWP before knitting this row	←
Row 3	Colour 2	RB	K S K S K S K S K	Push end needle at left to UWP before knitting this row	→
Row 2	Colour 1	RB	S K S K S K S K S	Automatic	←
Row 1	Colour 1	RB	S K S K S K S K S	Automatic	→

It is important to realize that this sequence refers only to straight pieces of knitting. Where shaping occurs, the different number of stitches as the work progresses must be taken into account. After the first and after every alternate shaping when increasing or decreasing 1 stitch on both beds, colour 1 is pushed up at the carriage end, not colour 2 as in the instructions for straight knitting.

Other Brother / Knitmaster Ribbers

Set the rib carriage to slip in both directions. Follow the row sequence for Brother 850, selecting alternate rib bed needles with needle pusher. Push knit needles – K in the above table – to upper working position before each row. Auto Drive on Knitmaster SRP 60 is not used in this stitch. You may think that this is too slow for a complete garment, but it could be used for trims and small pieces of individual garments.

Toyota

This stitch can be knitted using a Double Jacquard punch card and changing colour manually, setting the main bed to empty. This could be a worthwhile project for trims.

Variations for Brother/Knitmaster Machines

1. The rib bed can be set to tuck instead of to slip, with the main bed also tucking to balance the fabric.
2. Other stripe formations can be knitted using different needle pushers.
3. Broken stripes can be knitted as follows on the Brother 850 ribber, knitting 2 rows colour 1, 2 rows colour 2 throughout and using an odd number of rib bed needles:

Rows 9–16 push end needle at carriage end to UWP when knitting colour 1
Rows 1–8 Push end needle at carriage end to UWP when knitting colour 2

Broken stripes can be as long or as short as you wish. If they are knitted using any other ribber the same effect is achieved by pushing up alternate needles on every row with a needle pusher. In rows 1–8, push up the first and alternate needles from the carriage end when knitting colour 1, and the second and alternate needles when knitting colour 2. Reverse this for rows 9–16. Use an odd number of rib bed needles.

In the Brother/Knitmaster garment shown in colour photograph 64 the stripes are knitted in sets of 8 rows as above, giving 4 rows of each colour arrangement. Take care to keep the correct continuity of the broken stripes when shaping the shoulders. This is easy for the left front and the back, as the shaping is at the right. All you need to remember is that if the colour of the last stitch is the same as the yarn threaded, you must push up the end needle before knitting to the left unless you are reversing colours of stripes. The sleeve decreasing varies with the size and has been worked out in detail in the pattern. This stitch is the reverse side of card 1, Figure 24.

Vertical Stripes Reversing to Vertical Stripes

Brother/Knitmaster Machines

Vertical 1 × 1 Stripes Both Sides, Slip or Tuck
Use the following pattern, which is a basic one for most machines. Set the main bed for Double Jacquard. Alternatively card 1, Figure 24, can be used double length.

Fig. 141 *Use this punch card, or Figure 24 double length, for 1 × 1 vertical stripes on both sides of the fabric as seen in colour photograph 60.*

or   **used double length**

Fig. 142 *Electronic chart for 1 × 1 reversible stripes.*

Start at the left and knit 2 rows in colour 1, 2 rows in colour 2. The rib bed method for all machines is the same as in the previous example – that is, using lılı buttons on Brother 850 and a needle pusher on other ribbers. It is necessary to be very careful about placing the work on the needle bed. Knitting should be arranged so that colour 1 is behind colour 2 and vice versa.

As long as your pattern is punched or marked out exactly as above and you have an even number of stitches both sides of centre, making the total number of stitches divisible by four, the main bed, as you look at it on the machine, will knit in this order from left to right:

Rows 3 and 4	Main bed will knit	S	K	S	K	S	K	S				
		–	2	–	2	–	2	–	Colour 2		←
	Rib bed will knit	K	S	K	S	K	S	K				
		2	–	2	–	2	–	2	Colour 2		→
Rows 1 and 2	Main bed will knit	K	S	K	S	K	S	K				
		1	–	1	–	1	–	1	Colour 1		←
	Rib bed will knit	S	K	S	K	S	K	S				
		–	1	–	1	–	1	–	Colour 1		→

Tuck could be used instead of slip. The stripes on the main bed could be wider than those on the rib bed by using a different punch card. For example:

Fig. 143 *Punch card repeats for wider stripes.*

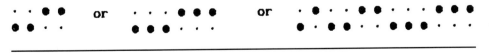

Fig. 144 *Electronic charts for wider stripes.*

Use all these patterns double length, starting at the left. If you have the first pattern in full-length form in your basic set, use it without double length setting. For Knitmaster 500 560, mark each line twice.

Toyota

This stitch can be knitted in the same way as the previous example.

Vertical Stripes Reversing to Plain

Method 1

Brother/Knitmaster

Use any of the patterns in the previous section to knit stripes on the main bed, or make similar patterns with wider stripes. Set the main carriage for Double Jacquard and the rib carriage to slip one of the colours.

Toyota

Use 1 row of any punch card locked and knit in Simulknit. Remember that the chosen row will be knitted on the right side. The jacket uses card 1, Figure 24.

Method 2

Brother/Knitmaster

Revise the settings for plain Double Jacquard

Main bed row sequence 1: Start right Slip Knit Knit Slip (see Chapter 3, page 32).
Main bed row sequence 2: Start left Slip Slip Knit Knit (see Chapter 4, page 56).

Punch Card Machines Use a plain Double Jacquard punch card on the main bed, using sequence 2. Colour 1 will show on main bed side. Rib bed knits as in Sample 1 (see previous page).

Fig. 145 *The method of knitting a plain fabric that reverses to vertical stripes with a Brother 850.*

```
RB  K S K S K S K S K ........      Rows 3 4  Colour 2 alternate stitches
MB  · · · · · · · · ........        Row  4    Slips
MB  · · · · · · · · ........        Row  3    Slips
MB  ● ● ● ● ● ● ● ● ........        Row  2    Colour 1
MB  ● ● ● ● ● ● ● ● ........        Row  1    Colour 1
RB  S K S K S K S K S ........      Rows 1 2  Colour 1 alternate stitches
```

Electronic Machines Find the following sequence from a mylar sheet and work from the left, using double length, setting the machine for slip not Double Jacquard. Knit the rib bed as for punch card machines in Sample 1.

Fig. 146 *An electronic chart for the same method.*

Toyota
Use card 1, Figure 24, locked on row 1 for main bed. Knit in Simulknit. The rib bed will knit in whichever yarn is in the S feed, and the main bed will knit 1 × 1 stripes. Alternatively, make the 1-line card used for the sample in colour photograph 61.

· · · · · ●●●● · · · ●●●● · · · · · ·

Fig. 147 *The locked punch card line for the Toyota fabric, plain one side reversing to wide vertical stripes, shown in colour photograph 61.*

Horizontal Stripes Reversing to Horizontal Stripes

All Brother/Knitmaster Punch Card and Electronic Machines

Use a plain Double Jacquard pattern, starting as specified for the particular sample, and knit the following row sequences to achieve various effects.

Sample 1: Narrow Stripes
Work 1 row stripes main bed; 2 row stripes rib bed. Start at left on row 1 of pattern, and knit row sequence 1 given below.

Row number	Main bed	Rib bed	Colour	Direction
4	Slip	Knit	2	←
3	Knit	Knit	2	→
2	Knit	Knit	1	←
1	Slip	Knit	1	→

Sample 2: Stripes of Any Width
These are knitted by changing colour less frequently – every 4 rows, for example. Use a Double Jacquard pattern and knit row sequence 2 given below. The number of rows in a stripe must be divisible by 4. Electronic machines should use Figure 137, slip setting, on the main bed.

Row number	Main bed	Rib bed	Colour	Direction
8	Knit	Knit	2	←
7	Knit	Knit	2	→
6	Slip	Knit	2	←
5	Slip	Knit	2	→
4	Knit	Knit	1	←
3	Knit	Knit	1	→
2	Slip	Knit	1	←
1	Slip	Knit	1	→

Do you see the way this sequence works? The 2 rows when the rib bed knits alone come immediately after a change of colour. The extra 2 rows on the rib bed make slight ridges on the side that is the right side of the fabric. This is Pattern 2 in the Brother/Knitmaster jacket illustrated on page 178.

For wider stripes on the main bed, change colour less frequently, but always have groups of rows divisible by 4. Should you wish to knit this stitch reversing the beds, you would not need patterning on the main bed because it would knit all the time. You would then use the front levers to control the rib bed. This can be done automatically with the Auto Drive of the Knitmaster SRP 60.

Toyota

Narrow stripes are time consuming without a colour changer, but wide stripes are quite practicable changing colours by hand. Knit the sequence giving above using the plain Double Jacquard punch card. Try some really wide stripes.

Horizontal Stripes Reversing to Plain Double Jacquard

All Brother/Knitmaster Punch Card and Electronic Machines

Knit as Sample 1 on page 183, but start at the right, using row sequence 1, as follows:

Row number	Main bed	Rib bed	Colour	Direction
4	Slip	Knit	1	→
3	Knit	Knit	2	←
2	Knit	Knit	2	→
1	Slip	Knit	1	←

Look carefully at this sequence. Notice that the main bed only knits in colour 2. If you want colour 1 to be the plain side, start with 1 row of colour 2.

Toyota

Set the change-over slots in horizontal position so that the end needles are not selected. Cast on using main yarn, knitting the last row of selvedge or welt from left to right, at the same time programming the punch card. Change to Simulknit setting. Use the extended length method to give 4-row stripes. If wider stripes are required punch a special card with blanks rows for the main yarn stripes and punched rows for the contrast yarn ones.

Plain Double Jacquard Reversing to Second Plain Colour

All Brother/Knitmaster Punch Card and Electronic Machines

Use plain Double Jacquard pattern, row sequence 1. Start from the right, knitting the following sequence and changing rib bed setting manually.

Row number	Main bed	Rib bed	Colour	Direction	Manual control changes
4	Tuck	Knit	1	→	
					Left rib bed front lever ↓
3	Knit	Slip	2	←	
					Right rib bed front lever ↓ ; cancel tuck
2	Knit	Tuck	2	→	
					Rib bed front levers ↑ ; set to tuck
1	Slip	Knit	1	←	

Have you worked this one out? This is what happens:

On the rib bed, colour 1 is knitted; colour 2 is slipped for 1 row and tucked for 1 row.

On the main bed, colour 2 is knitted; colour 1 is slipped for 1 row and tucked for 1 row.

Only knitted rows will show on the two surfaces of the fabric. Colour 1 will show on the rib bed side, and colour 2 will show on the main bed side. Care must be taken in the choice of yarn. Textured yarn, such as industrial poodle yarn, is very suitable. With plain yarns the reverse side may show through. Try very low tensions – from 0/0 to 1/1 for industrial yarns. You will be amazed at the width of the fabric, though, of course, it will need a great many rows. This stitch produces a very soft, springy fabric, and it is worth the effort. You will soon get into the rhythm of the control changes.

Toyota

This machine needs an entirely different method. Tuck on the rib bed cannot be combined with Simulknit. Design a punch card with as few holes (contrast yarn) as is practical to link the knitting of both beds together. The main bed will be predominantly colour 1, and the rib bed entirely colour 2. Here is an example. The change-over slots should be vertical to join up the ends.

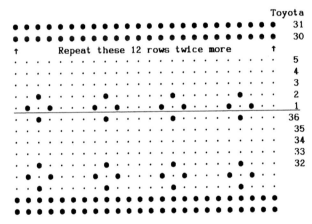

Fig. 148 *Use this for a Toyota fabric that is nearly plain on both sides; see colour photograph 56 on page 175.*

To Knit the Jackets

The following patterns are used in the garments:

Pattern 1

Brother/Knitmaster Chapter 4, pattern (Figures 52 or 54, 55 or 56) with broken vertical 1 × 1 stripes using Brother 850 or 1 × 1 needle pusher.

Toyota Chapter 4 pattern with striped reverse side (Figures 139 or 140).

Pattern 2

Brother/Knitmaster Two 2-row stripes reversing to 4-row stripes (see page 183).

Toyota 1 × 1 vertical stripes reversing to plain.

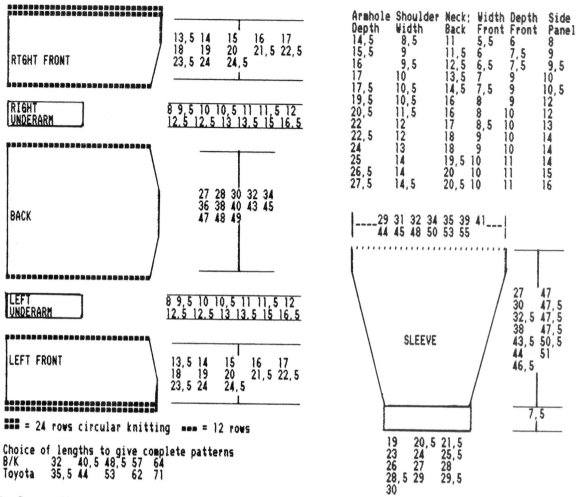

RIGHT FRONT

13,5	14	15	16	17
18	19	20	21,5	22,5
23,5	24	24,5		

RIGHT UNDERARM

| 8 | 9,5 | 10 | 10,5 | 11 | 11,5 | 12 |
| 12,5 | 12,5 | 13 | 13,5 | 15 | 16,5 | |

BACK

27	28	30	32	34
36	38	40	43	45
47	48	49		

LEFT UNDERARM

| 8 | 9,5 | 10 | 10,5 | 11 | 11,5 | 12 |
| 12,5 | 12,5 | 13 | 13,5 | 15 | 16,5 | |

LEFT FRONT

13,5	14	15	16	17
18	19	20	21,5	22,5
23,5	24	24,5		

▄▄▄ = 24 rows circular knitting   ▄▄▄ = 12 rows

Choice of lengths to give complete patterns
| B/K | 32 | 40,5 | 48,5 | 57 | 64 |
| Toyota | 35,5 | 44 | 53 | 62 | 71 |

Armhole Depth	Shoulder Width	Neck; Back	Width Front	Depth Front	Side Panel
14,5	8,5	11	5,5	6	8
15,5	9	11,5	6	7,5	9
16	9,5	12,5	6,5	7,5	9,5
17	10	13,5	7	9	10
17,5	10,5	14,5	7,5	9	10,5
19,5	10,5	16	8	9	12
20,5	11,5	16	8	10	12
22	12	17	8,5	10	13
22,5	12	18	9	10	14
24	13	18	9	10	14
25	14	19,5	10	11	14
26,5	14	20	10	11	15
27,5	14,5	20,5	10	11	16

| ---- | 29 | 31 | 32 | 34 | 35 | 39 | 41 | --- |
| | 44 | 45 | 48 | 50 | 53 | 55 | | |

SLEEVE

27	47
30	47,5
32,5	47,5
38	47,5
43,5	50,5
44	51
46,5	

7,5

19	20,5	21,5
23	24	25,5
26	27	28
28,5	29	29,5
30		

Fig. 149 *Garment blocks for the reversible jacket shown in colour photographs 64–67.*

All machines The yoke pattern is used for the first 3 sizes, the main pattern for the remainder.

After you have tried out these patterns you may wish to use different ones for another garment. You will need to work out the rows for each pattern again. The amount of Pattern 1 depends on the length of Pattern 2.

| Sizes to fit chest in centimetres | 61 | 66 | 71 | 76 | 81 | 86 | 91 | 96 | 102 | 107 | 112 | 117 | 122 |
| in inches | 24 | 26 | 28 | 30 | 32 | 34 | 36 | 38 | 40 | 42 | 44 | 46 | 48 |

N.B. Toyota colours (grey 1, maroon 2) are given in this order: Feeder O/Feeder S. All circular knitting, casting on, casting off is knitted in colour 1 by both machines.
Tensions Full needle rib – all machines 4/4. Circular – Brother/Knitmaster 5··/6, Toyota 5/4··. Brother/Knitmaster: Pattern 1 5/4, Pattern 2 6/7. Toyota: Patterns 1 and 2 5/6.

Left front

Brother/Knitmaster Carriage left. **Toyota** Carriage right. Cast on for full needle rib over width of following main bed needles

98 98 122 122 146 146 146 170 170 170 170 192 192

Knit 2 rows circular at each of following tensions: 1/1, 2/2, 3/3, 4/4. **Brother/Knitmaster** Knit 24 rows. **Toyota** Knit 30 rows. **All machines** Knit 1 row full needle rib programming Pattern 1. Knit 2 small diamonds sizes 1–3, 1 large diamond other sizes. RC 000. **Toyota** Continue at *.

Brother/Knitmaster Tension 5/4.
Pattern 1. Knit to RC

88 88 88 96 96 96 96 96 96 96 96 96 96

Tension 6/7. Pattern 2. Knit to RC

96 100 104 116 120 124 132 136 144 152 156 160 168

At same time commence shoulder decreasing on right at RC

48 48 48 64 64 64 72 80 80 80 88 88 96

Decrease 1 stitch 8 times both beds next row and at following row intervals

6 6 6 8 8 8 9 10 10 10 11 11 12

N.B. Keep continuity of rib side during decreasing.
* **Toyota** Pattern 1. Tension 5/6. Knit to RC

44 44 44 48 48 48 48 48 48 48 48 48 48

Pattern 2. Knit to RC

52 54 58 62 66 68 72 76 82 86 90 92 96

At same time commence shoulder decreasing on right at RC

20 22 22 26 26 28 28 32 34 38 38 40 40

Decrease 1 stitch 8 times both beds next row and at following row intervals

4 4 4/5 4/5 5 5 5/6 5/6 6 6 6/7 6/7 7

Change to Pattern 1. Colours 2/1. Knit to RC

52 52 58 62 66 68 72 76 82 86 90 92 94

All machines Stitches remaining

90 90 114 114 138 138 138 162 162 162 162 184 184

* Knit 1 row full needle rib, 12 rows circular, 1 row full needle rib. Transfer stitches to main bed. Tension 10. Knit 1 row. Cast off with latch tool.*

Right front

Knit in same way as left front, except that shoulder decreasing is at left.

Pockets

Knit 2 pieces alike, fixed to 1 side only. Make to match chosen side.
All machines Number of main bed stitches – choose one of these to suit length of garment:
26 (1 pattern), 38 (1½ patterns) or 50 (2 patterns) Cast on in full needle rib. Knit selvedge. Knit to match patterns 1 and 2 on fronts. There are 2 ways of finishing depending on whether the opening chosen is at top or side.

Top opening

Brother/Knitmaster garment as shown. Transfer to main bed. Tension 10. Knit 1 row. Cast off with latch tool. Pick up side loops for heading. Tension 7. Knit 8 rows stocking stitch. Release on waste knitting. Main bed needles for heading

Hem heading to inside. Oversew to bottom edge. Mattress stitch sides to edge of pattern.

40	42	44	46	50	52	56	58	62	66	70	72	74

Side opening

Toyota garment as shown. Knit from * to * as on left front. Oversew bottom edge. Mattress stitch front edge and top.

Underarm pieces

Knit 2 pieces alike.

Brother/Knitmaster Number of main bed stitches
Toyota Number of main bed stitches
†Cast on for full needle rib. Knit selvedge. Knit 12 rows circular knitting. Knit 1 row full needle rib programming Pattern 2.†
Brother/Knitmaster Knit to RC
Toyota Knit to RC
††**All machines** Knit 1 row full needle rib, 12 rows circular, 1 row full needle rib. Transfer stitches to main bed. Tension 10. Knit 1 row. Cast off with latch tool.††

46	46	66	62	84	78	76	96	94	90	86	82	78
58	56	78	74	98	92	90	110	108	104	102	120	116
44	52	56	56	60	64	68	68	68	72	76	84	92
30	36	38	40	42	44	46	48	48	50	52	58	64

Back

All machines Cast on and knit circular as for underarm pieces, † to †. Number of stitches
Brother/Knitmaster Tension 6/7. Pattern 2. Knit to RC
Tension 5/4. Pattern 1. Knit to RC
Tension 6/7. Pattern 2. Knit to RC
At same time commence increasing at right edge for shoulder at RC
Increase 1 stitch 8 times at following row intervals
RC at end of increasing
Continue in pattern as given above. *At same time* commence shoulder decreasing as on left front at RC
Toyota Tension 5/6. Pattern 2. Knit to RC
Pattern 1. Knit to RC
Pattern 2. Knit to RC
At same time commence increasing at right edge for shoulder at RC
Increase 1 stitch 8 times following row intervals
RC at end of increasing
Continue in pattern as given above. *At same time* commence shoulder decreasing as on left front at RC

90	90	114	114	138	138	138	162	162	162	162	184	184
8	12	16	20	24	28	36	40	48	56	60	64	72
184	188	192	212	216	220	228	232	240	248	252	256	264
192	200	208	232	240	248	264	272	288	304	312	320	336
6	6	6	8	8	8	9	10	10	10	11	11	12
6	6	6	8	8	8	9	10	10	10	11	11	12
48	48	48	64	64	64	72	80	80	80	88	88	96
144	152	160	168	176	184	192	192	208	224	232	240	240
8	10	14	16	18	20	24	28	34	38	42	44	46
96	98	102	112	114	116	120	124	130	134	138	140	142
104	108	116	128	132	136	144	152	164	174	180	184	188
4	4	4	4	5	5	5	5	6	6	6	6	7
4	4	4/5	4/5	5	5	5/6	5/6	6	6	6/7	6/7	7
32	32	36	36	40	40	44	44	48	48	52	52	56
72	76	80	92	92	96	100	108	116	126	128	132	132

All machines Knit from †† to ††. Transfer stitches to main bed. Tension 10. Knit 1 row. Cast off with latch tool.

Sleeves

Knit sleeves from sleeve head to cuff. If using Brother 850 ribber, change rib bed setting for each stitch pattern.

All machines Cast on and knit hem as for underarm pieces.

Brother/Knitmaster Number of main bed needles
Pattern 2. Knit to RC
RC 000. Pattern 1. Knit without shaping to RC

88	94	96	102	106	118	124	132	136	144	150	160	166
24	28	28	28	32	32	36	36	36	36	36	44	48
16	16	16	—	16	24	24	—	—	—	—	—	—

Decrease 1 stitch both beds both ends at following row intervals.

8 ——→		16/8	16	16/8 ——————→				8/8/16 ——————→			

Number of stitches to be decreased at both ends
Continue in Pattern 1 to RC
Change to Pattern 2. Number of stitches after decreasing
Knit to RC

16	16	16	17	17	21	23	26	26	29	31	36	38
84	84	84	96	192	192	192	192	192	192	192	192	192
56	62	64	68	72	76	78	80	84	86	88	88	90
152	168	176	212	264	268	276	280	284	288	288	292	292

Frequency of decreasing and end stitch arrangements for Brother 850. Push up end needle at carriage end when knitting colours shown below:
Sizes 1–3 8th and every following 8th row. Colour 2 throughout.
Sizes 4 and 6–10 16th and 8th rows alternately. Rows 1–8 colour 2, rows 9–32 colour 1, rows 33–56 colour 2. Continue in this way: 24 rows for each colour after first 8 rows.
Size 5 16th and every following 16th row. Rows 1–8 colour 2, rows 9–24 colour 1, rows 25–40 colour 2. Continue in this way. 16 rows for each colour after first 8 rows.
Sizes 11–13 At following row intervals throughout: 8, 8, 16. Rows 1–24 colour 2. Rows 25–48 colour 1. 24 rows for each colour.
N.B. Knitters using needle pusher to knit this stitch must be careful to keep continuity of rib bed pattern.

Toyota Number of main bed needles
Knit without shaping to RC

78	84	86	92	96	106	112	120	122	130	136	144	150
16	18	20	20	22	22	24	24	24	26	26	30	32

Decrease 1 stitch on both beds at both ends of next row and at following row intervals
Number of stitches to be decreased both ends
Knit to RC
Stitches remaining over width of main bed needles

7	7/8	7/8	9	11	8	7/8	7/8	7	7	6	5/6	5
14	14	15	15	14	19	22	23	24	25	28	32	35
104	114	124	144	166	168	176	178	180	180	184	192	194
50	56	56	62	68	68	68	74	74	80	80	80	80

Transfer to main bed. Tension 10. Knit 1 row. Cast off with latch tool.

Cuffs

All machines Knit 2 alike. Cast on and knit 6 rows circular knitting as for fronts over following main bed needles
Knit 36 rows circular knitting *. Transfer stitches to main bed. Tension 10. Knit 1 row. Cast off with latch tool. Alternative cuffs, as shown in Toyota garment, are knitted as a double cuff in 2 × 2 (2 up 1 down) rib.

50	50	54	54	60	64	64	64	68	68	68	74	74

Waistband

Colour 1. Knit as cuffs. Joins between pieces must be so neat they are invisible. Back and 1 front combined
Front
Back
Knit back and 1 front piece combined and separate front piece for small sizes. Knit separate back and 2 front pieces for larger sizes. Knit 36 rows. Cast off as cuffs. Seam into 1 length.

145	154	166	175	187	196	—	—	—	—	—	—	—
64	70	76	79	85	88	94	97	103	106	112	118	124
81	84	90	96	102	108	114	120	126	135	141	144	147

Neckband

Knit to match cuffs. Following needles both beds
Knit as cuffs to *. Knit 1 row full needle rib. Knit 12 rows separately on both beds. Release separately on waste knitting.

84	88	94	98	106	114	114	120	124	126	136	138	140

To make up

Join shoulders by mattress stitching on one side and crocheting together on the other. Cut and sew round neckline. Depth of neck in table of measurements is cutting line. Measure and tack on this line. Sew 2 rows zigzag machining below line. Cut out neck. Back neck can also be curved in same way by 1–1.5cm if you wish. Place neckline between stocking stitch edges of collar. Tack into position, taking care that full needle rib row on collar fits against cut edge. Backstitch through stitches on both sides taking care not to sew through to the other side.

All long seams are joined by crocheting through the cast-off edges. Attach tops of sleeves to armhole edges of fronts and back. Join side pieces to fronts and back. Join sleeve seams as shoulders. Attach cuffs, easing sleeves into position. Sew straight piece of sleeves to top edges of side pieces using same method.

Attach pockets and waistband. Fasten fronts with buttons and loops (see colour photograph 68). Two sets are required so that the garment can be reversed.

Index

Page numbers in **bold** refer to illustrations.